RADISE RESIDENCE

Kosuke Fujishima

volume **2**

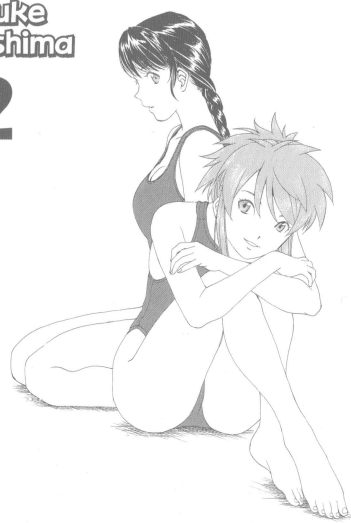

CONTENTS

episode.8

THE TYPHOON PASSES

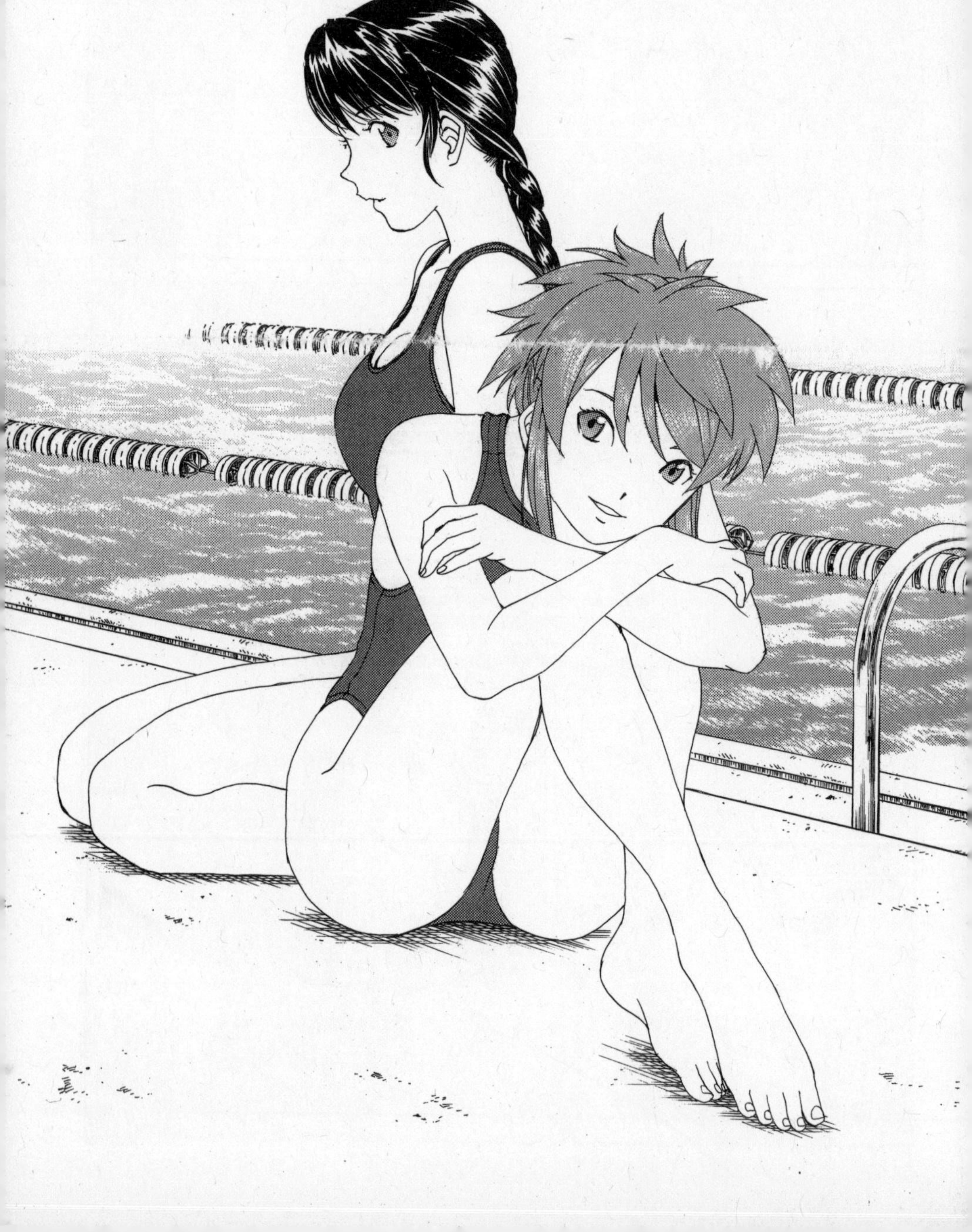

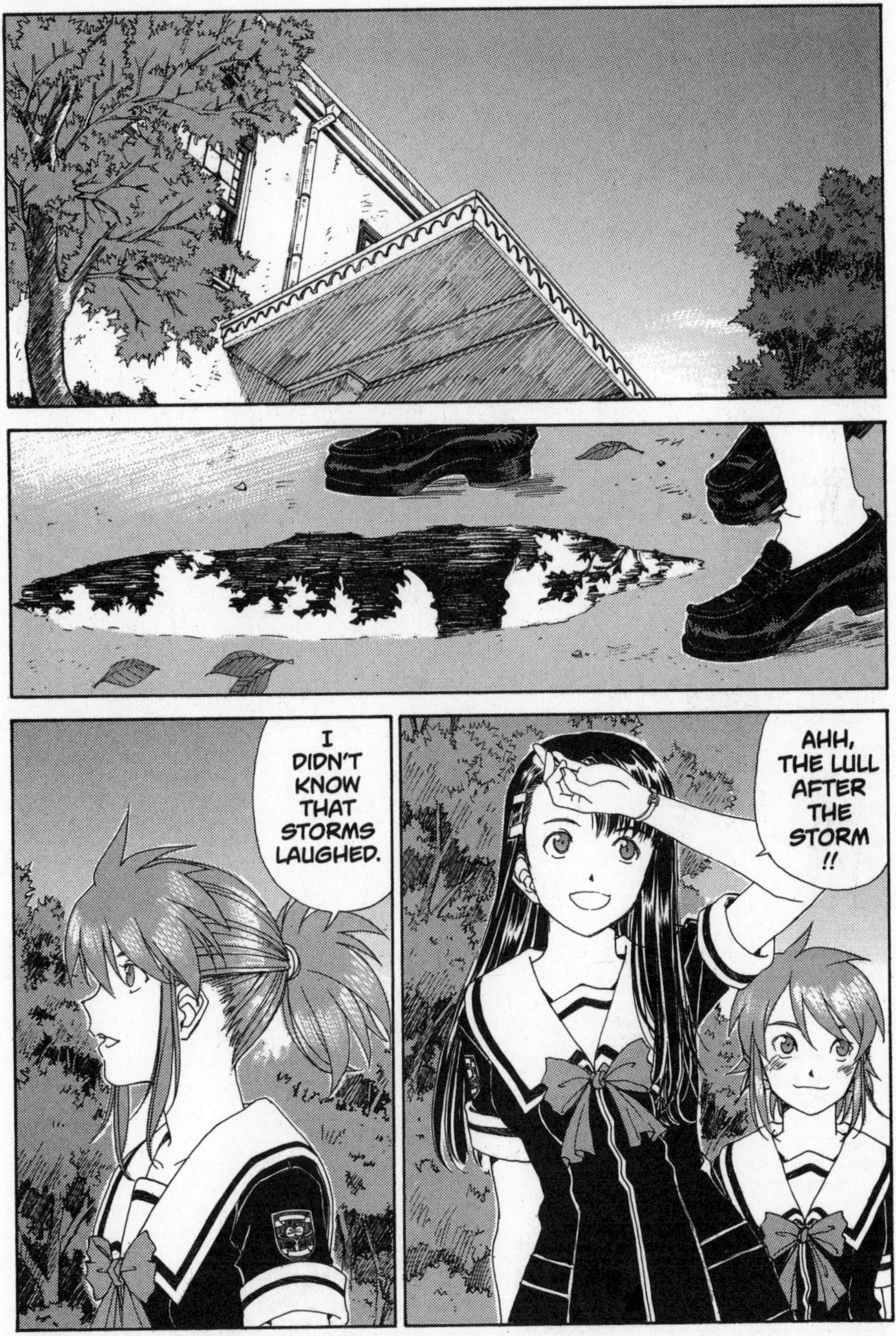
AHH, THE LULL AFTER THE STORM !!
I DIDN'T KNOW THAT STORMS LAUGHED.

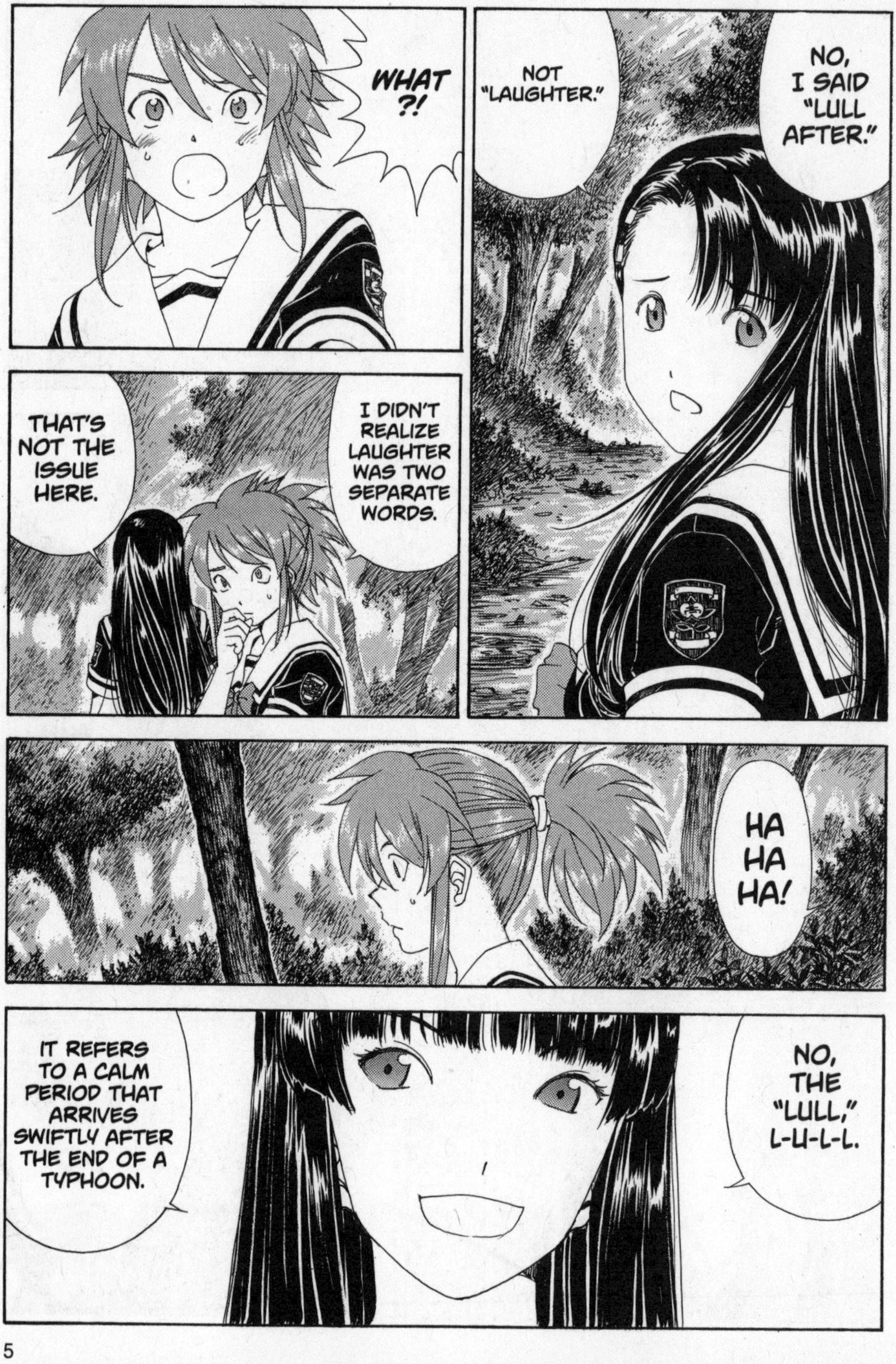
NO, I SAID "LULL AFTER."
NOT "LAUGHTER."
WHAT ?!
I DIDN'T REALIZE LAUGHTER WAS TWO SEPARATE WORDS.
THAT'S NOT THE ISSUE HERE.
HA HA HA!
NO, THE "LULL," L-U-L-L.
IT REFERS TO A CALM PERIOD THAT ARRIVES SWIFTLY AFTER THE END OF A TYPHOON.

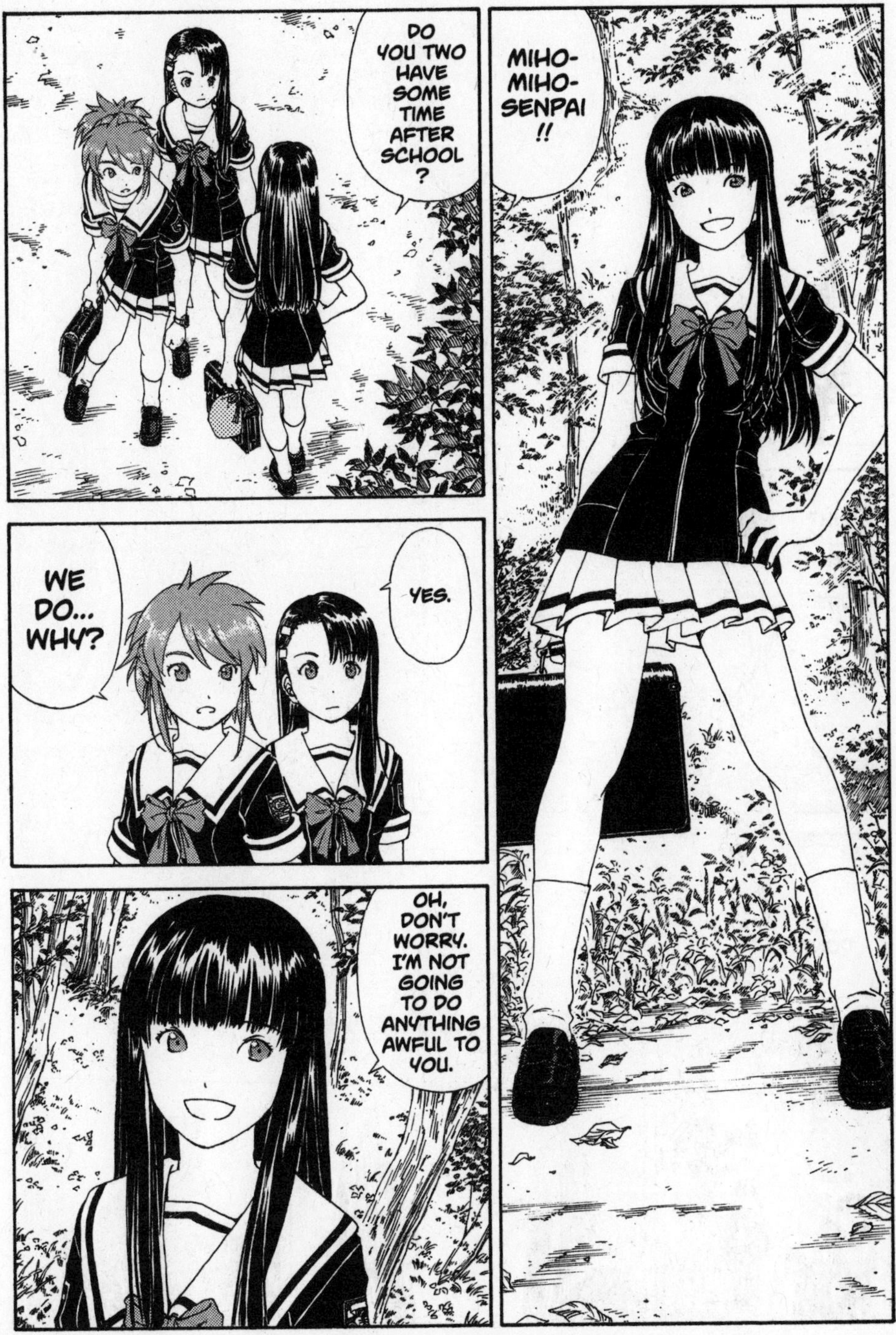
MIHO-MIHO-SENPAI!!
DO YOU TWO HAVE SOME TIME AFTER SCHOOL?
YES.
WE DO... WHY?
OH, DON'T WORRY. I'M NOT GOING TO DO ANYTHING AWFUL TO YOU.

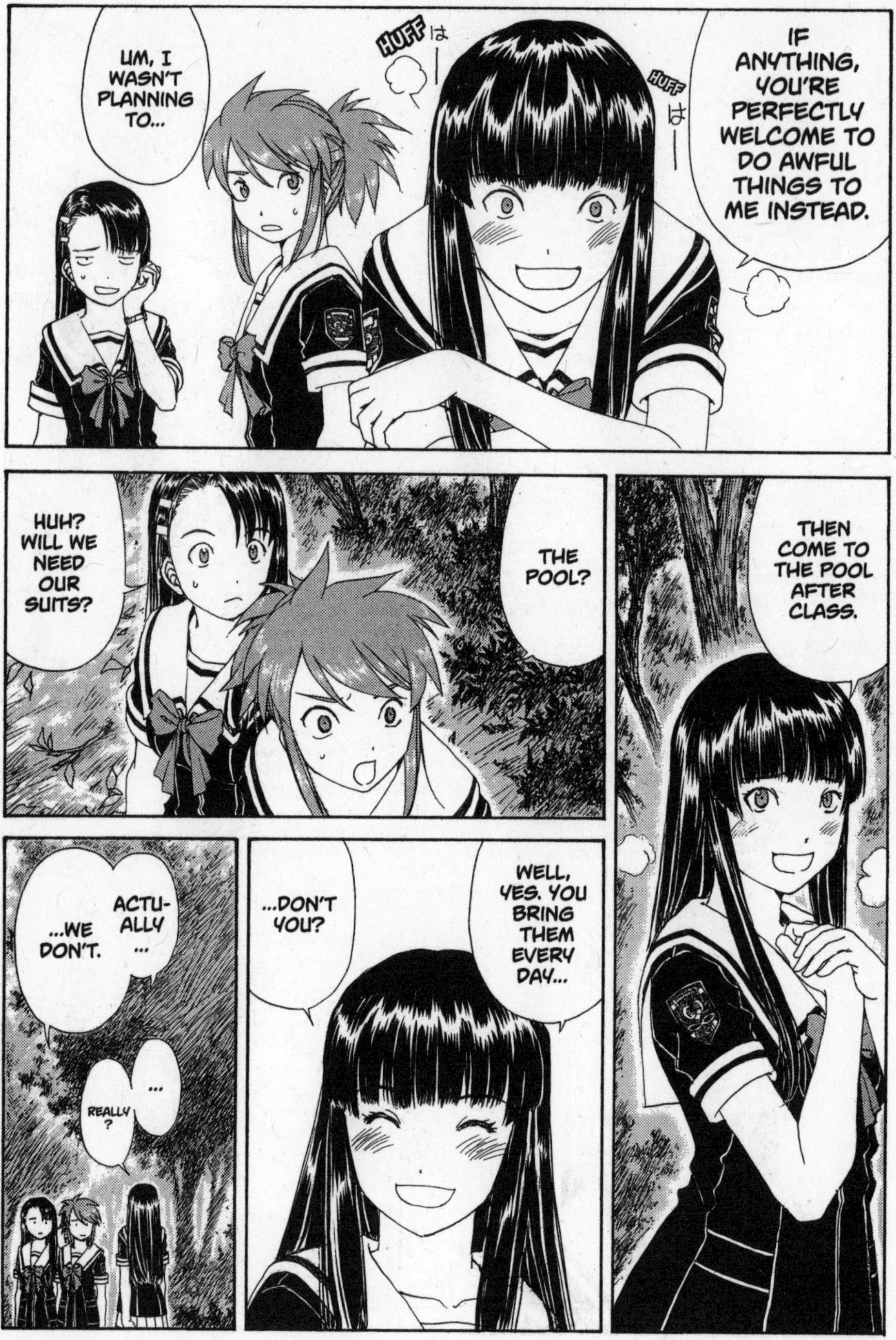
IF ANYTHING, YOU'RE PERFECTLY WELCOME TO DO AWFUL THINGS TO ME INSTEAD.
HUFF はー
HUFF はー
UM, I WASN'T PLANNING TO...
THEN COME TO THE POOL AFTER CLASS.
THE POOL?
HUH? WILL WE NEED OUR SUITS?
WELL, YES. YOU BRING THEM EVERY DAY...
...DON'T YOU?
ACTU-ALLY ...
...WE DON'T.
...
REALLY ?

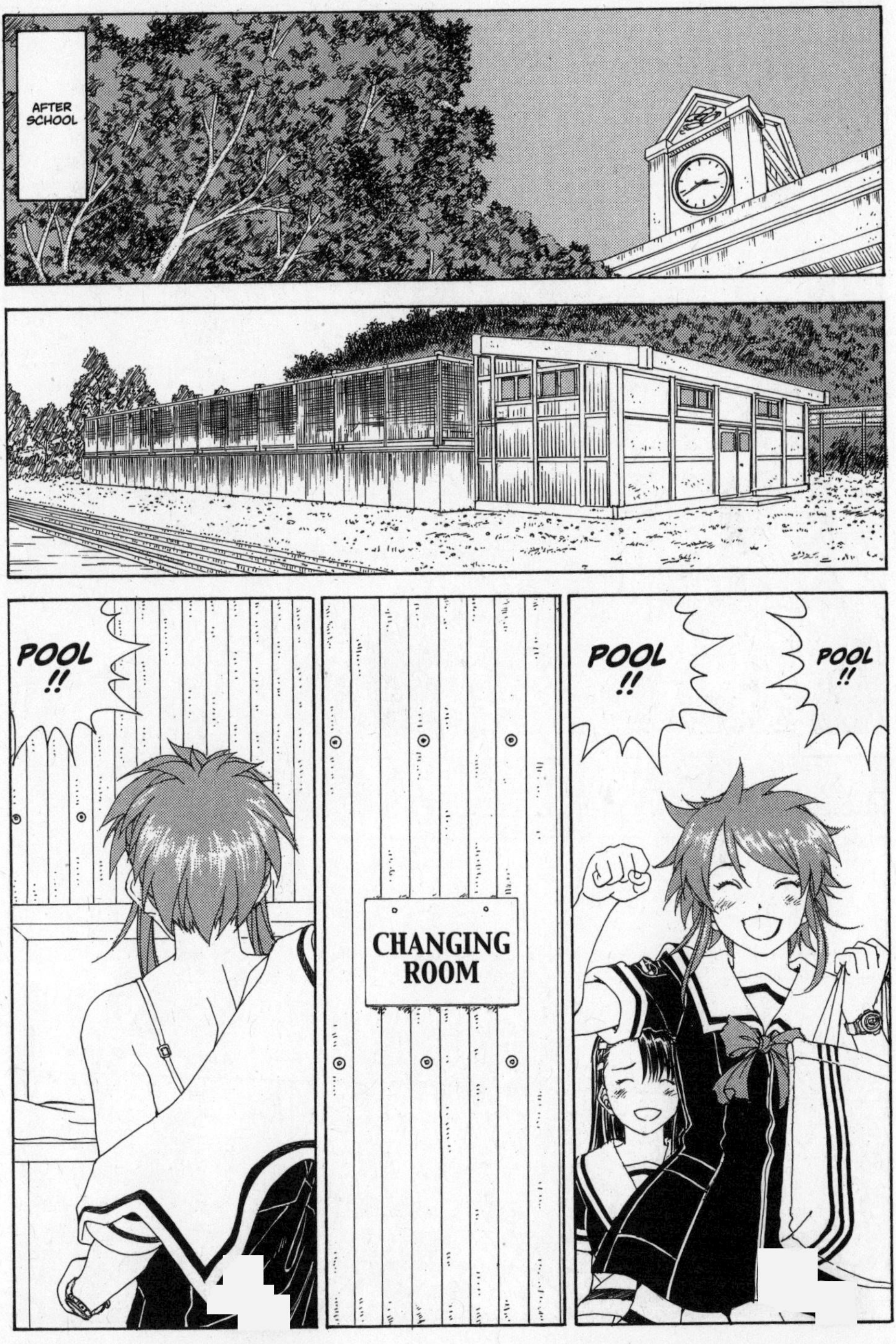
AFTER SCHOOL
POOL !!
POOL !!
CHANGING ROOM
POOL !!

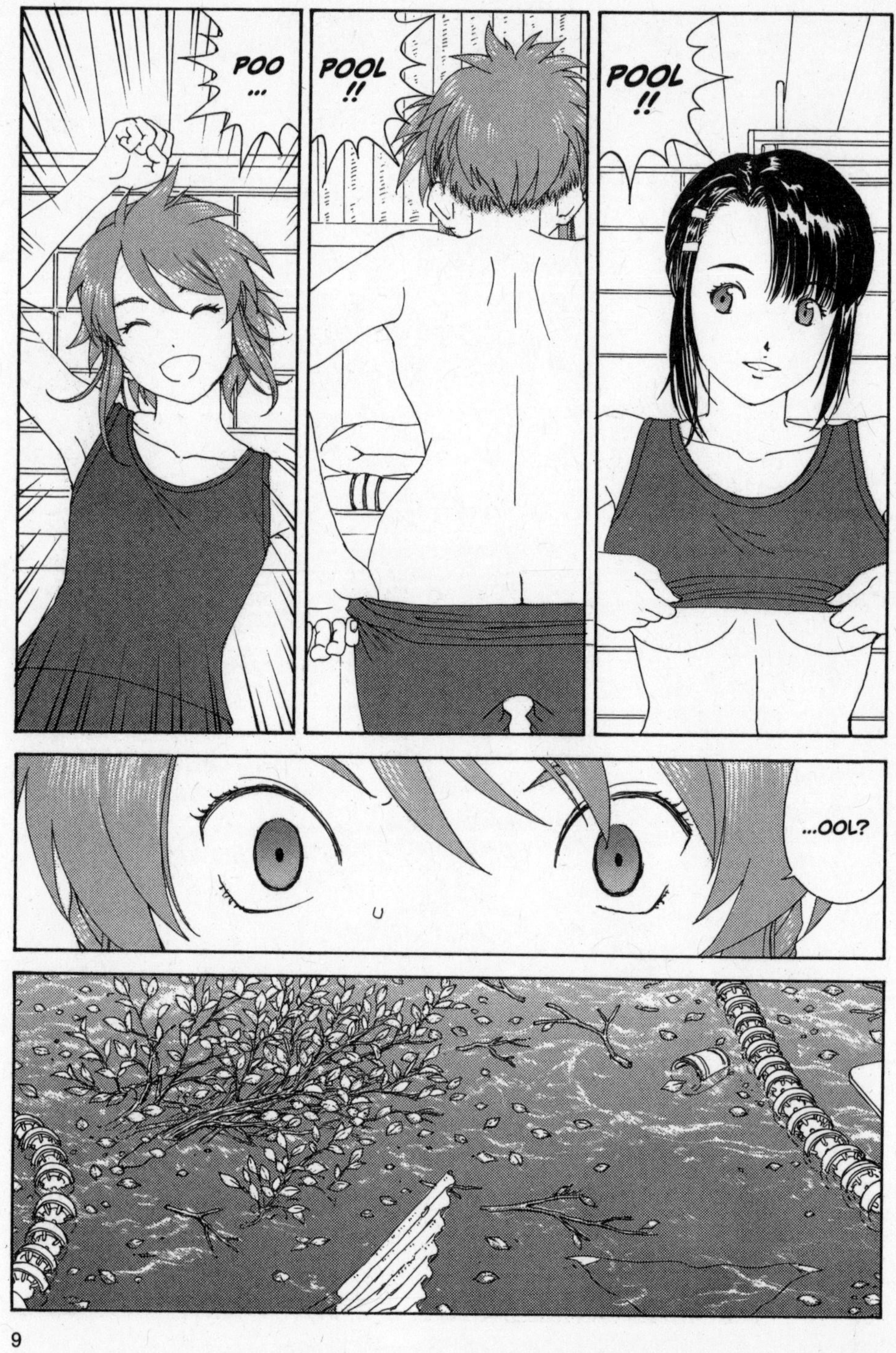
POOL !!
POOL !!
POO ...
...OOL?

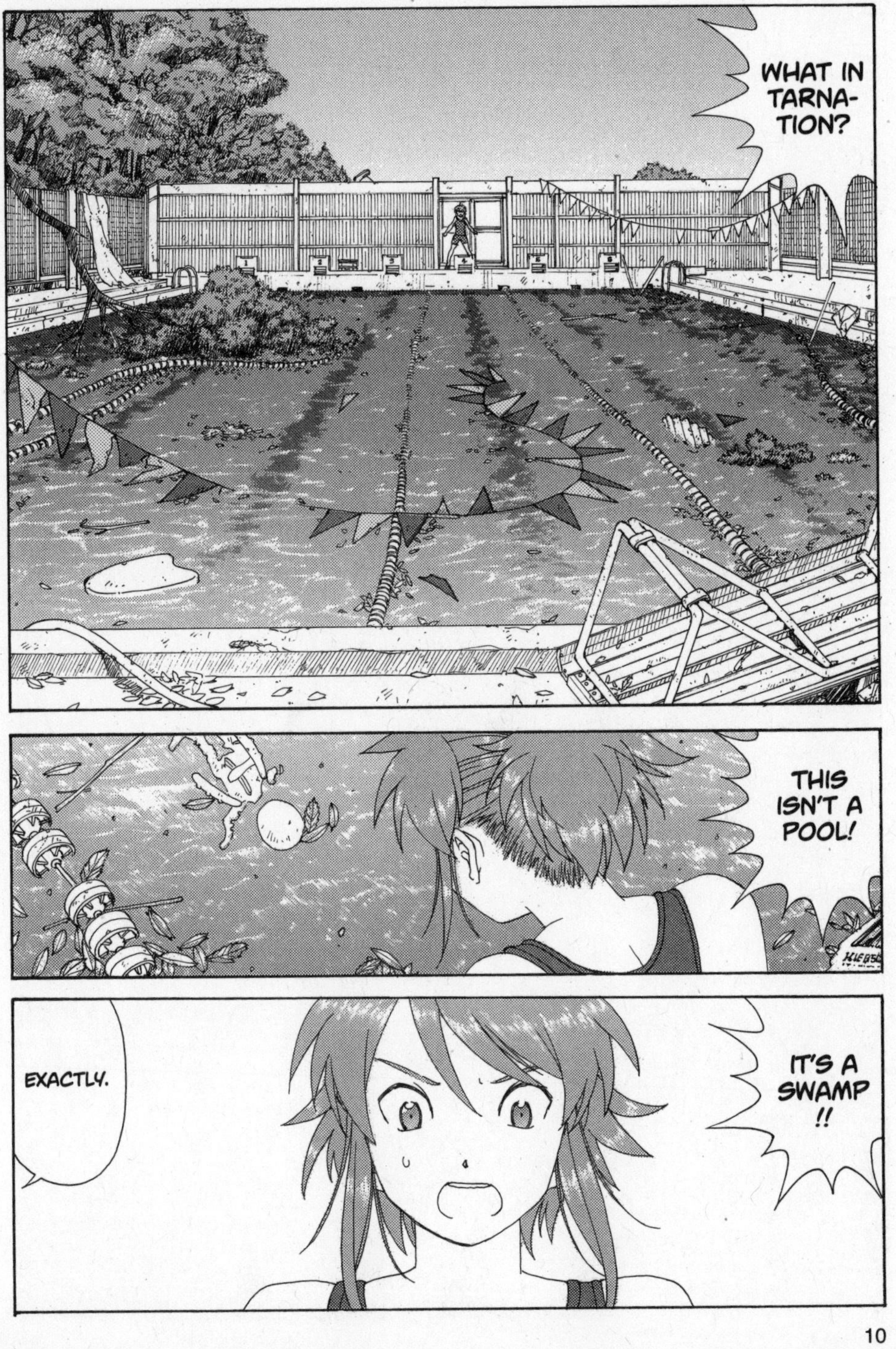
WHAT IN TARNATION?
THIS ISN'T A POOL!
IT'S A SWAMP !!
EXACTLY.

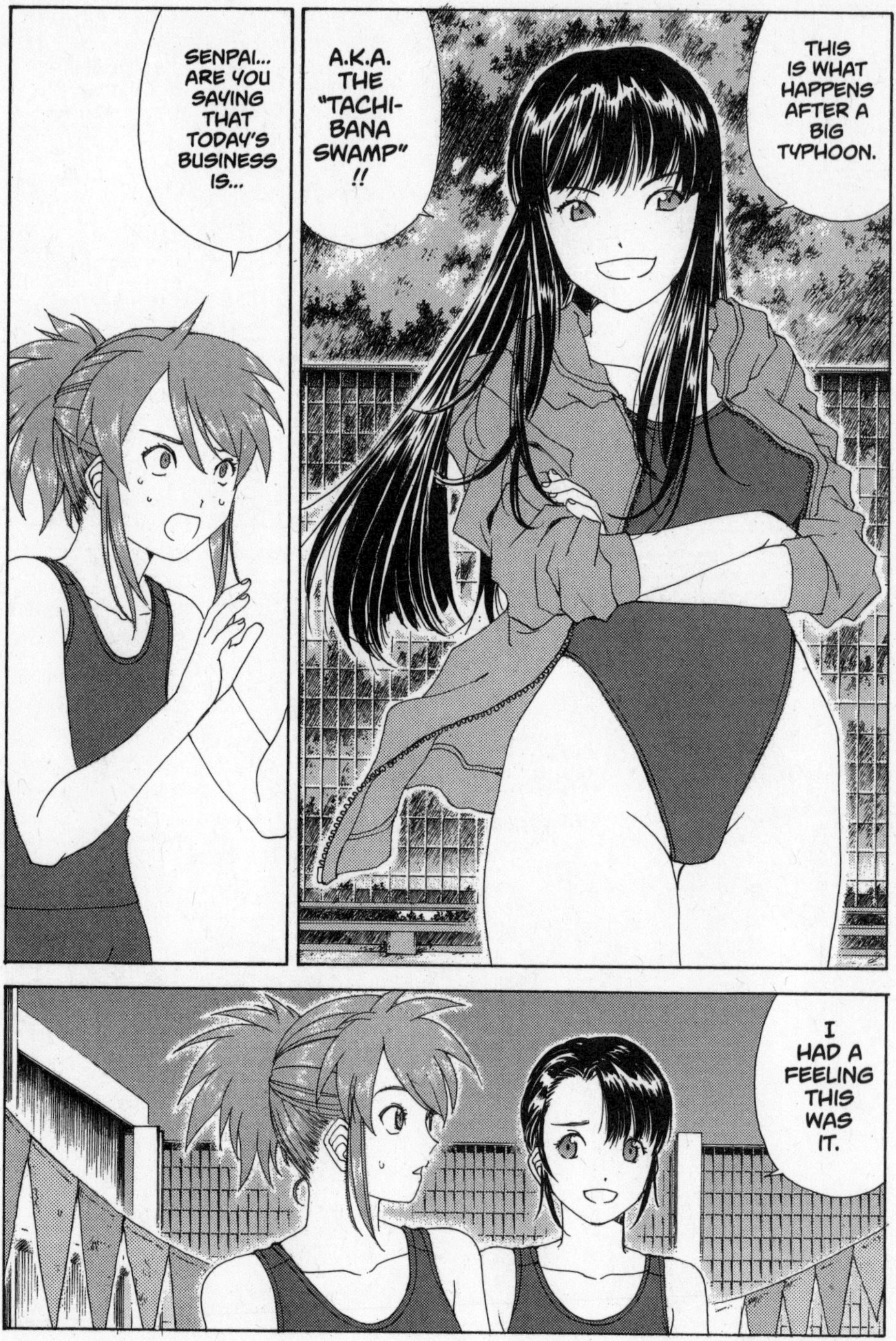
THIS IS WHAT HAPPENS AFTER A BIG TYPHOON.
A.K.A. THE "TACHI-BANA SWAMP" !!
SENPAI... ARE YOU SAYING THAT TODAY'S BUSINESS IS...
I HAD A FEELING THIS WAS IT.

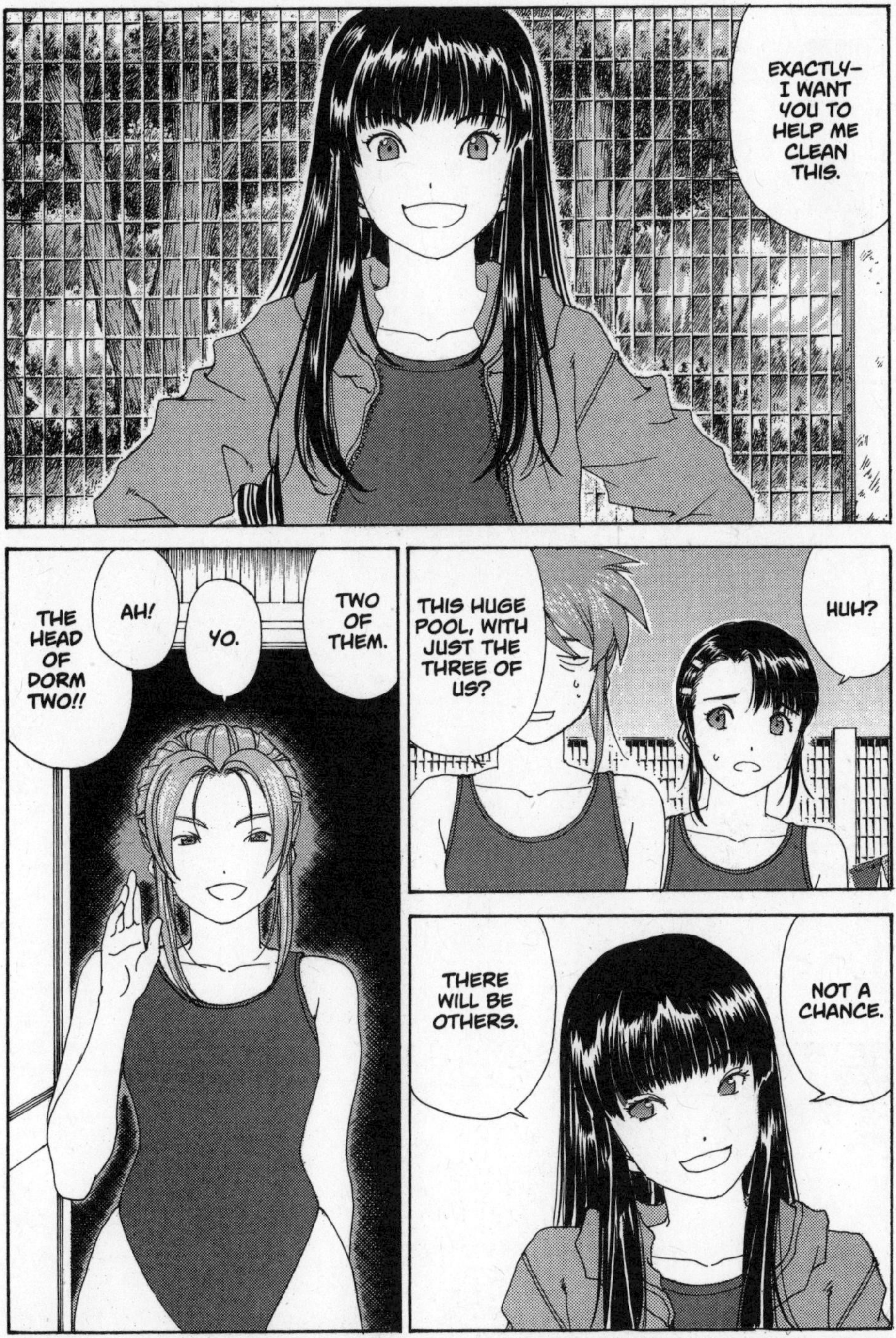
EXACTLY— I WANT YOU TO HELP ME CLEAN THIS.
HUH?
THIS HUGE POOL, WITH JUST THE THREE OF US?
NOT A CHANCE.
THERE WILL BE OTHERS.
TWO OF THEM.
YO.
AH!
THE HEAD OF DORM TWO!!

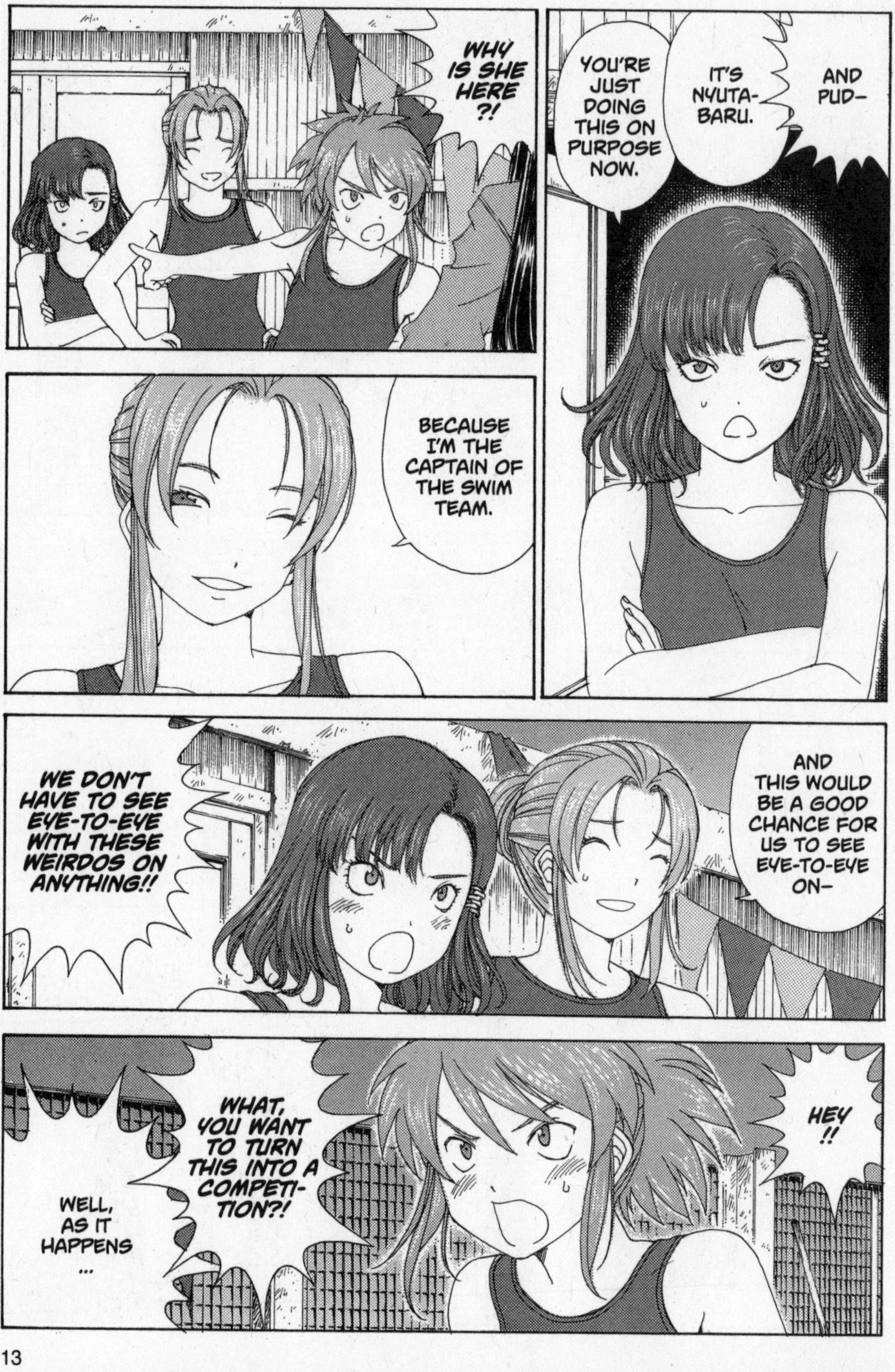
AND PUD–
IT'S NYUTA-BARU.
YOU'RE JUST DOING THIS ON PURPOSE NOW.
WHY IS SHE HERE?!
BECAUSE I'M THE CAPTAIN OF THE SWIM TEAM.
AND THIS WOULD BE A GOOD CHANCE FOR US TO SEE EYE-TO-EYE ON–
WE DON'T HAVE TO SEE EYE-TO-EYE WITH THESE WEIRDOS ON ANYTHING!!
HEY!!
WHAT, YOU WANT TO TURN THIS INTO A COMPETI-TION?!
WELL, AS IT HAPPENS ...

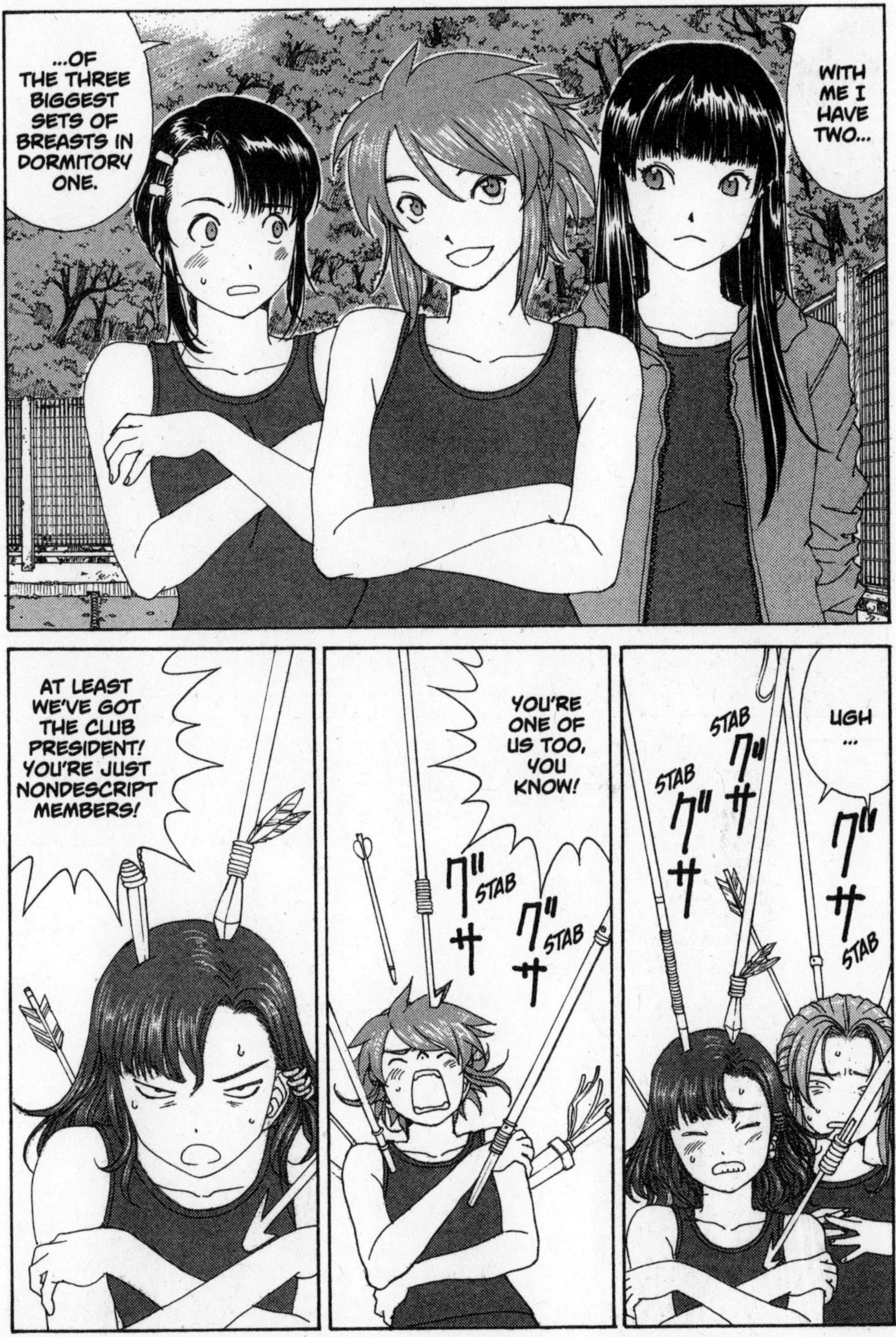
WITH ME I HAVE TWO...
...OF THE THREE BIGGEST SETS OF BREASTS IN DORMITORY ONE.
UGH ...
STAB
グサ
STAB
グサ
グサ
STAB
YOU'RE ONE OF US TOO, YOU KNOW!
グサ
STAB
グサ
STAB
AT LEAST WE'VE GOT THE CLUB PRESIDENT! YOU'RE JUST NONDESCRIPT MEMBERS!

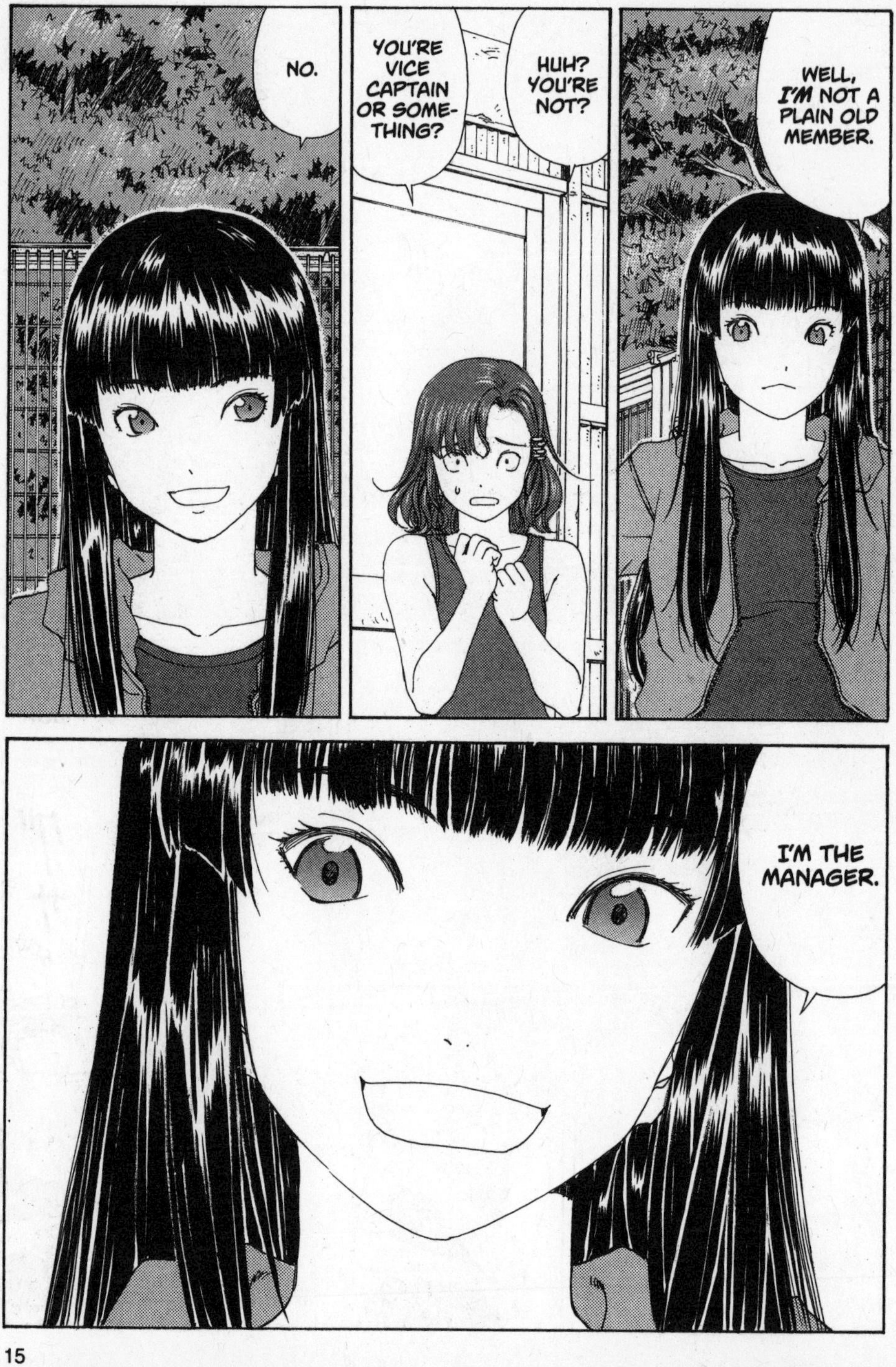
WELL, I'M NOT A PLAIN OLD MEMBER.
HUH? YOU'RE NOT?
YOU'RE VICE CAPTAIN OR SOME-THING?
NO.
I'M THE MANAGER.

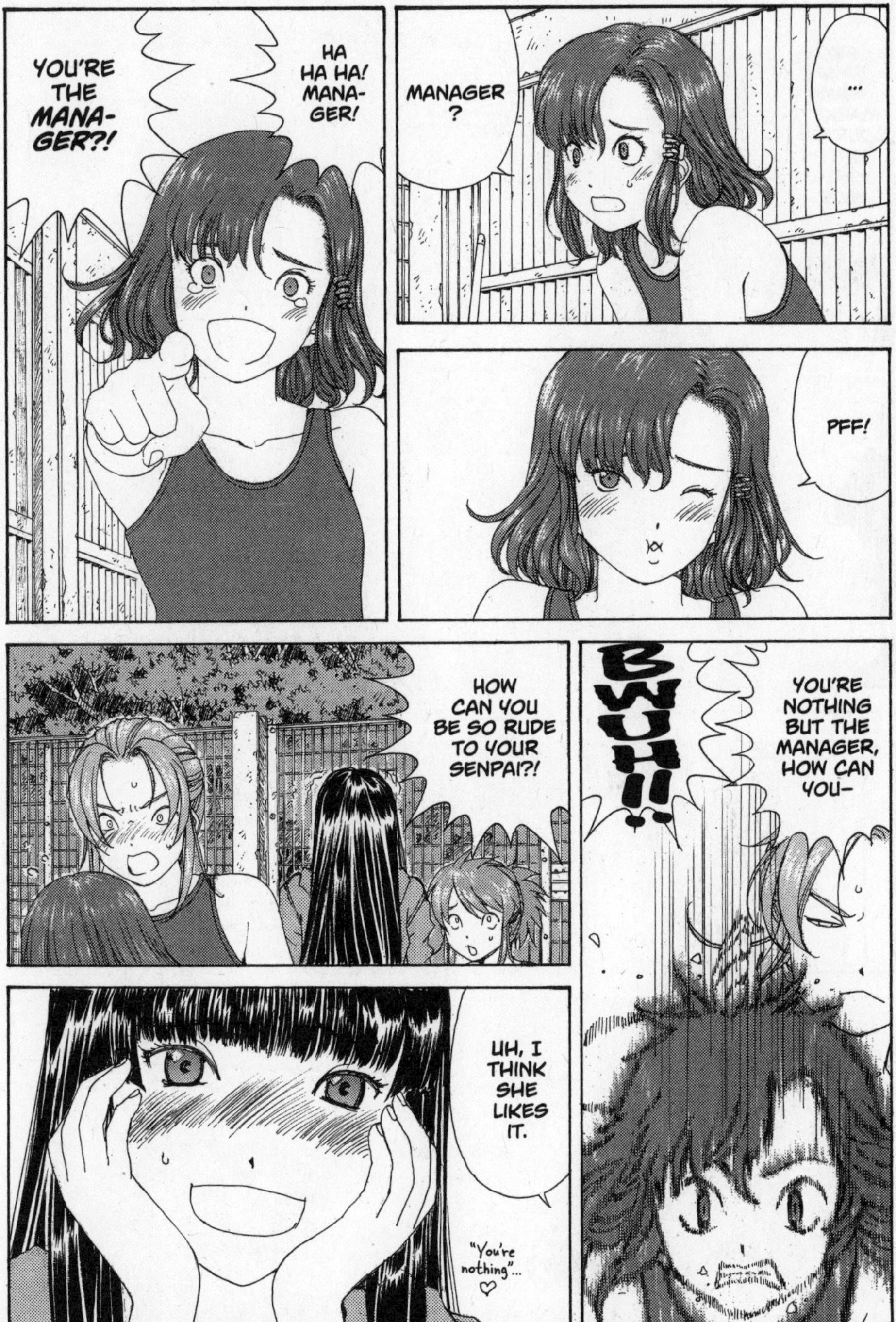
...
MANAGER ?
PFF!
HA HA HA! MANAGER!
YOU'RE THE MANAGER?!
YOU'RE NOTHING BUT THE MANAGER, HOW CAN YOU-
BWUH!!
HOW CAN YOU BE SO RUDE TO YOUR SENPAI?!
UH, I THINK SHE LIKES IT.
"You're nothing"... ♡

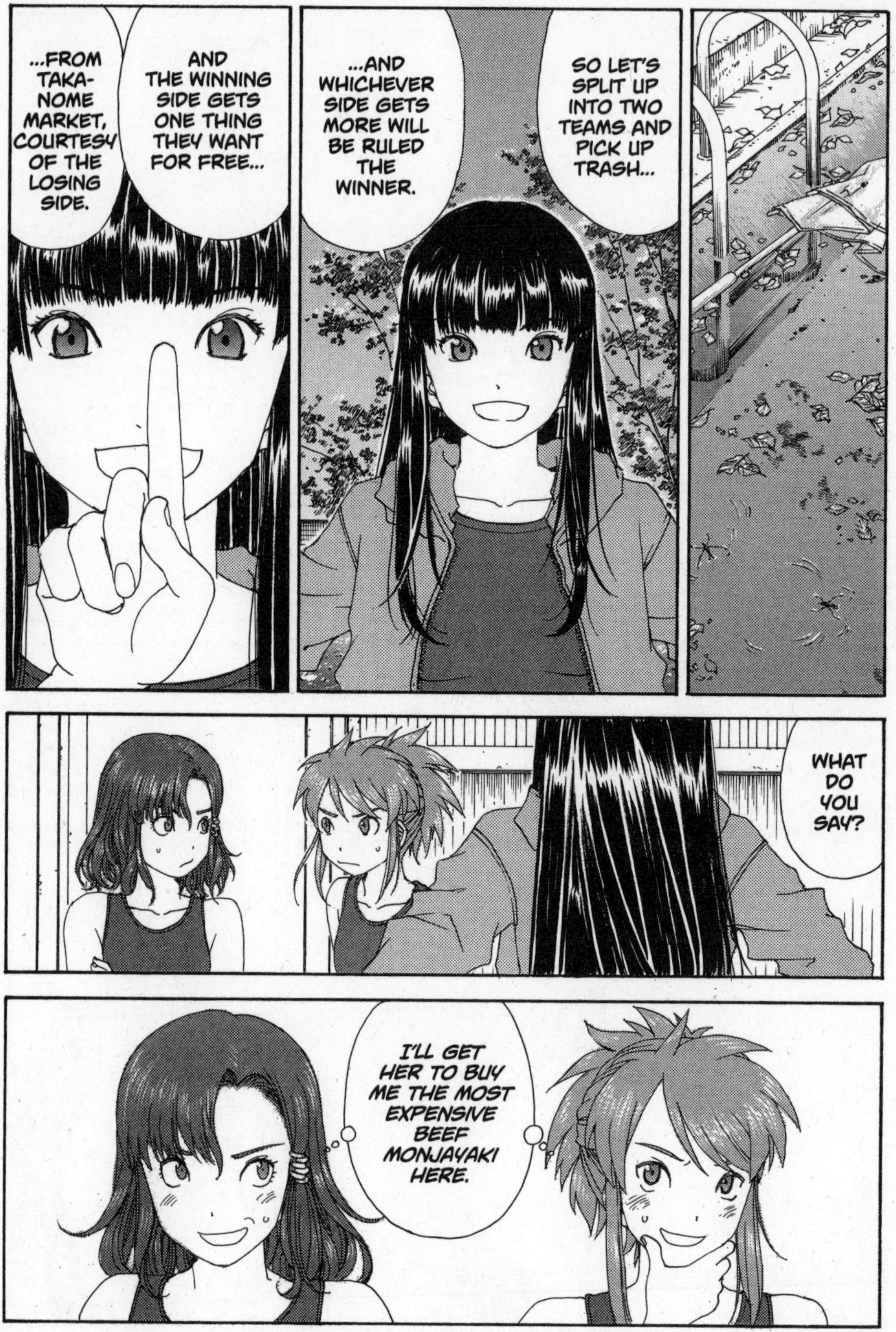
SO LET'S SPLIT UP INTO TWO TEAMS AND PICK UP TRASH...
...AND WHICHEVER SIDE GETS MORE WILL BE RULED THE WINNER.
AND THE WINNING SIDE GETS ONE THING THEY WANT FOR FREE...
...FROM TAKA-NOME MARKET, COURTESY OF THE LOSING SIDE.
WHAT DO YOU SAY?
I'LL GET HER TO BUY ME THE MOST EXPENSIVE BEEF MONJAYAKI HERE.

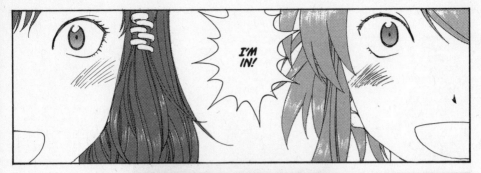

I'M IN!

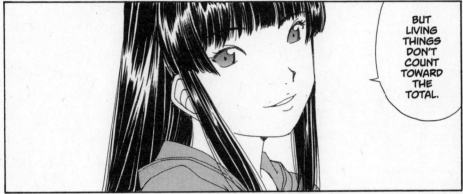

BUT LIVING THINGS DON'T COUNT TOWARD THE TOTAL.

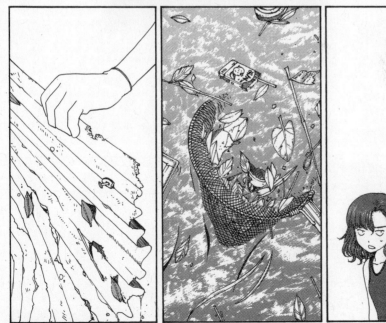

LIVING THINGS?

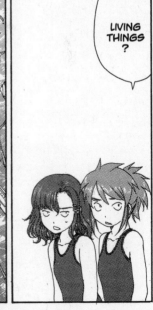

18

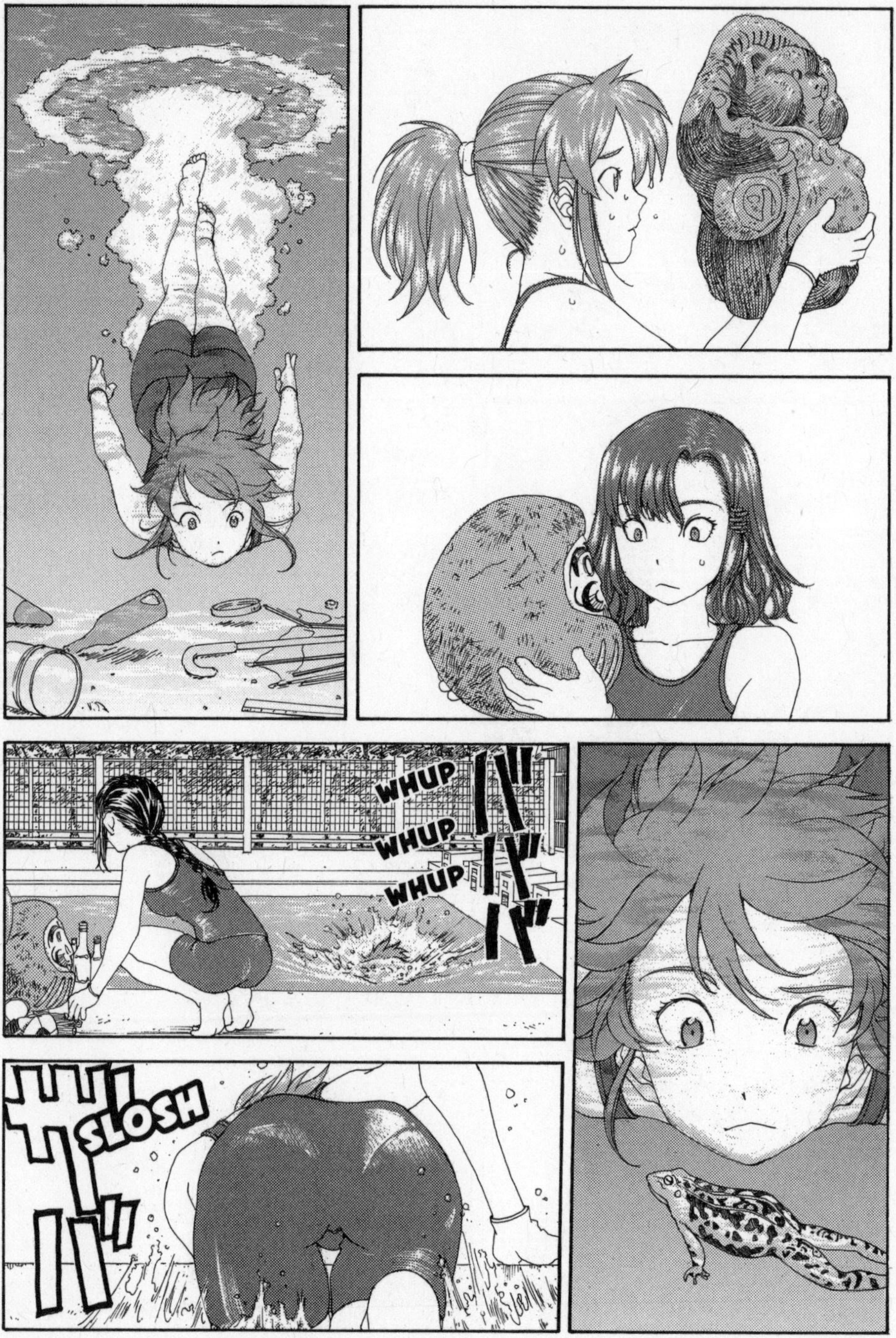
WHUP
WHUP
WHUP
SLOSH

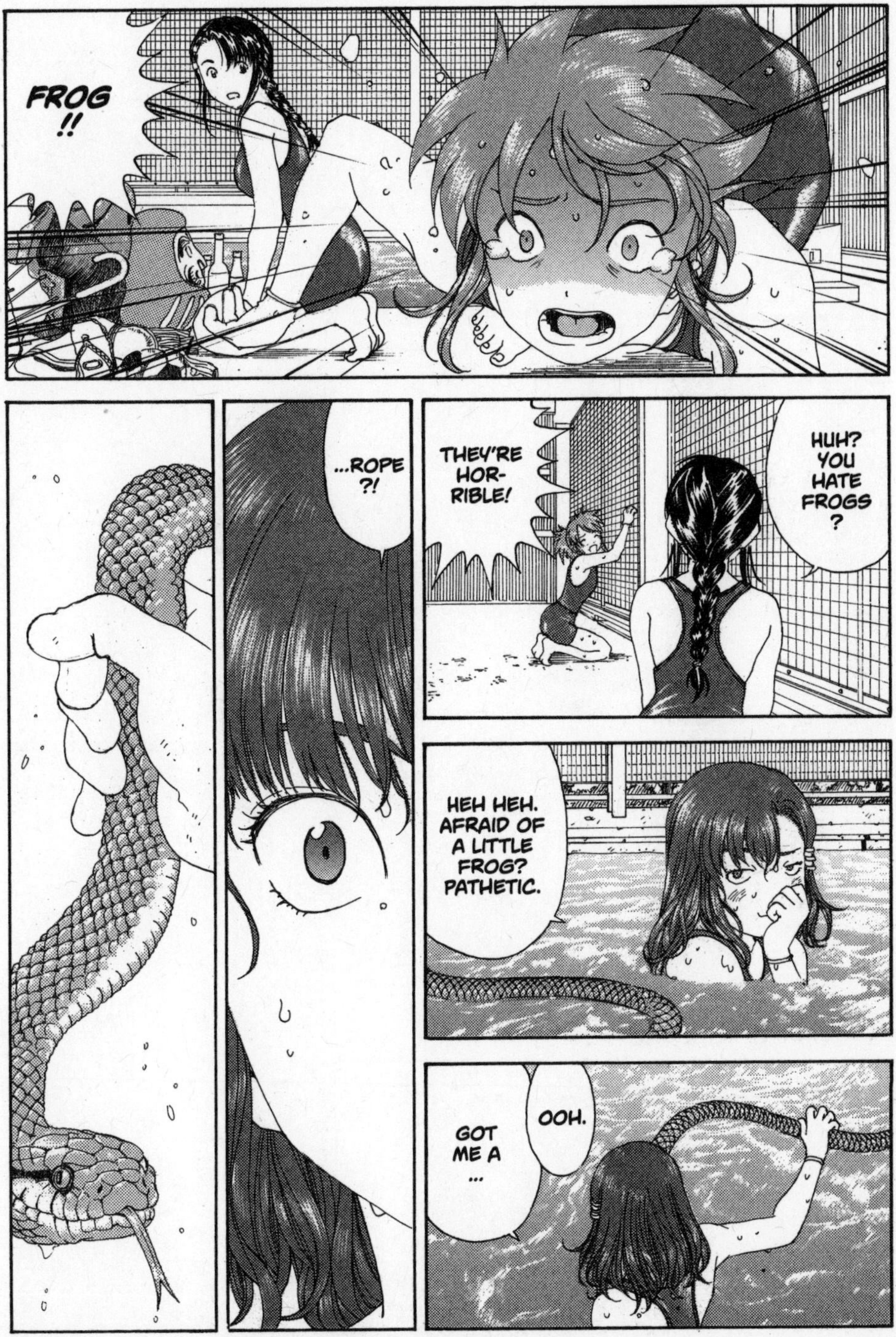

FROG!!
HUH? YOU HATE FROGS?
THEY'RE HOR-RIBLE!
HEH HEH. AFRAID OF A LITTLE FROG? PATHETIC.
OOH.
GOT ME A ...
...ROPE?!

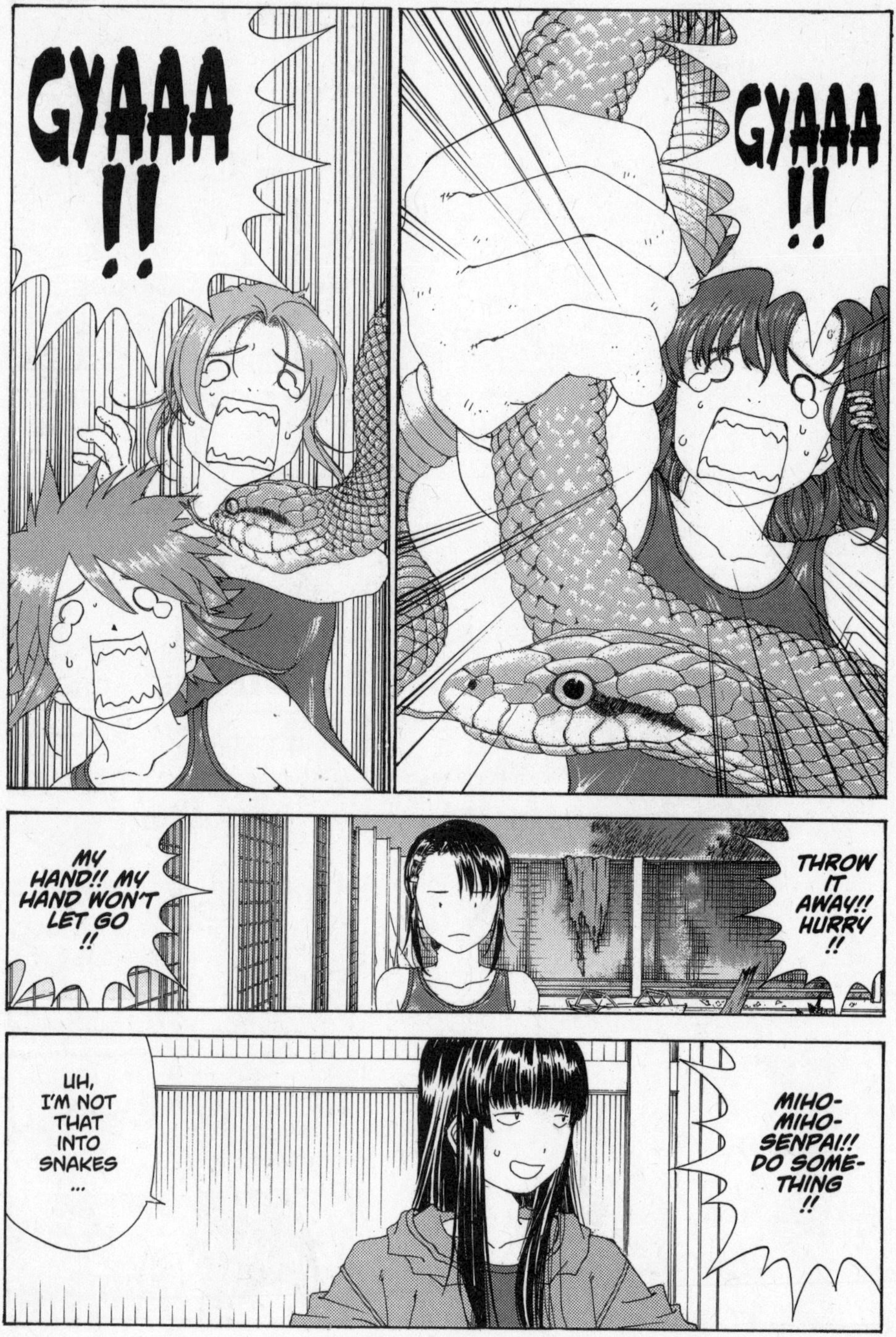
GYAAA !!
GYAAA !!
THROW IT AWAY!! HURRY !!
MY HAND!! MY HAND WON'T LET GO !!
MIHO-MIHO-SENPAI!! DO SOME-THING !!
UH, I'M NOT THAT INTO SNAKES ...

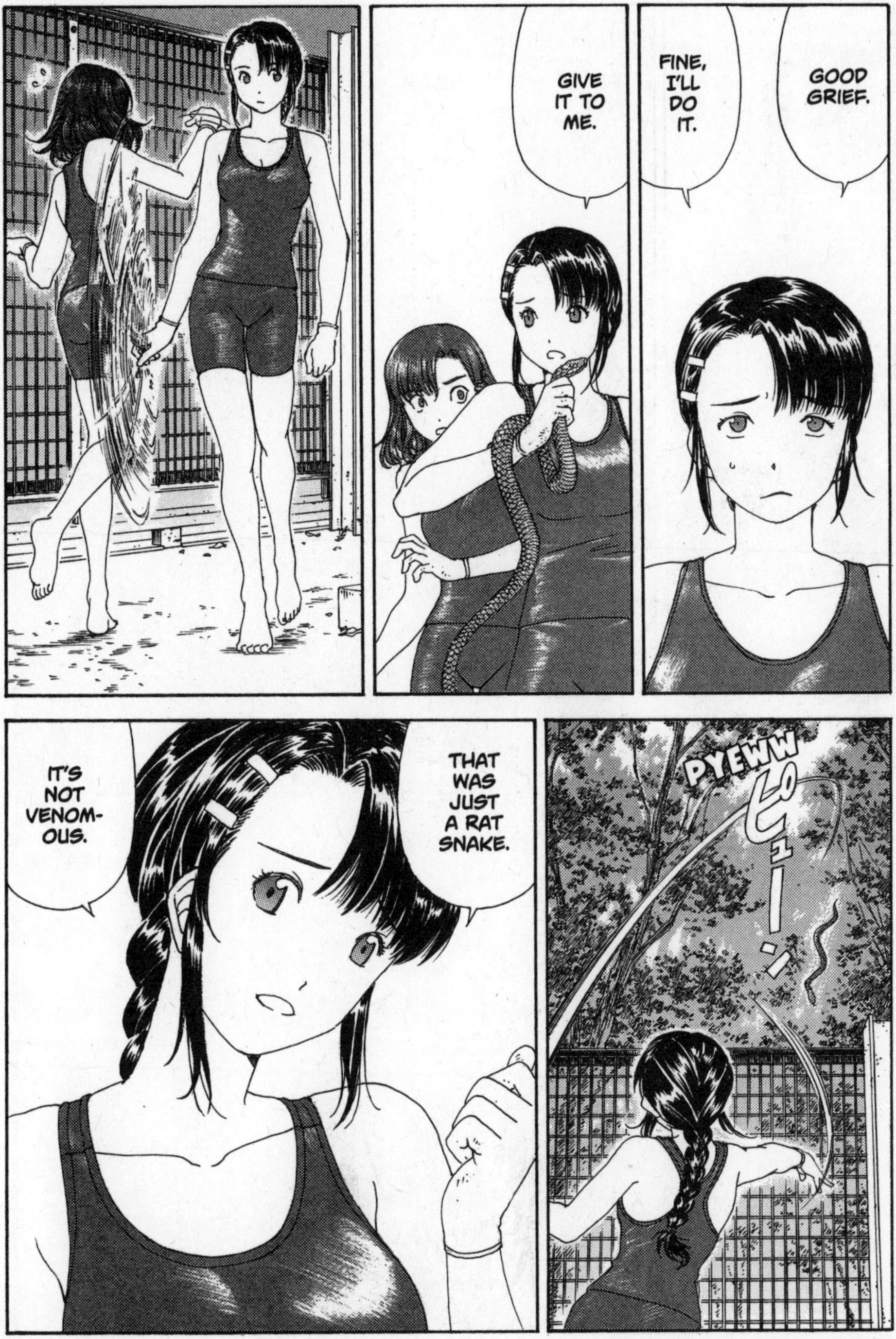
GOOD GRIEF.
FINE, I'LL DO IT.
GIVE IT TO ME.
PYEWW
THAT WAS JUST A RAT SNAKE.
IT'S NOT VENOMOUS.

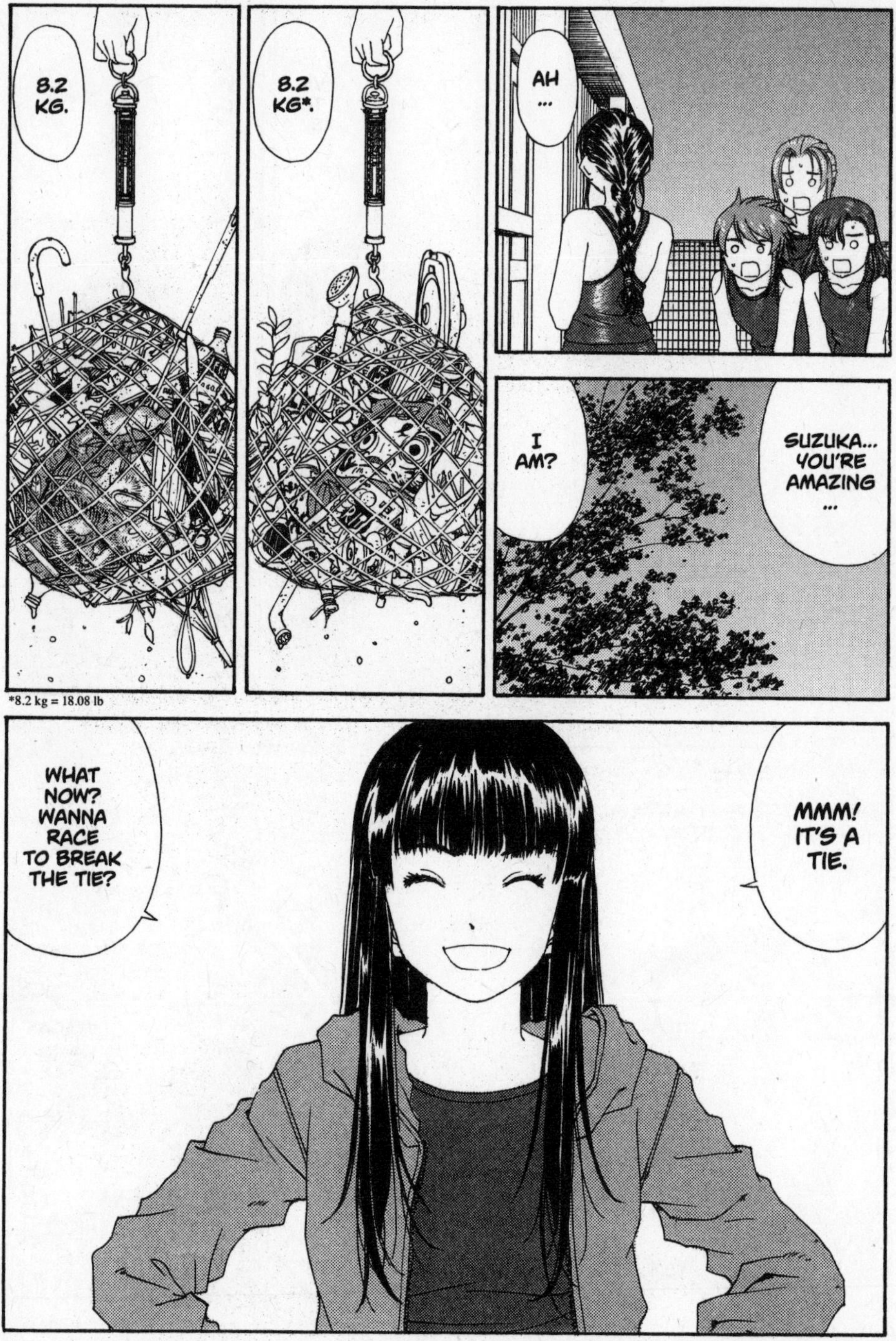
AH ...
SUZUKA... YOU'RE AMAZING ...
I AM?
8.2 KG*.
8.2 KG.
MMM! IT'S A TIE.
WHAT NOW? WANNA RACE TO BREAK THE TIE?

*8.2 kg = 18.08 lb

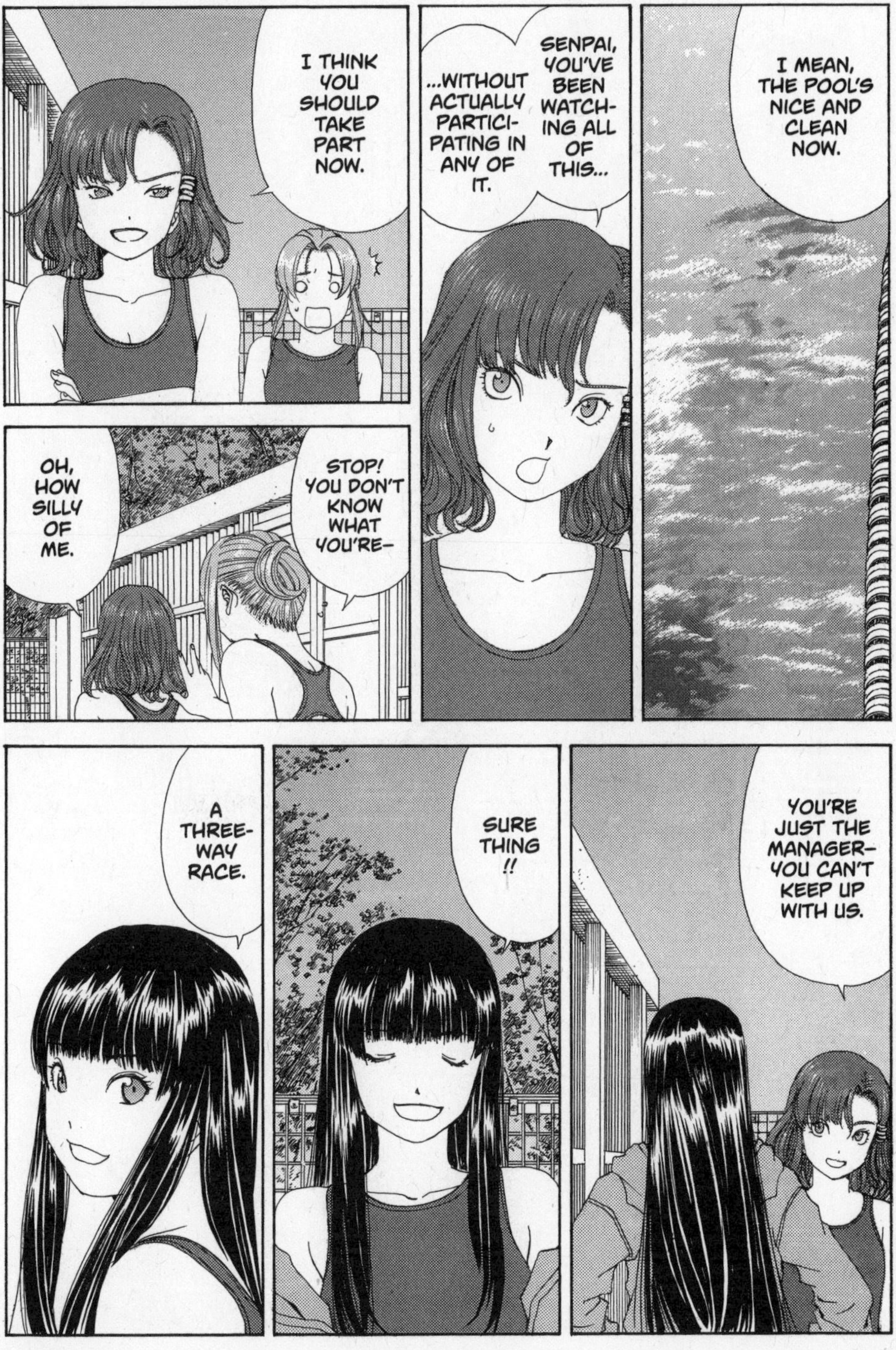
I MEAN, THE POOL'S NICE AND CLEAN NOW.
SENPAI, YOU'VE BEEN WATCHING ALL OF THIS...
...WITHOUT ACTUALLY PARTICIPATING IN ANY OF IT.
I THINK YOU SHOULD TAKE PART NOW.
STOP! YOU DON'T KNOW WHAT YOU'RE–
OH, HOW SILLY OF ME.
YOU'RE JUST THE MANAGER– YOU CAN'T KEEP UP WITH US.
SURE THING !!
A THREE-WAY RACE.

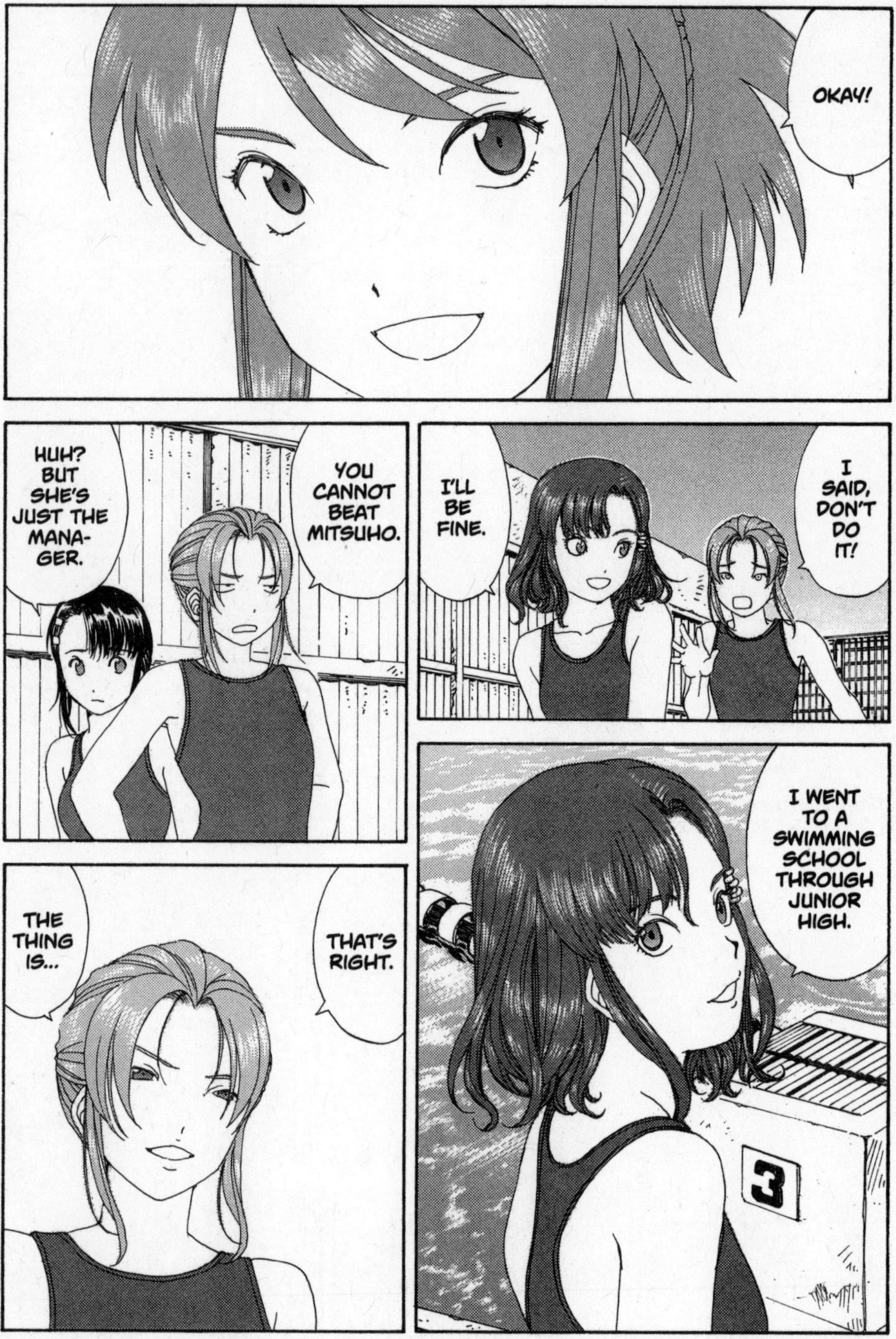
OKAY!
I SAID, DON'T DO IT!
I'LL BE FINE.
YOU CANNOT BEAT MITSUHO.
HUH? BUT SHE'S JUST THE MANA-GER.
I WENT TO A SWIMMING SCHOOL THROUGH JUNIOR HIGH.
THAT'S RIGHT.
THE THING IS...

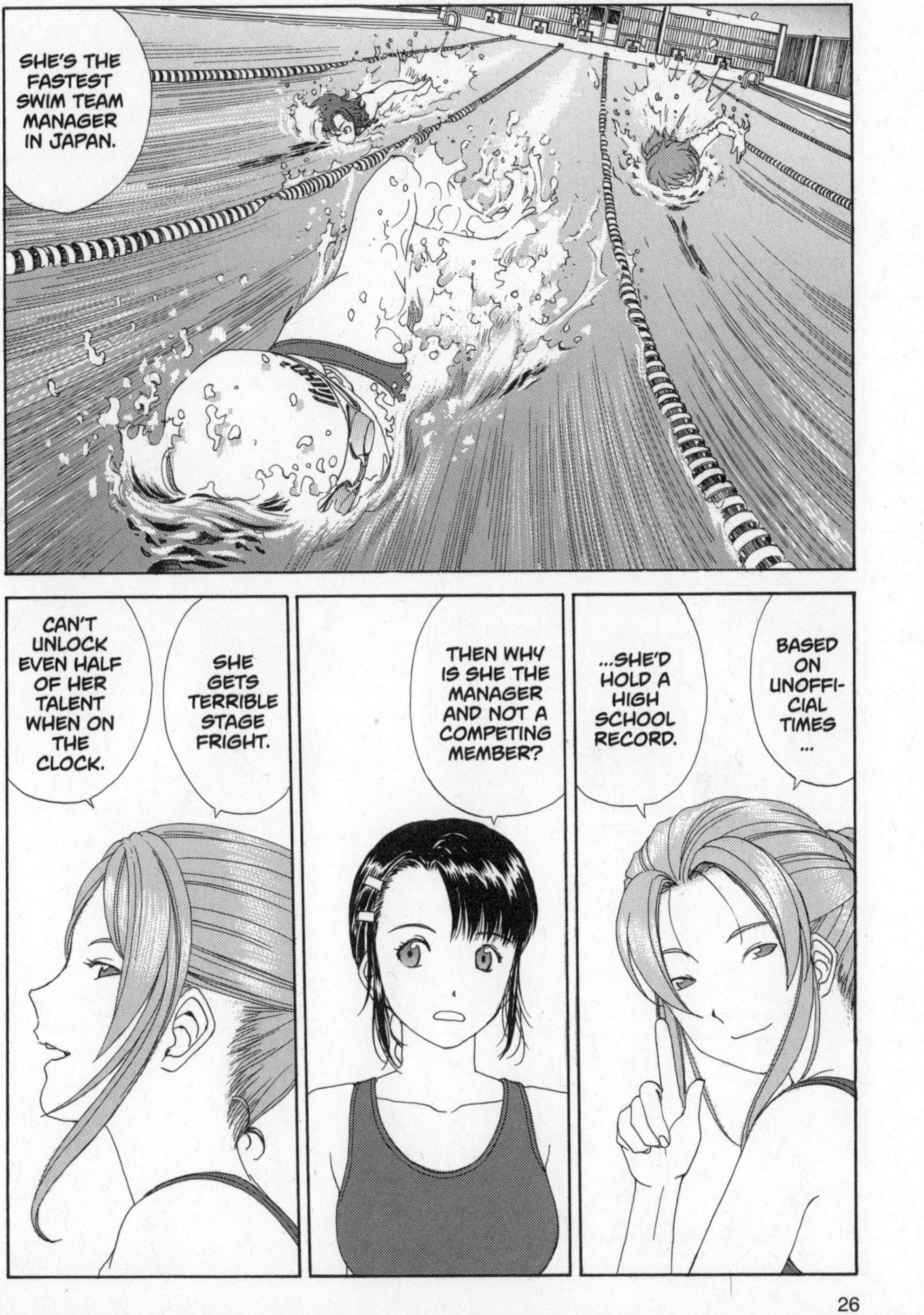
SHE'S THE FASTEST SWIM TEAM MANAGER IN JAPAN.
BASED ON UNOFFICIAL TIMES ...
...SHE'D HOLD A HIGH SCHOOL RECORD.
THEN WHY IS SHE THE MANAGER AND NOT A COMPETING MEMBER?
SHE GETS TERRIBLE STAGE FRIGHT.
CAN'T UNLOCK EVEN HALF OF HER TALENT WHEN ON THE CLOCK.

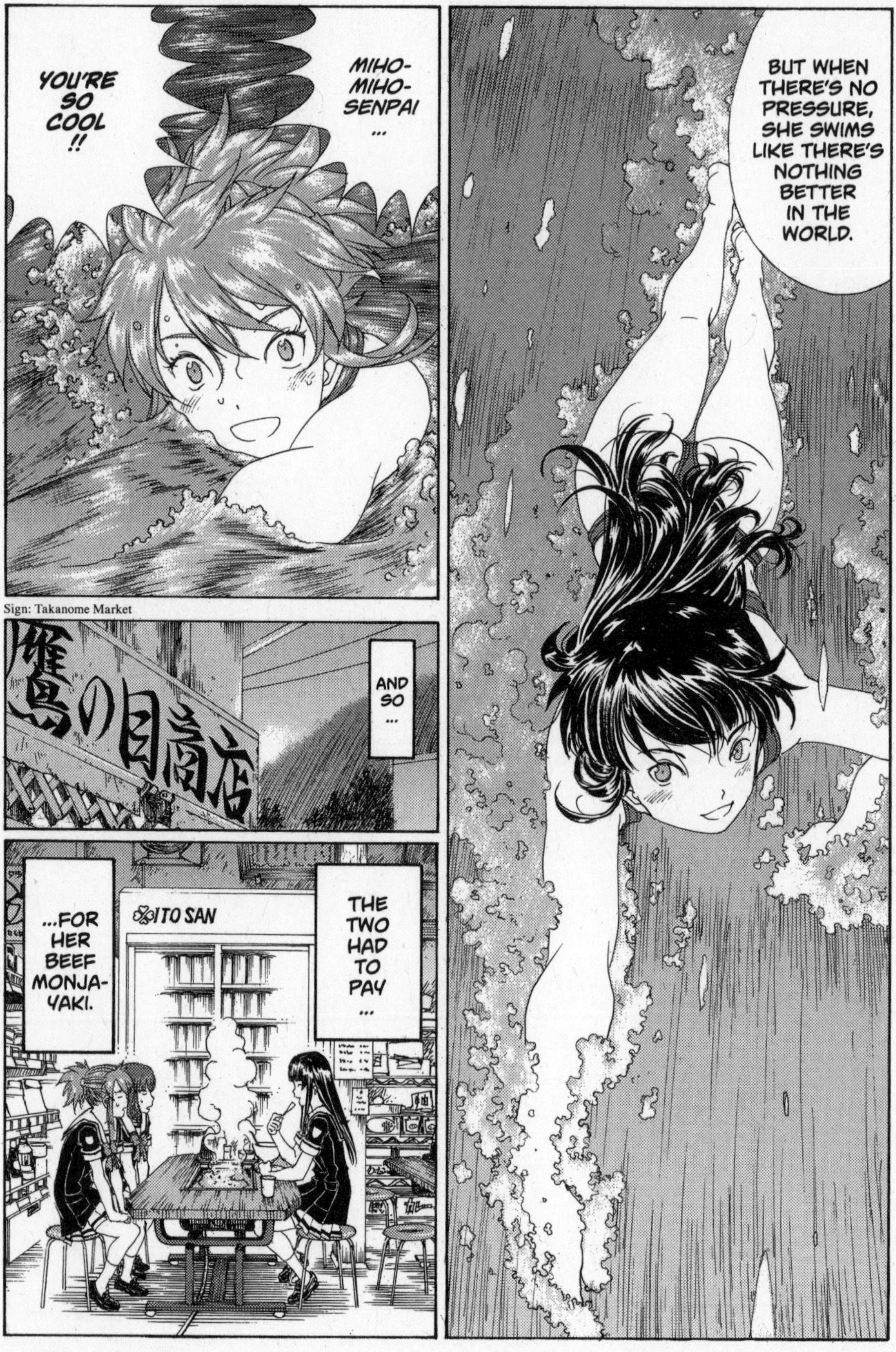
BUT WHEN THERE'S NO PRESSURE, SHE SWIMS LIKE THERE'S NOTHING BETTER IN THE WORLD.
MIHO-MIHO-SENPAI ...
YOU'RE SO COOL !!
Sign: Takanome Market
AND SO ...
THE TWO HAD TO PAY ...
...FOR HER BEEF MONJA-YAKI.
ITO SAN

episode.8 / **END**

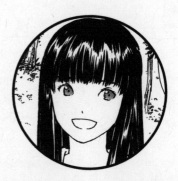

episode.9

TAKANASHI'S
SIMPLE RECIPE!

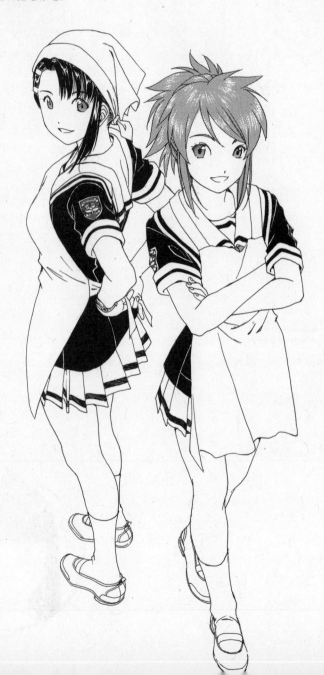

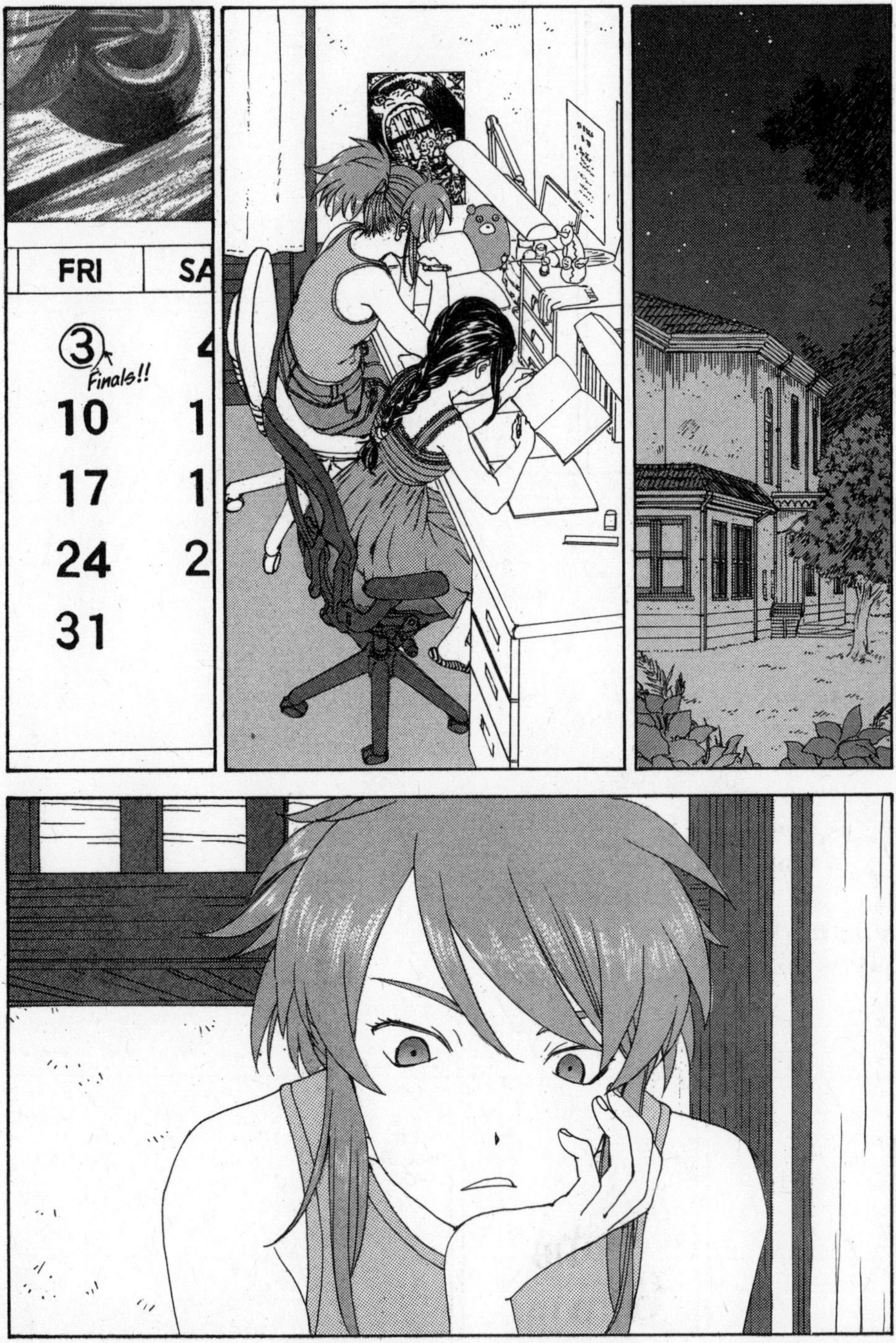
FRI SA
3 4
Finals!!
10 1
17 1
24 2
31

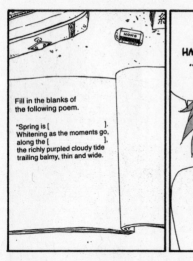

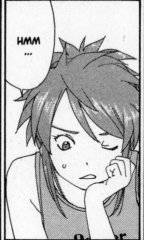

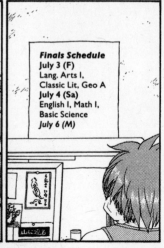

Finals Schedule
July 3 (F)
Lang. Arts I, Classic Lit, Geo A
July 4 (Sa)
English I, Math I, Basic Science
July 6 (M)
HMM ...
HONO
Fill in the blanks of the following poem.
"Spring is [ ].
Whitening as the moments go,
along the [ ],
the richly purpled cloudy tide
trailing balmy, thin and wide.
HUH? HOW DOES IT GO AGAIN?
UMM ...
UMM ...
the blanks of
following poem.
is [ ].
ning as the moments go,
along the [ ],
the richly purpled cloudy tide
trailing balmy, thin and wide.
D...
DA.
DA BOMB, YO...
AHA!
he blanks of
owing poem.
is [da bomb, yo
ng as the mom
e [
y purpled clou
balmy, thin and

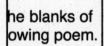

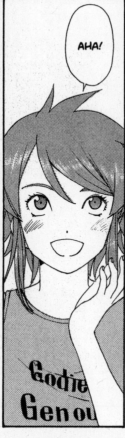

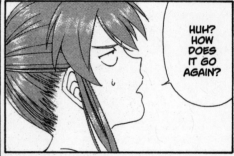

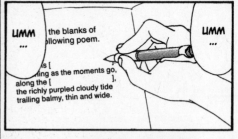

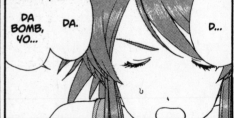

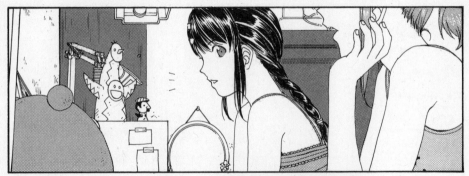

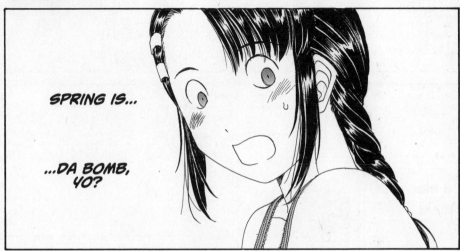

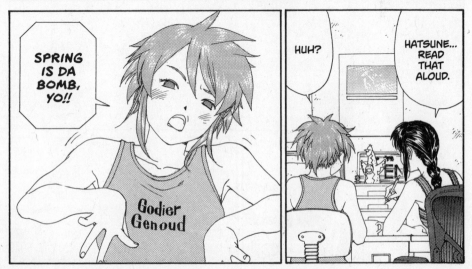

SPRING IS...
...DA BOMB, YO?
HATSUNE... READ THAT ALOUD.
HUH?
SPRING IS DA BOMB, YO!!
Godier Genoud

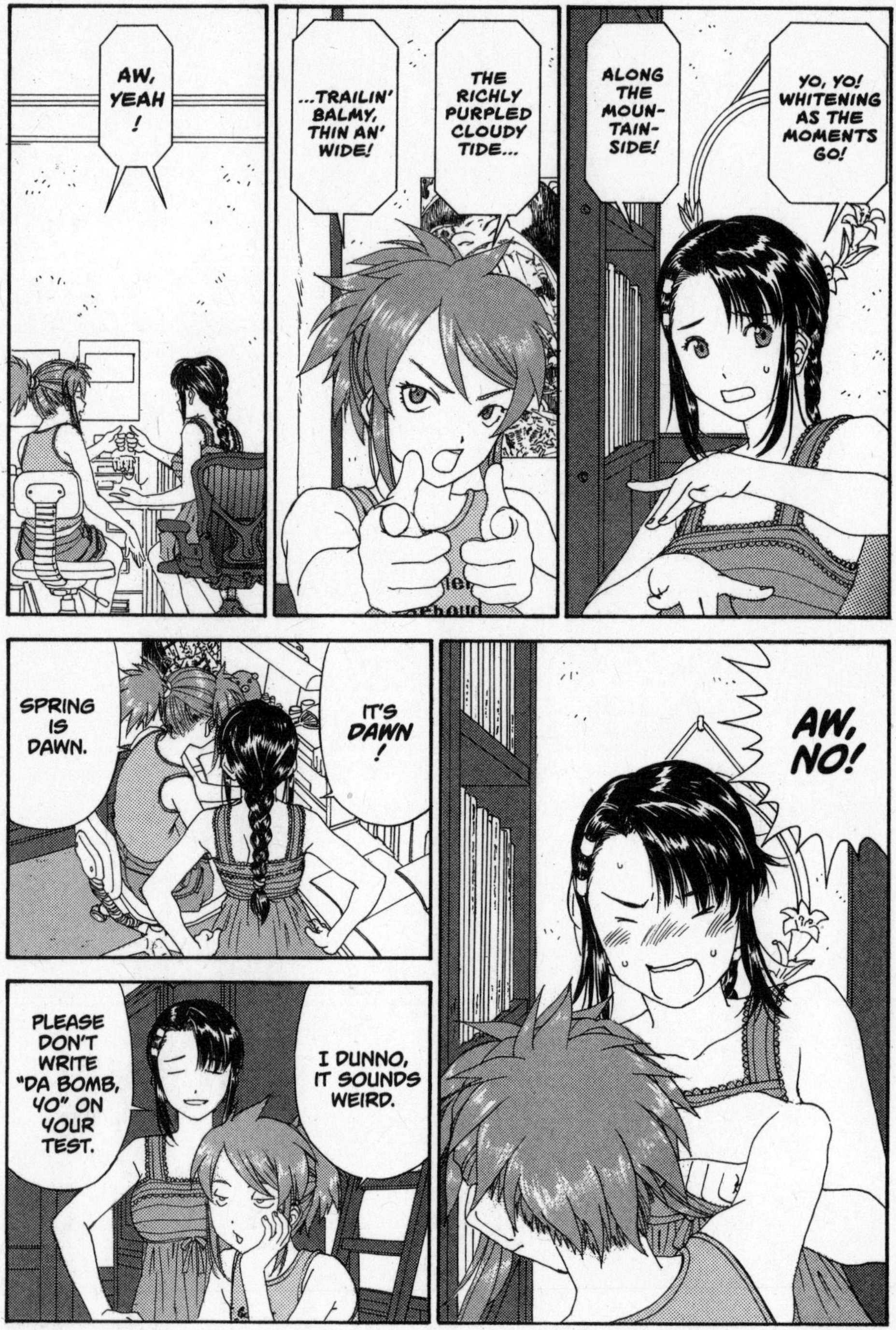
YO, YO! WHITENING AS THE MOMENTS GO!
ALONG THE MOUNTAIN-SIDE!
THE RICHLY PURPLED CLOUDY TIDE...
...TRAILIN' BALMY, THIN AN' WIDE!
AW, YEAH!
AW, NO!
IT'S DAWN!
SPRING IS DAWN.
I DUNNO, IT SOUNDS WEIRD.
PLEASE DON'T WRITE "DA BOMB, YO" ON YOUR TEST.

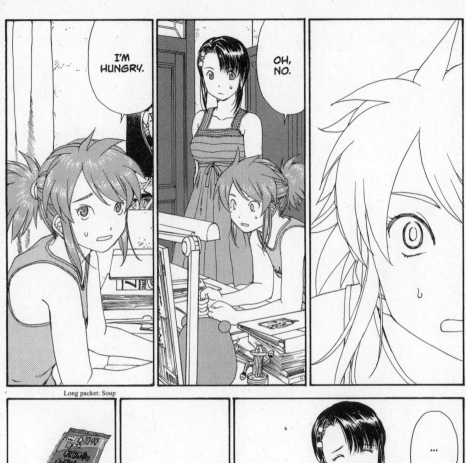

OH, NO.
I'M HUNGRY.
...
ACTUAL-LY...
...NOW THAT YOU MENTION IT...

Long packet: Soup

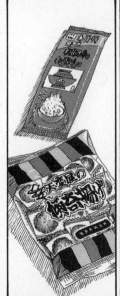

Striped package: Kabuki-age (a brand of deep-fried rice crackers)

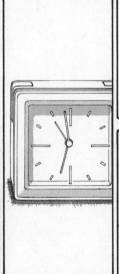

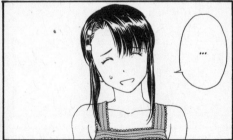

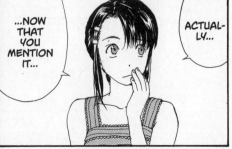

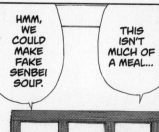

THIS ISN'T MUCH OF A MEAL...
HMM, WE COULD MAKE FAKE SENBEI SOUP.
FAKE SENBEI SOUP?
YEAH.
YOU KNOW HOW WE HAVE THAT HOT WATER POT FOR TEA?
BRING THAT HERE.
IF YOU SAY SO.
...
Packets: Soup

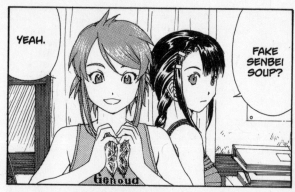

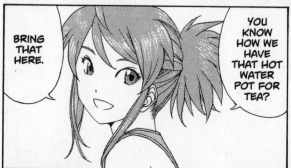

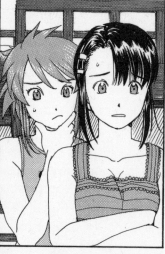

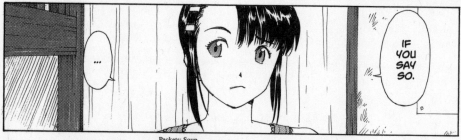

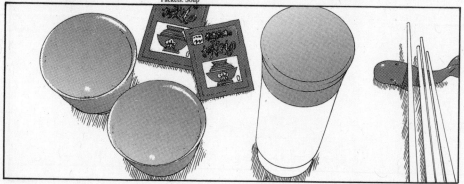

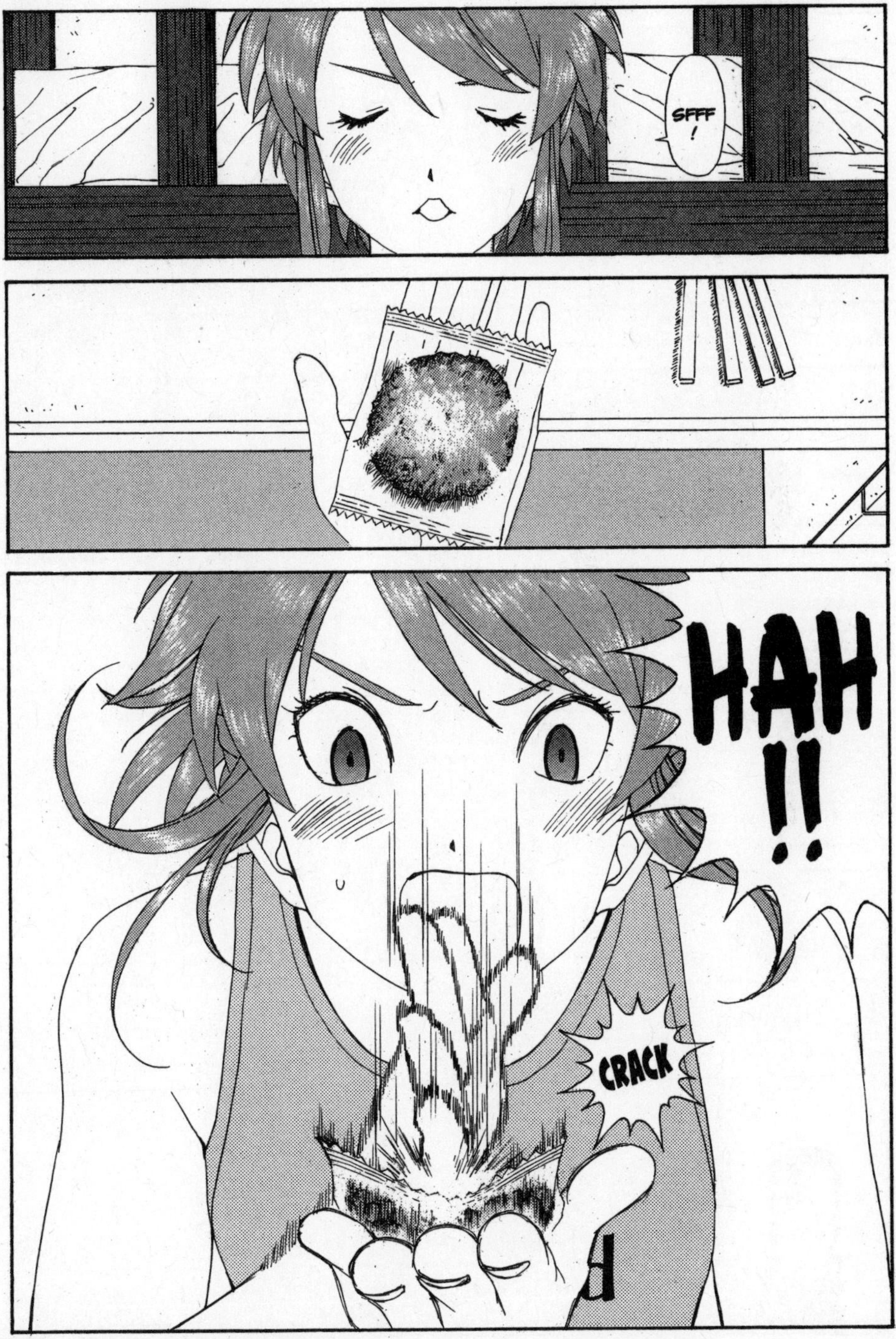
SFFF !
HAH !!
CRACK

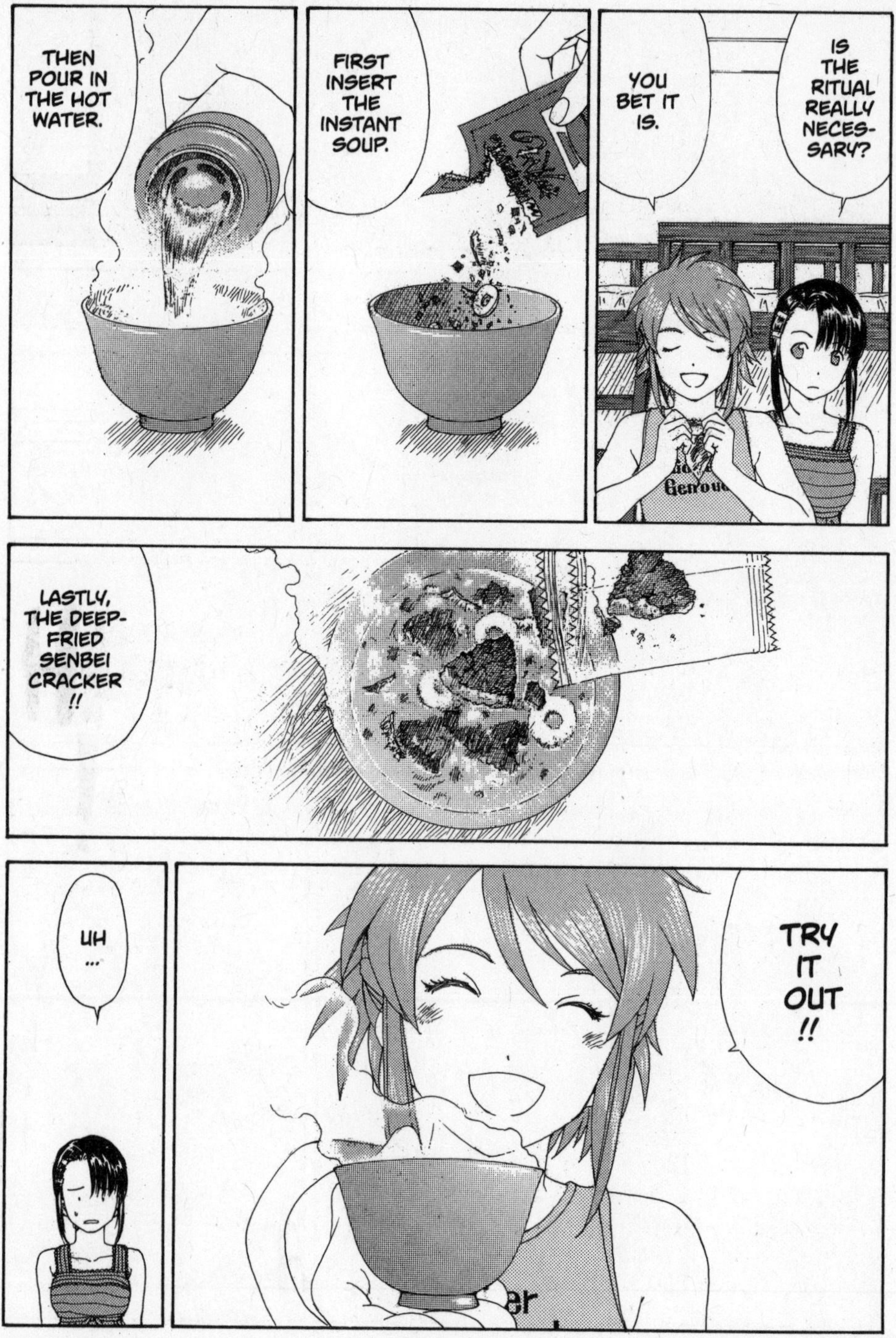
IS THE RITUAL REALLY NECES-SARY?
YOU BET IT IS.
FIRST INSERT THE INSTANT SOUP.
THEN POUR IN THE HOT WATER.
LASTLY, THE DEEP-FRIED SENBEI CRACKER !!
TRY IT OUT !!
UH ...

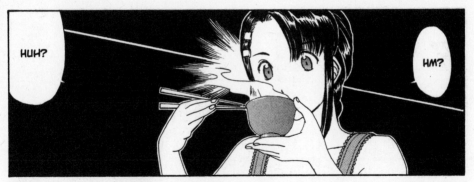

HM?
HUH?
THE CRACKER SOFTENS UP...
...AND IT BECOMES A BIT CHEWY. IT TASTES SURPRISINGLY GOOD.
AND THE OIL FROM THE SENBEI FLOATS ON THE BROTH, GIVING IT MORE BODY.
WHADDAYA THINK?!
Godier Genoud
ACTUALLY...

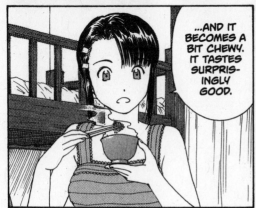

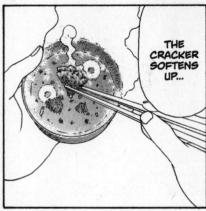

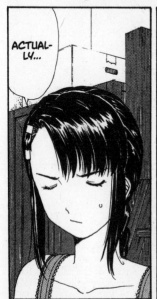

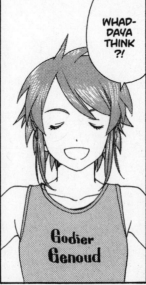

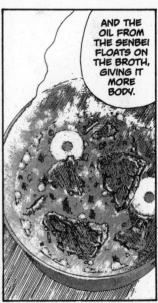

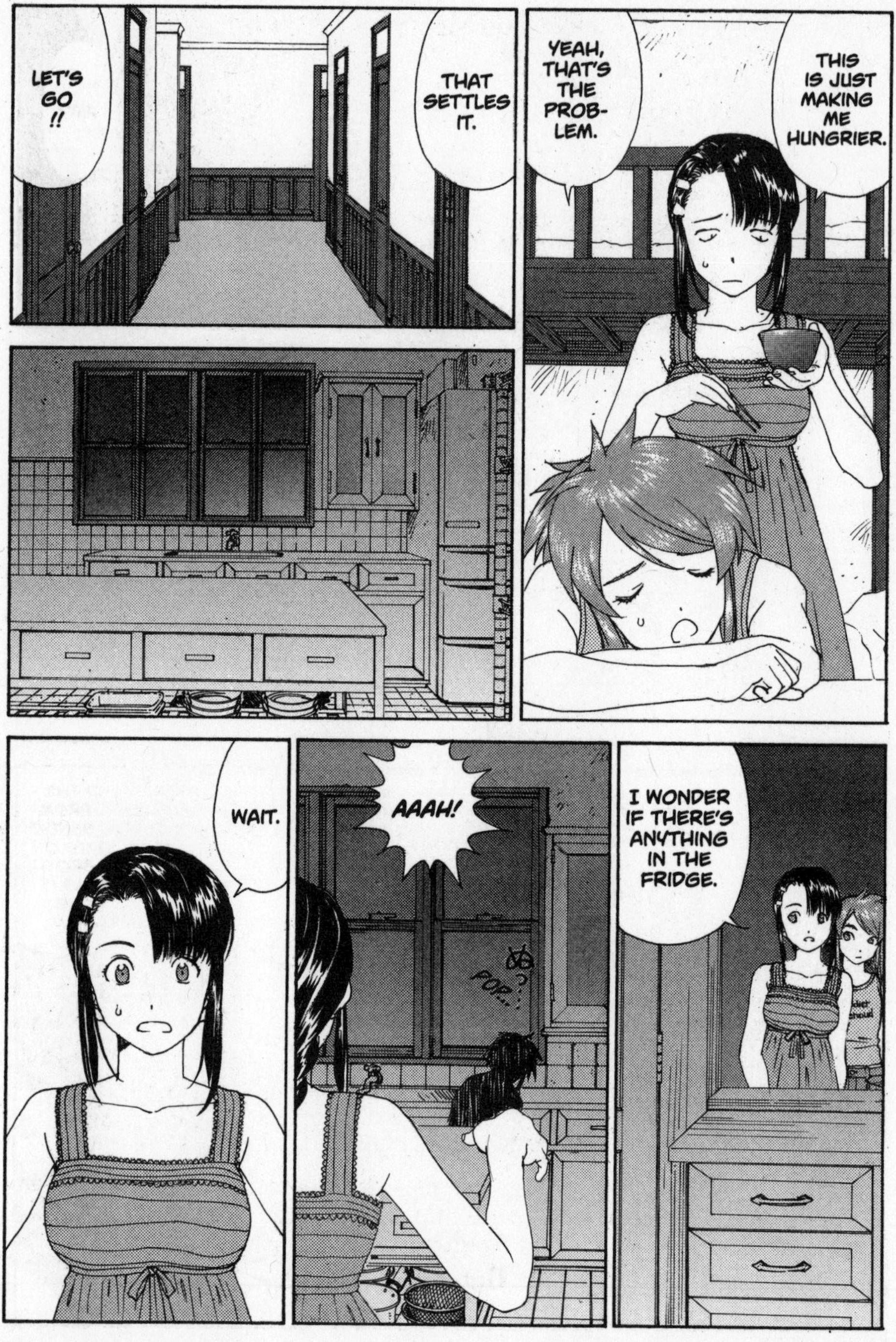
THIS IS JUST MAKING ME HUNGRIER.
YEAH, THAT'S THE PROB-LEM.
THAT SETTLES IT.
LET'S GO !!
I WONDER IF THERE'S ANYTHING IN THE FRIDGE.
AAAH!
POP...
WAIT.

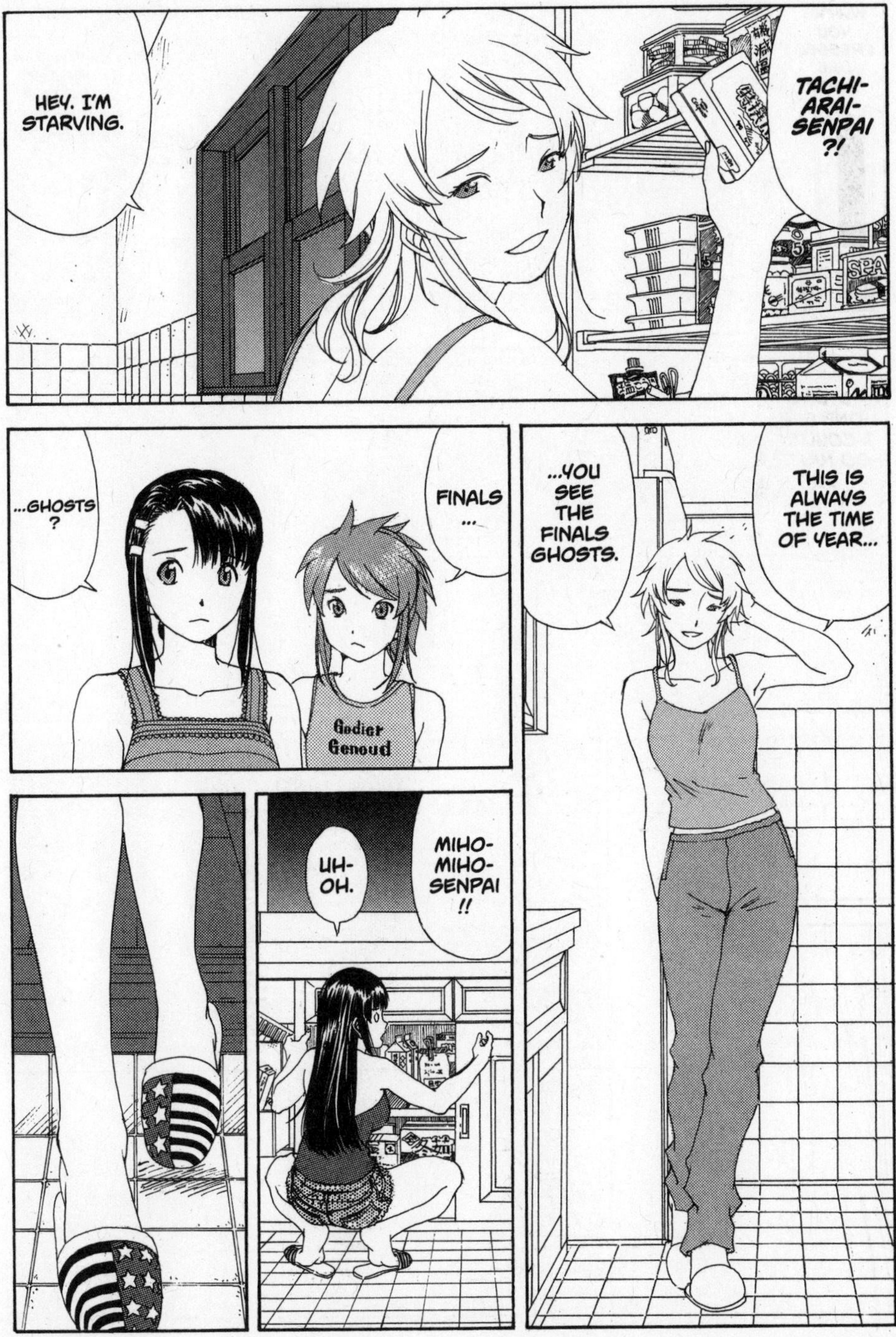
TACHI-ARAI-SENPAI?!
HEY. I'M STARVING.
THIS IS ALWAYS THE TIME OF YEAR...
...YOU SEE THE FINALS GHOSTS.
FINALS...
...GHOSTS?
MIHO-MIHO-SENPAI!!
UH-OH.
Godier Genoud

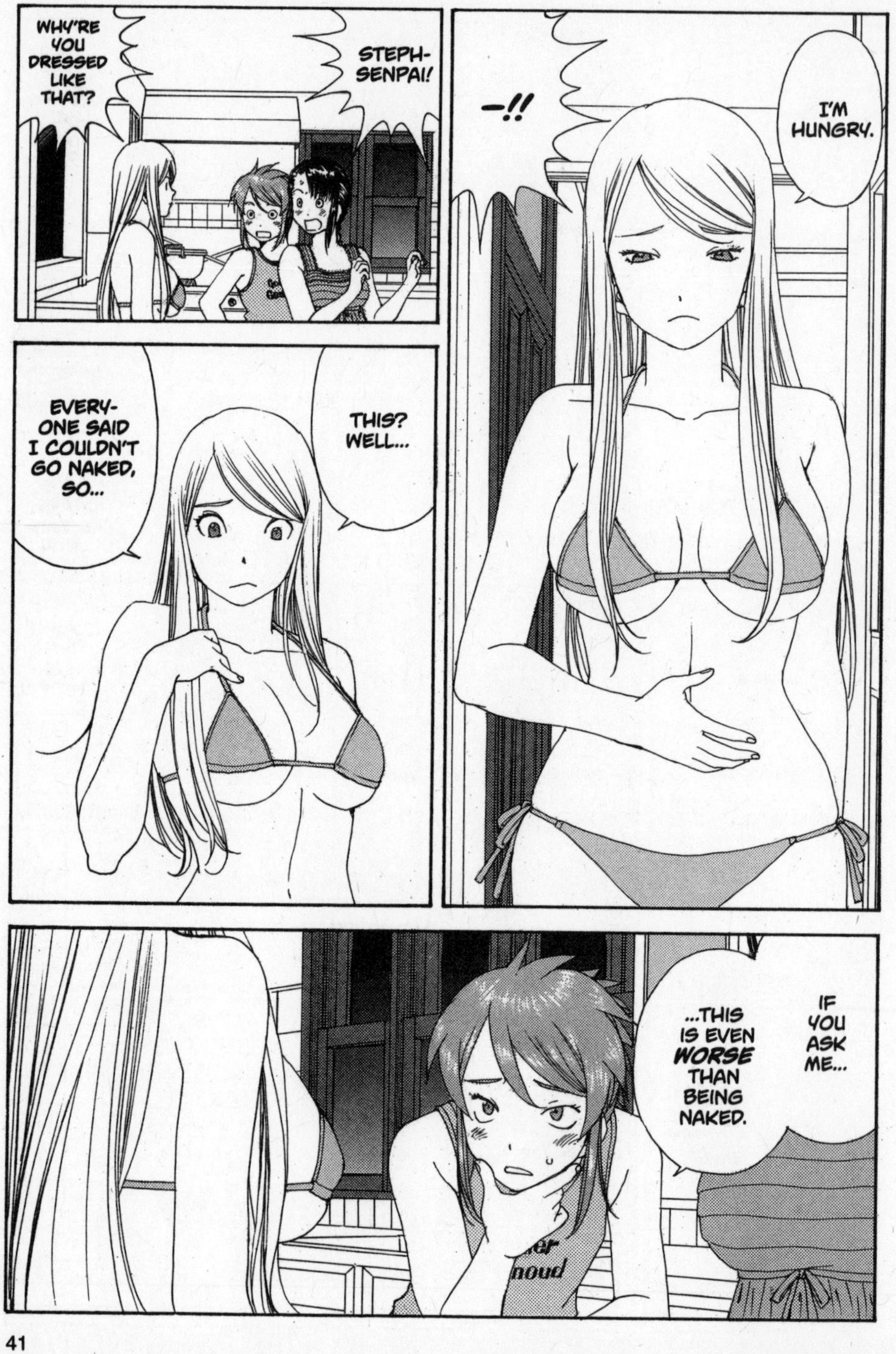
I'M HUNGRY.
—!!
STEPH-SENPAI!
WHY'RE YOU DRESSED LIKE THAT?
THIS? WELL...
EVERY-ONE SAID I COULDN'T GO NAKED, SO...
IF YOU ASK ME...
...THIS IS EVEN *WORSE* THAN BEING NAKED.

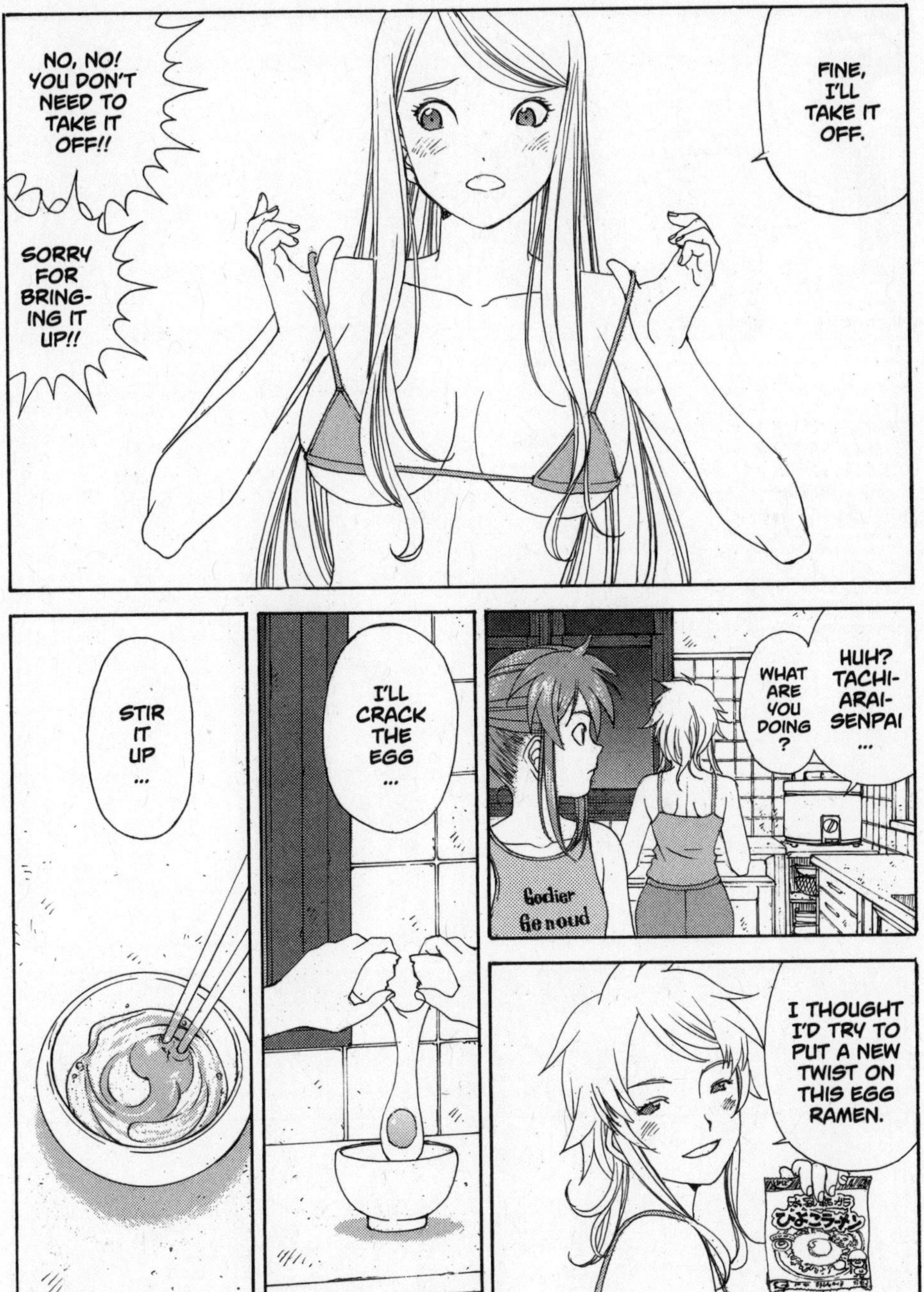
FINE, I'LL TAKE IT OFF.
NO, NO! YOU DON'T NEED TO TAKE IT OFF!!
SORRY FOR BRINGING IT UP!!
HUH? TACHIARAI-SENPAI...
WHAT ARE YOU DOING?
Godier Genoud
I THOUGHT I'D TRY TO PUT A NEW TWIST ON THIS EGG RAMEN.
ひよこラーメン
I'LL CRACK THE EGG...
STIR IT UP...

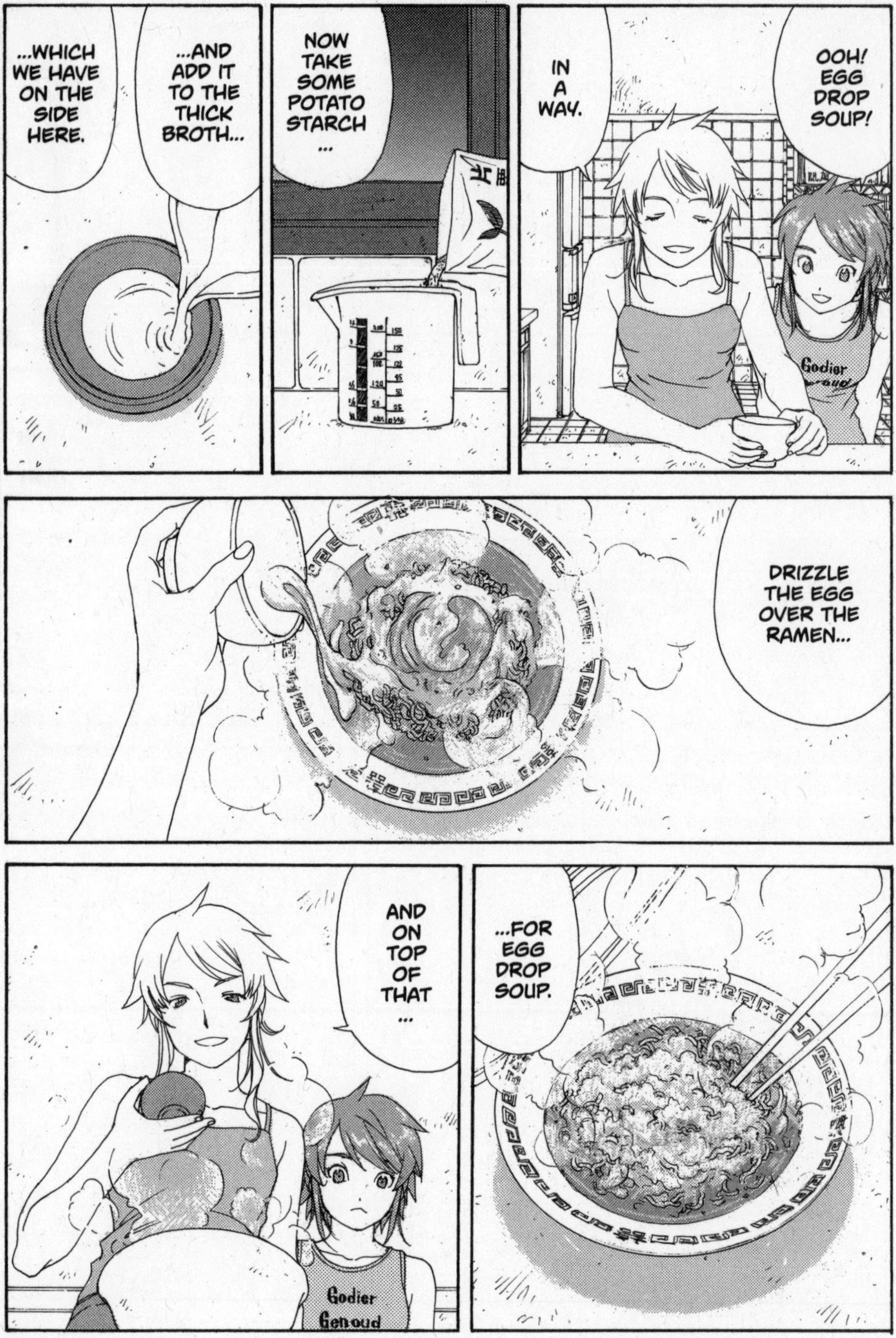
OOH! EGG DROP SOUP!
IN A WAY.
Godier
NOW TAKE SOME POTATO STARCH ...
...AND ADD IT TO THE THICK BROTH...
...WHICH WE HAVE ON THE SIDE HERE.
DRIZZLE THE EGG OVER THE RAMEN...
...FOR EGG DROP SOUP.
AND ON TOP OF THAT ...
Godier Genoud

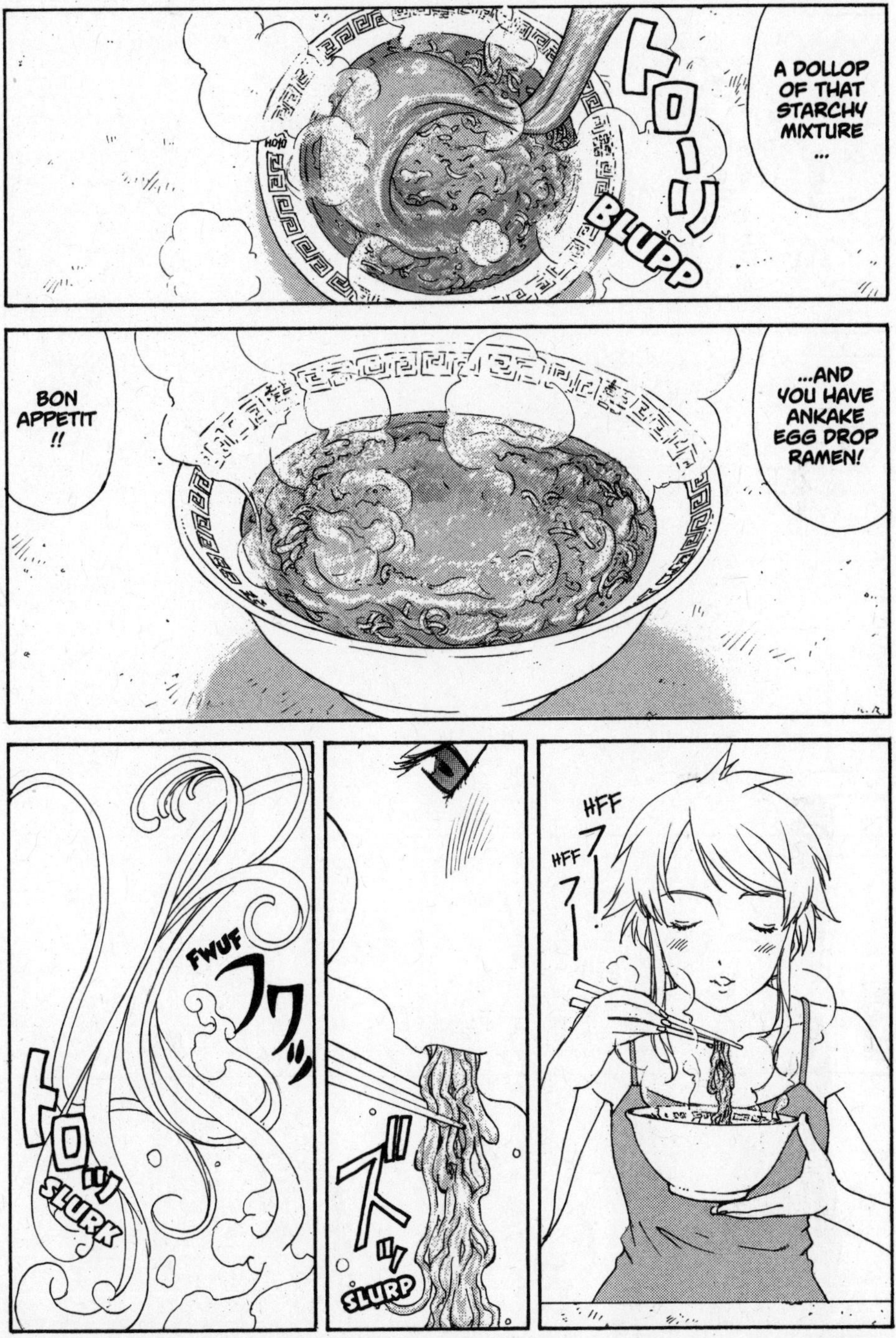

A DOLLOP OF THAT STARCHY MIXTURE ...
トローリ
BLUPP
...AND YOU HAVE ANKAKE EGG DROP RAMEN!
BON APPETIT !!
HFF
フー
HFF
フー
ズッ
SLURP
FWUF
フワッ
トロッ
SLURK

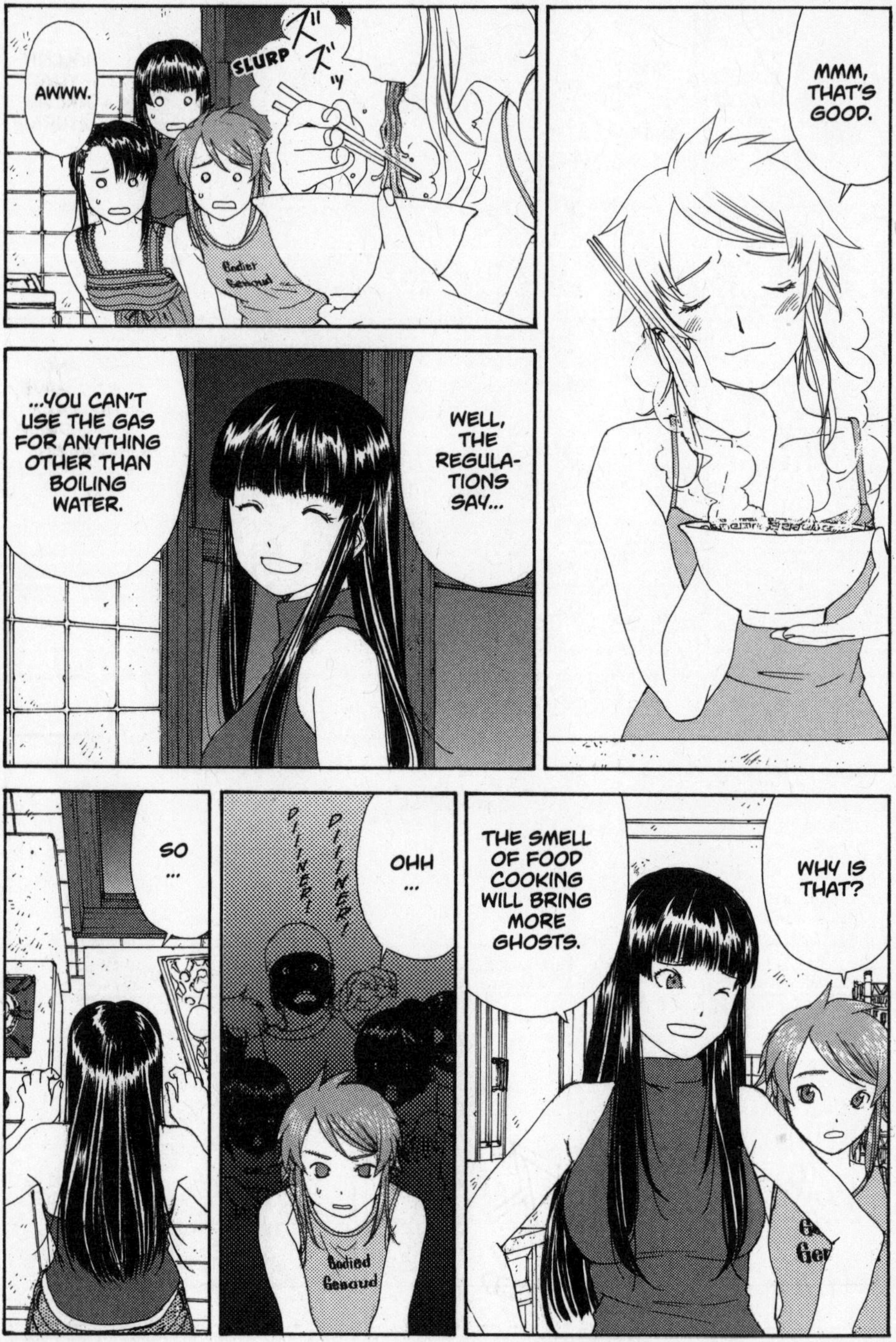
MMM, THAT'S GOOD.
SLURP
ズズッ
AWWW.
WELL, THE REGULA-TIONS SAY...
...YOU CAN'T USE THE GAS FOR ANYTHING OTHER THAN BOILING WATER.
WHY IS THAT?
THE SMELL OF FOOD COOKING WILL BRING MORE GHOSTS.
OHH ...
DIIINER!
DIIINER!
SO ...

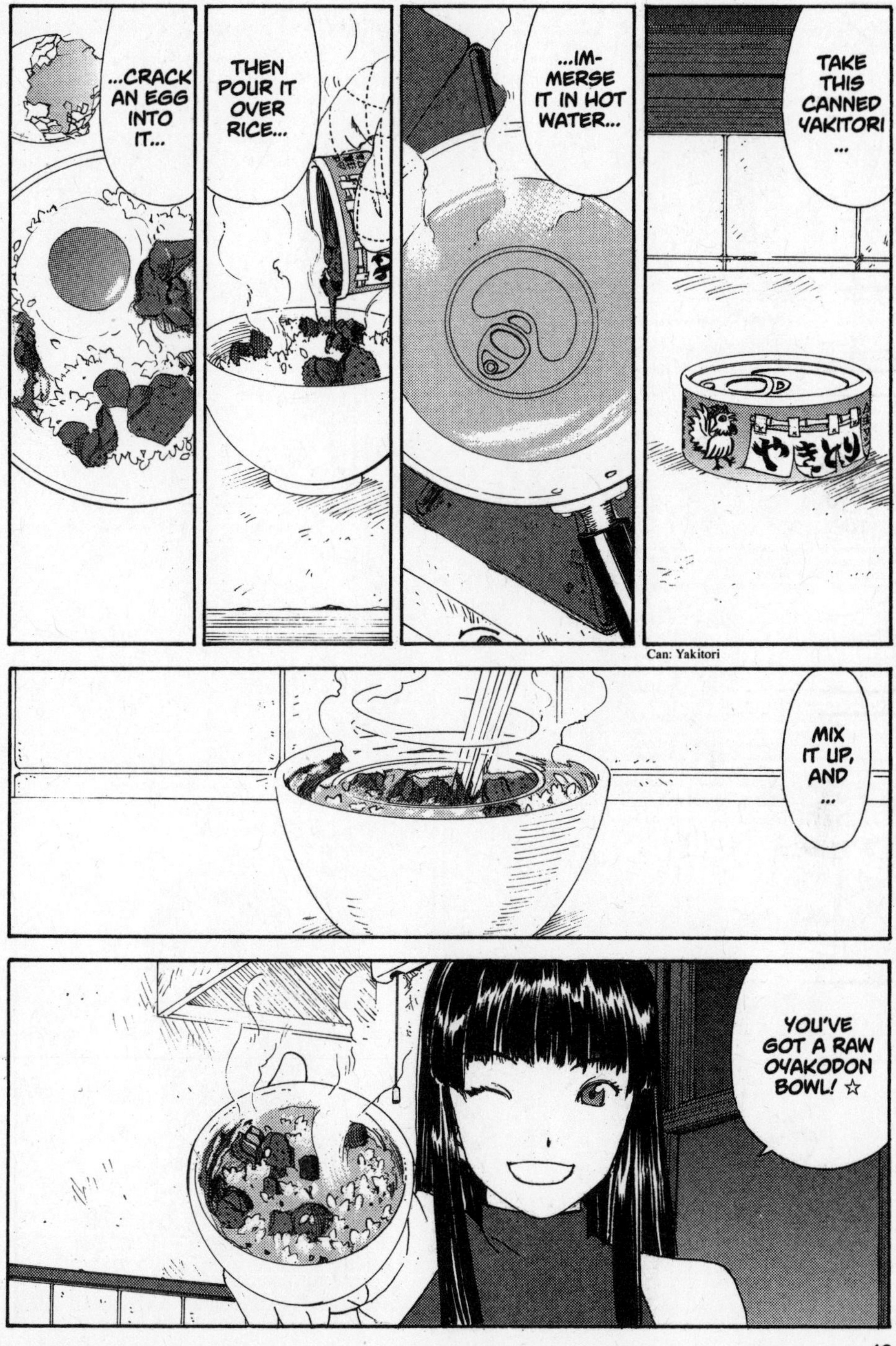
TAKE THIS CANNED YAKITORI ...
やきとり
...IM-MERSE IT IN HOT WATER...
THEN POUR IT OVER RICE...
...CRACK AN EGG INTO IT...
MIX IT UP, AND ...
YOU'VE GOT A RAW OYAKODON BOWL! ☆

Can: Yakitori

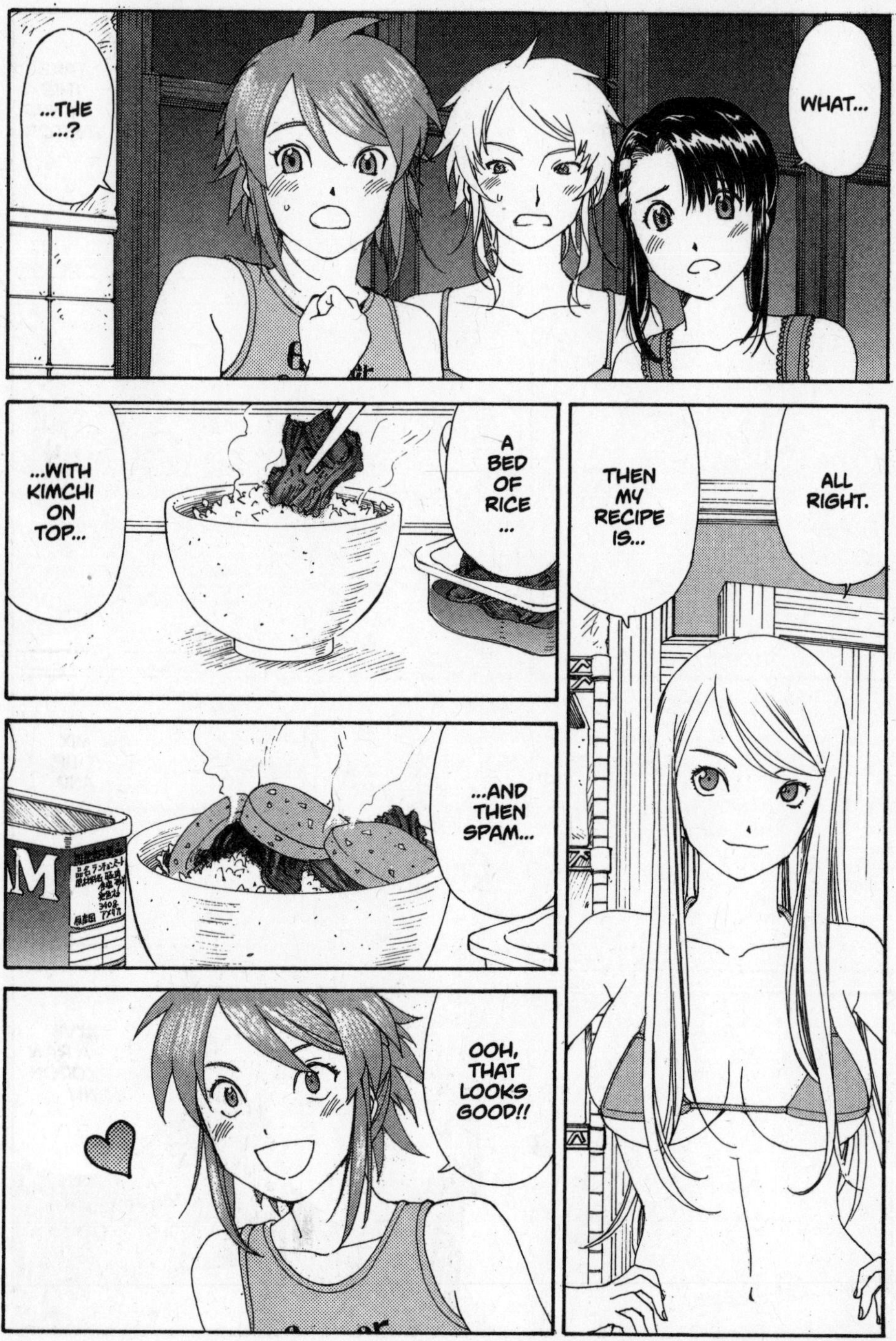
WHAT...
...THE ...?
ALL RIGHT.
THEN MY RECIPE IS...
A BED OF RICE ...
...WITH KIMCHI ON TOP...
...AND THEN SPAM...
OOH, THAT LOOKS GOOD!!

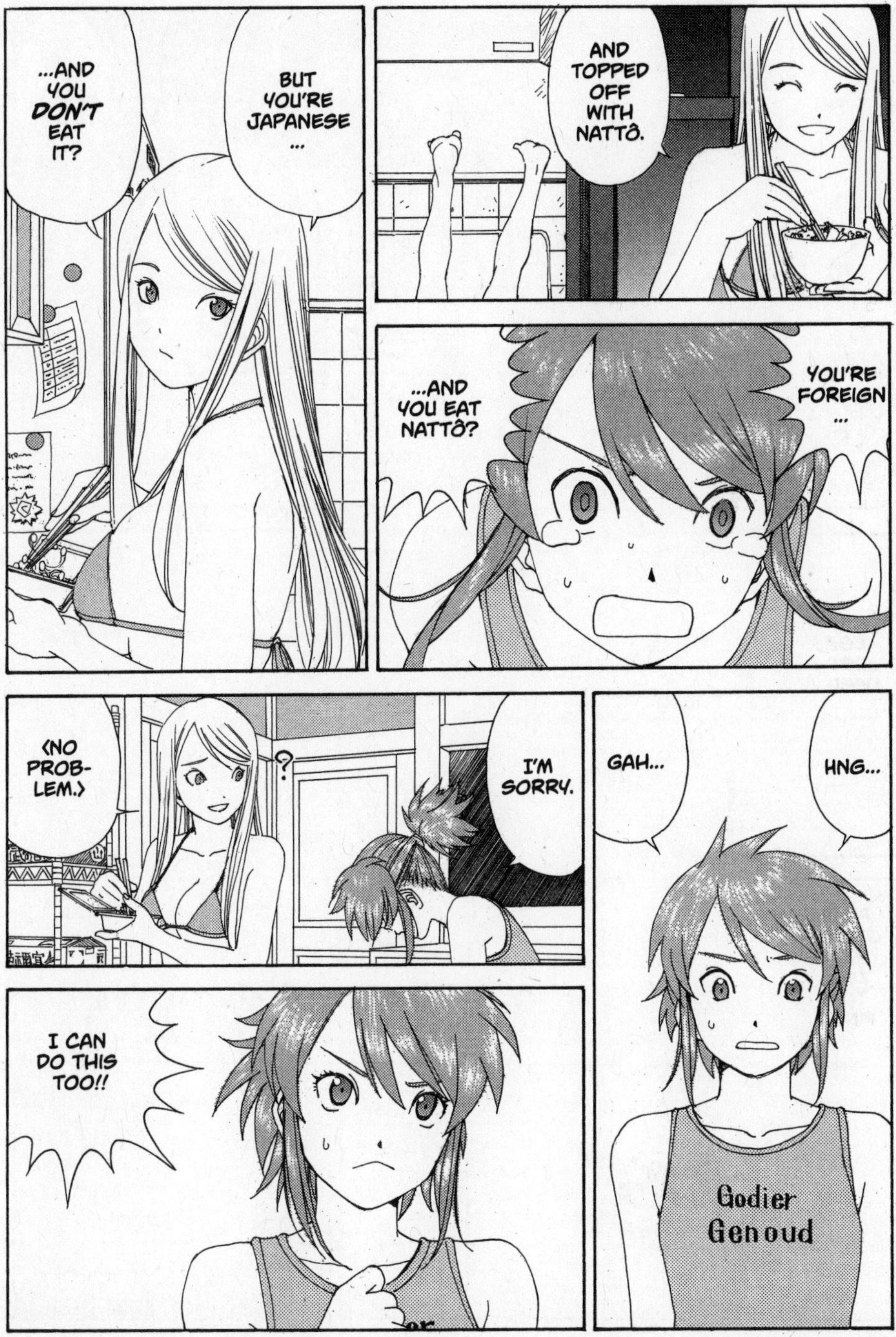
AND TOPPED OFF WITH NATTŌ.
YOU'RE FOREIGN ...
...AND YOU EAT NATTŌ?
BUT YOU'RE JAPANESE ...
...AND YOU **DON'T** EAT IT?
HNG...
GAH...
Godier Genoud
I'M SORRY.
?
‹NO PROB-LEM.›
I CAN DO THIS TOO!!

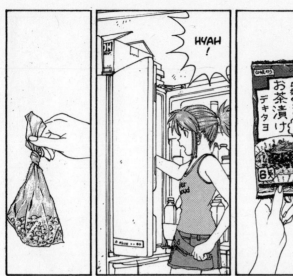

HYAH!
白娘のりの のり お茶漬け デキタヨ
HYAH !
ALL THAT'S LEFT IS RICE.
THE EGGS... JUST GOT USED UP...
SO THAT'S MY ONLY CHOICE.
POUR ON THE OCHA-ZUKE TOP-PING...

Packet: Nori (dried seaweed) Ochazuke

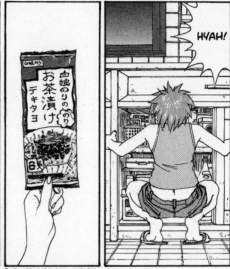

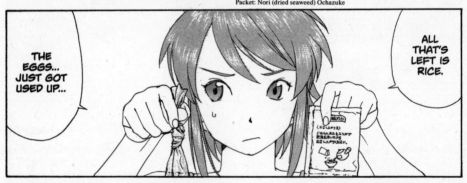

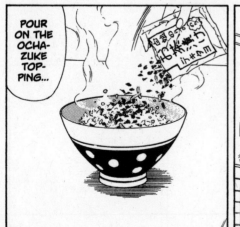

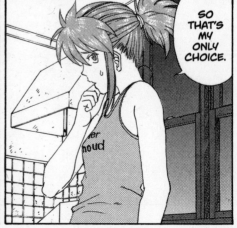

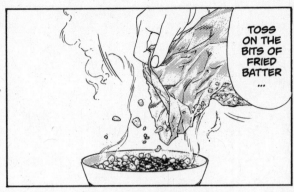

THEN ADD HOT WATER ...
TOSS ON THE BITS OF FRIED BATTER ...
...AND A DAB OF WASABI.
IT'S BEYOND SIMPLE!
TANUKI TEMPURA OCHA-ZUKE!!

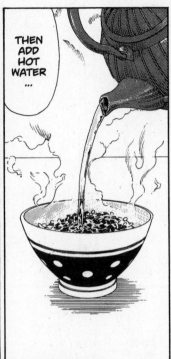

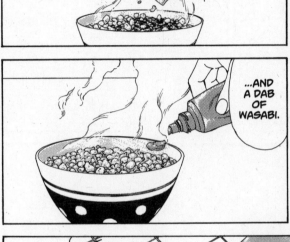

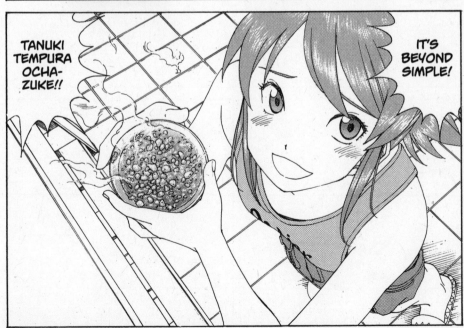

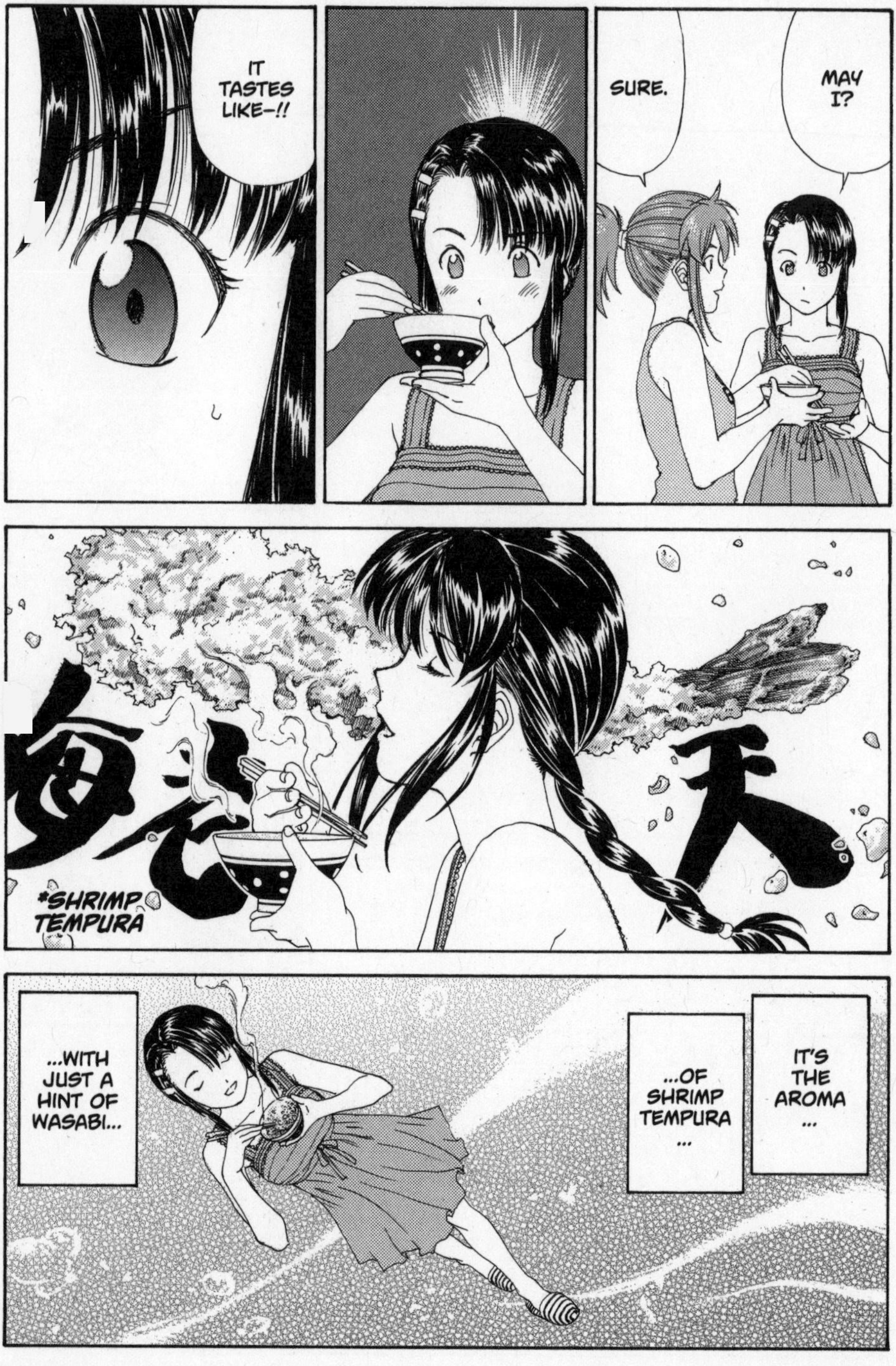
MAY I?
SURE.
IT TASTES LIKE–!!
*SHRIMP TEMPURA
IT'S THE AROMA ...
...OF SHRIMP TEMPURA ...
...WITH JUST A HINT OF WASABI...

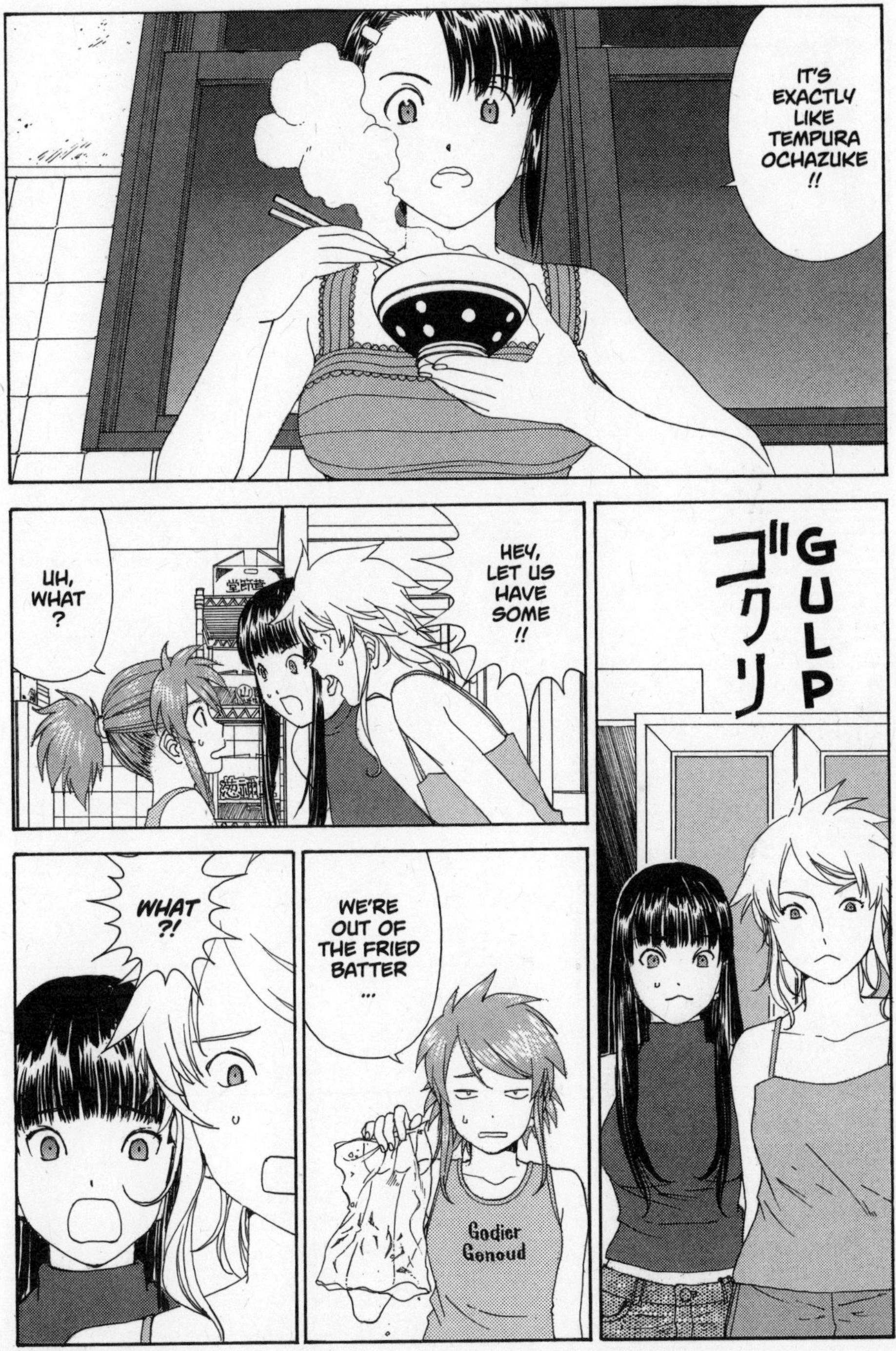
IT'S EXACTLY LIKE TEMPURA OCHAZUKE !!
ゴクリ
GULP
HEY, LET US HAVE SOME !!
UH, WHAT ?
WE'RE OUT OF THE FRIED BATTER ...
Godier Genoud
WHAT ?!

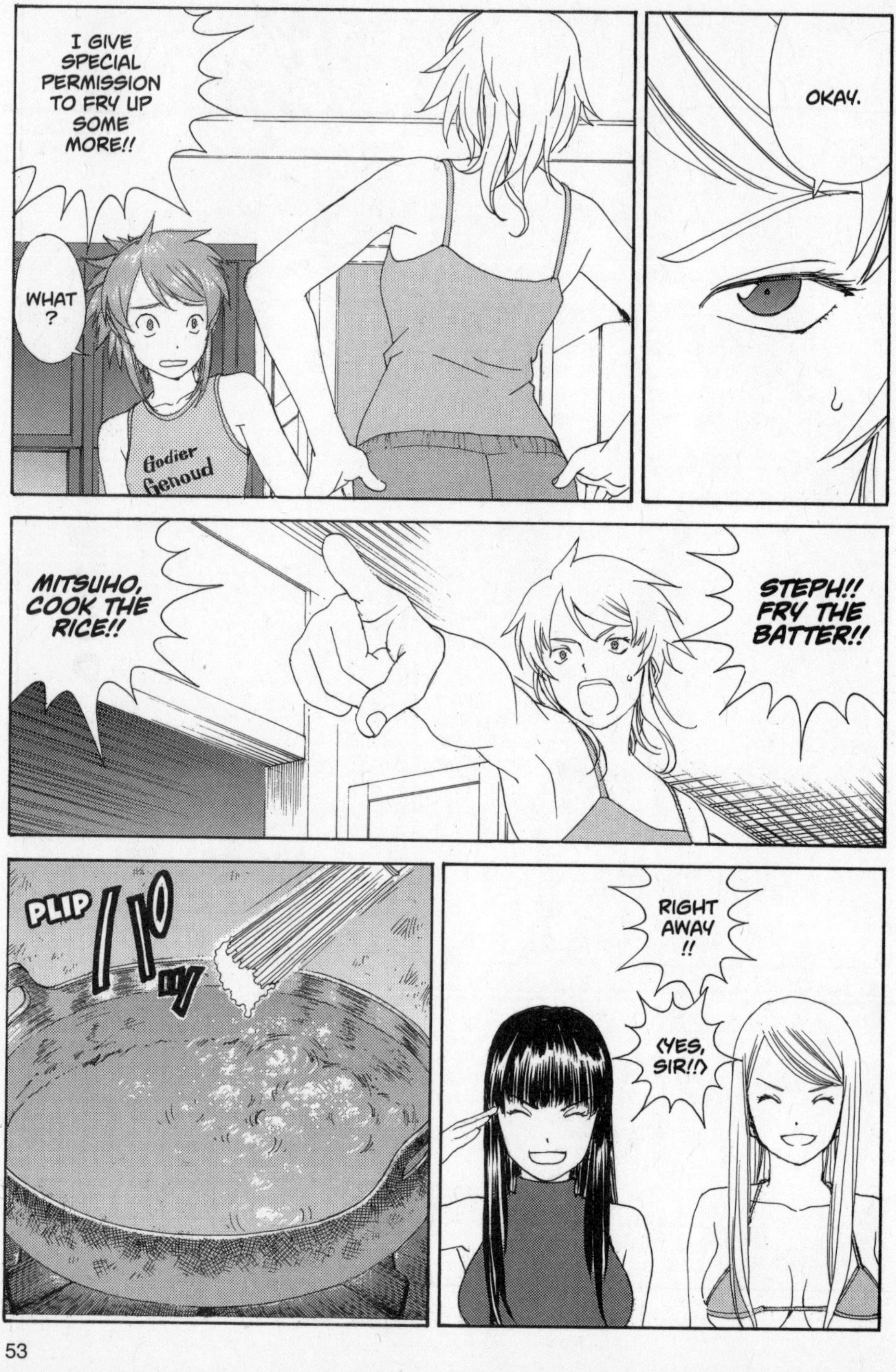
OKAY.
I GIVE SPECIAL PERMISSION TO FRY UP SOME MORE!!
WHAT?
Godier Genoud
STEPH!! FRY THE BATTER!!
MITSUHO, COOK THE RICE!!
RIGHT AWAY!!
‹YES, SIR!!›
PLIP

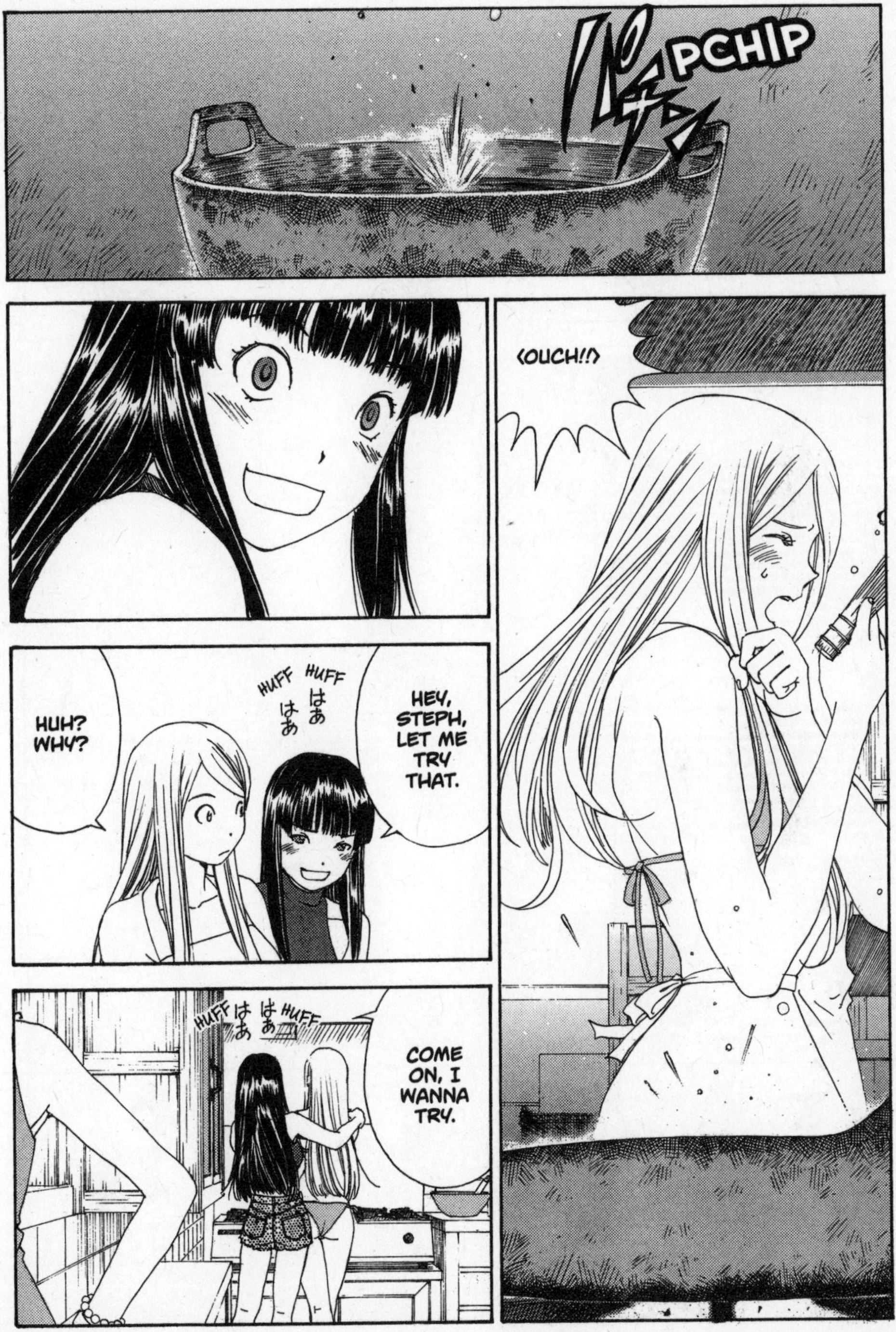
パチッ
PCHIP
‹OUCH!!›
HEY, STEPH, LET ME TRY THAT.
HUFF はあ HUFF はあ
HUH? WHY?
COME ON, I WANNA TRY.
HUFF はあ はあ HUFF

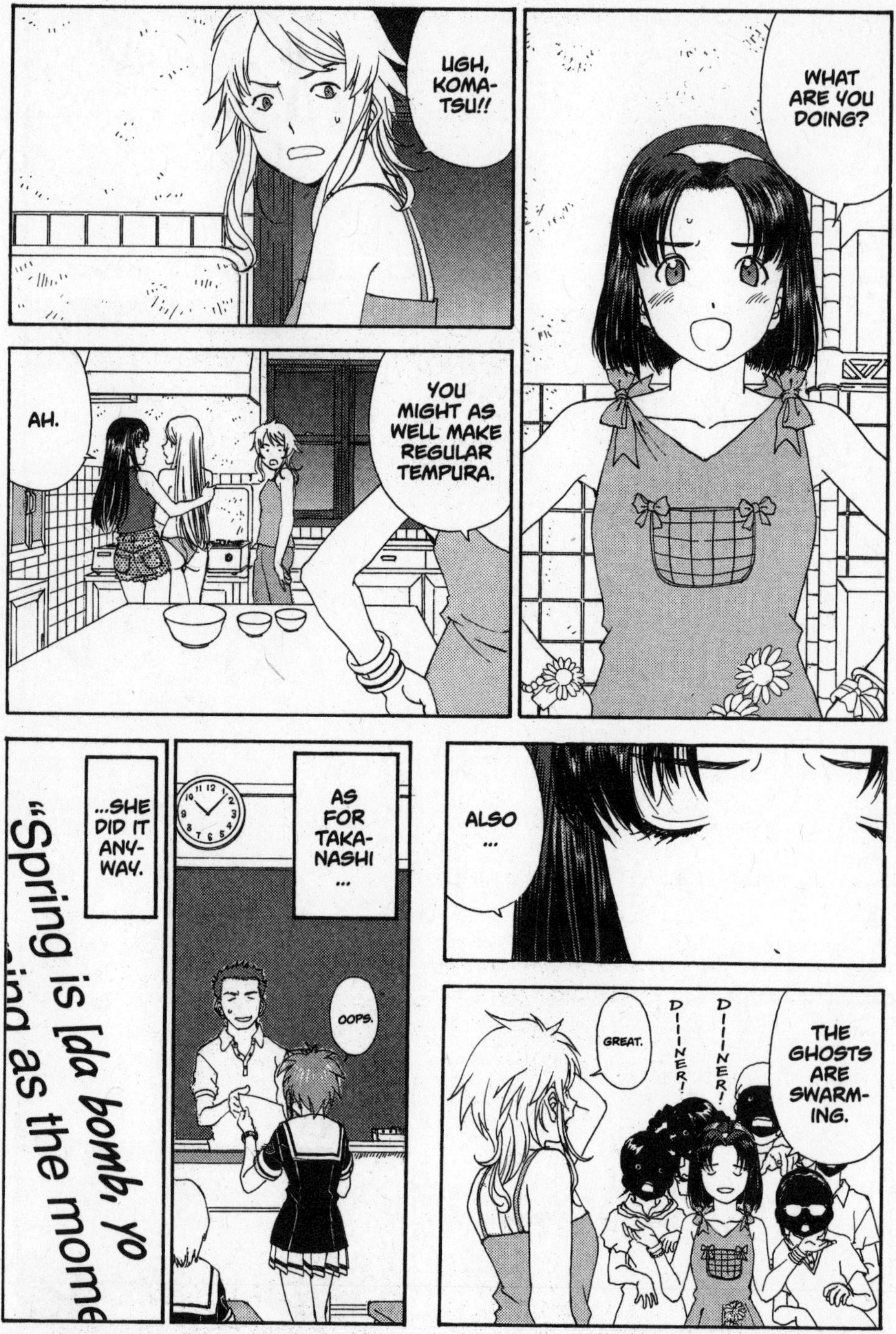
WHAT ARE YOU DOING?
UGH, KOMATSU!!
YOU MIGHT AS WELL MAKE REGULAR TEMPURA.
AH.
ALSO ...
THE GHOSTS ARE SWARMING.
DIIINER!
DIIINER!
GREAT.
AS FOR TAKANASHI ...
OOPS.
...SHE DID IT ANYWAY.
“Spring is [da bomb, yo

episode.9 / END

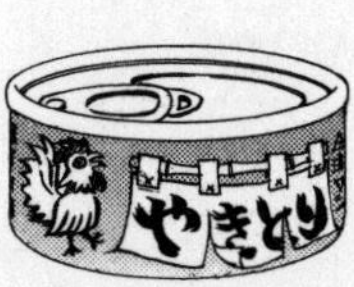
やきとり

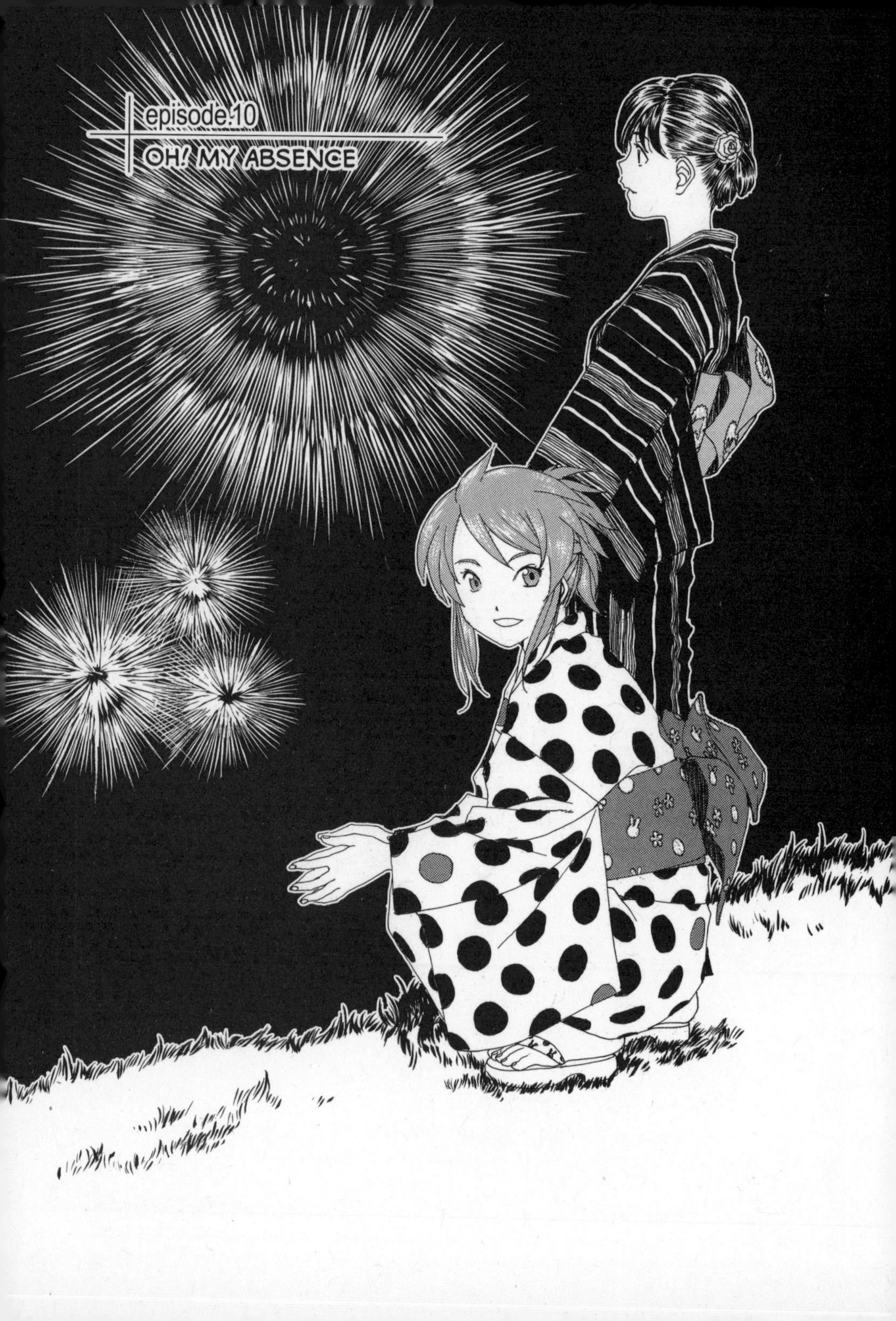
episode.10
OH! MY ABSENCE

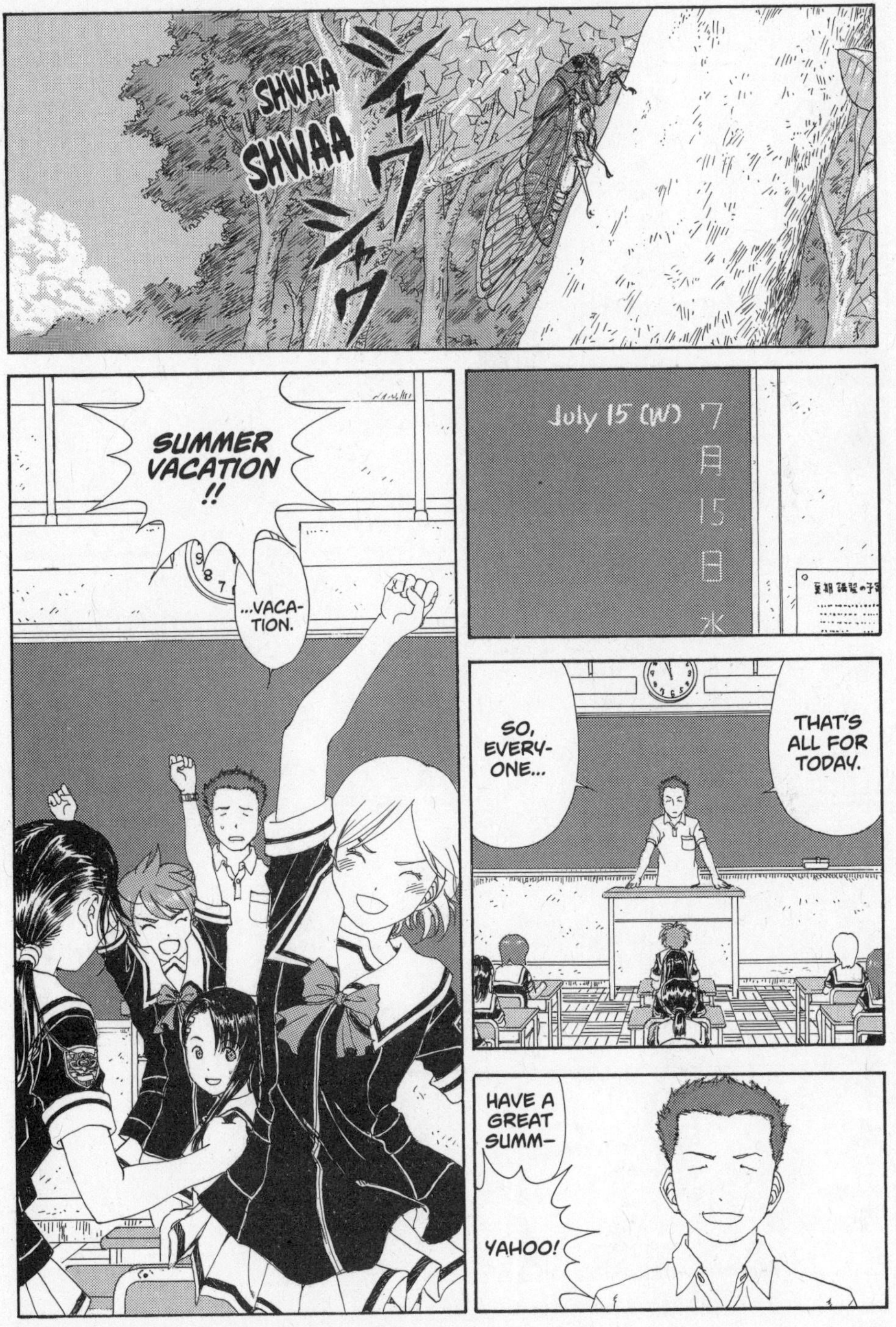
SHWAA SHWAA
July 15 (W)
7月15日水
THAT'S ALL FOR TODAY.
SO, EVERY-ONE...
HAVE A GREAT SUMM—
YAHOO!
SUMMER VACATION !!
...VACA-TION.

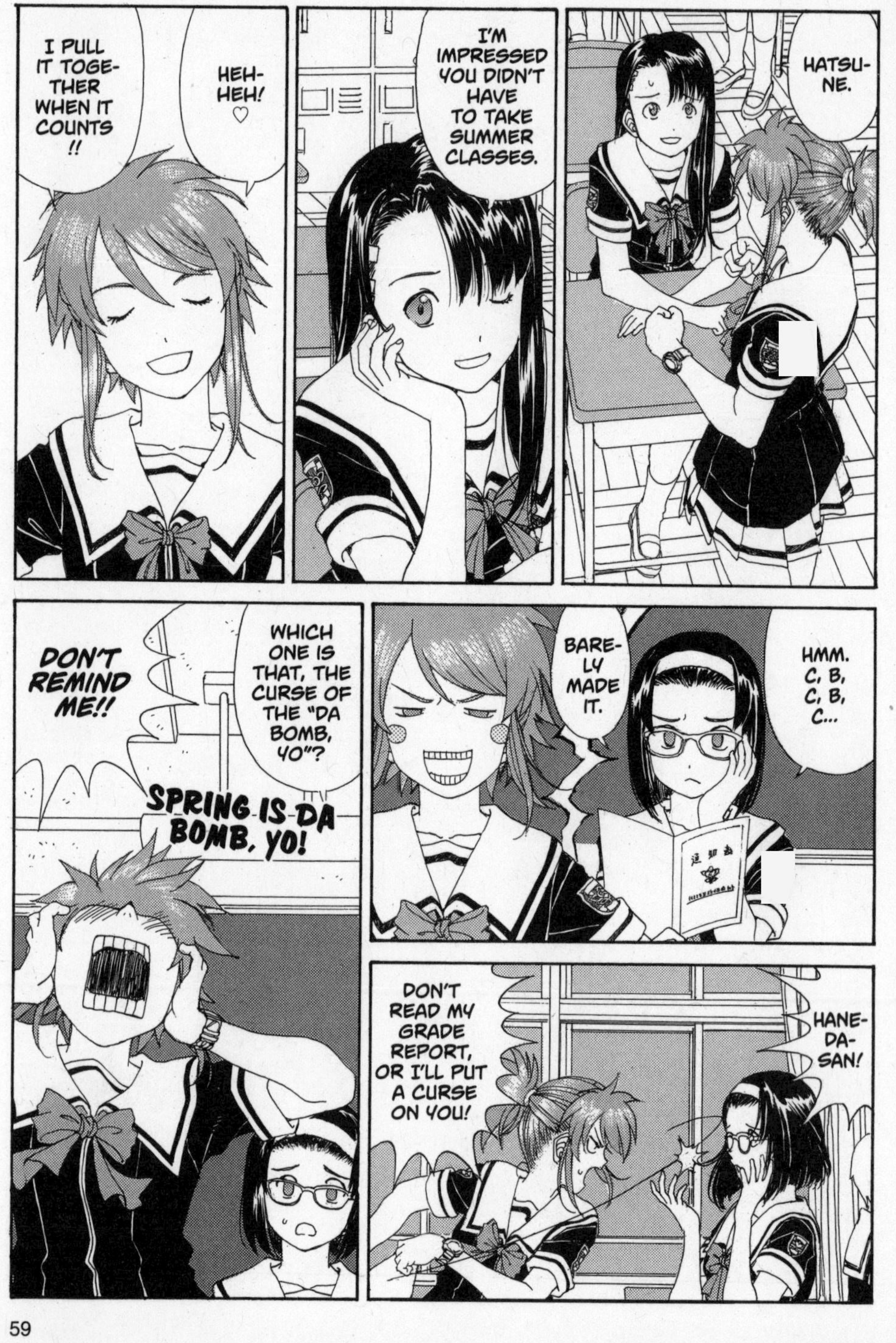
HATSU-NE.
I'M IMPRESSED YOU DIDN'T HAVE TO TAKE SUMMER CLASSES.
HEH-HEH! ♡
I PULL IT TOGE-THER WHEN IT COUNTS !!
HMM. C, B, C, B, C...
BARE-LY MADE IT.
HANE-DA-SAN!
DON'T READ MY GRADE REPORT, OR I'LL PUT A CURSE ON YOU!
WHICH ONE IS THAT, THE CURSE OF THE "DA BOMB, YO"?
DON'T REMIND ME!!
SPRING IS DA BOMB, YO!

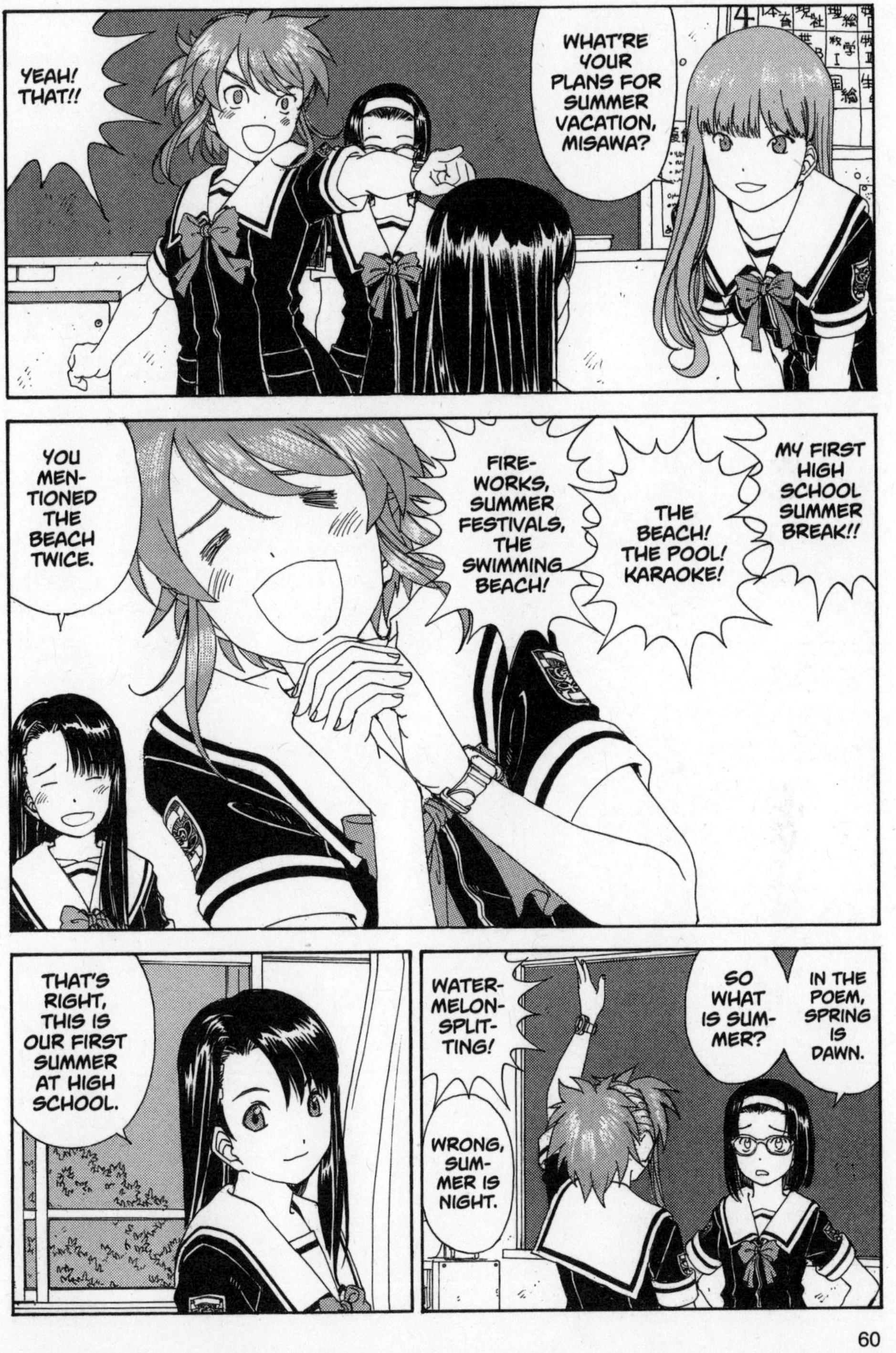
WHAT'RE YOUR PLANS FOR SUMMER VACATION, MISAWA?
YEAH! THAT!!
MY FIRST HIGH SCHOOL SUMMER BREAK!!
THE BEACH! THE POOL! KARAOKE!
FIRE-WORKS, SUMMER FESTIVALS, THE SWIMMING BEACH!
YOU MEN-TIONED THE BEACH TWICE.
IN THE POEM, SPRING IS DAWN.
SO WHAT IS SUM-MER?
WATER-MELON-SPLIT-TING!
WRONG, SUM-MER IS NIGHT.
THAT'S RIGHT, THIS IS OUR FIRST SUMMER AT HIGH SCHOOL.

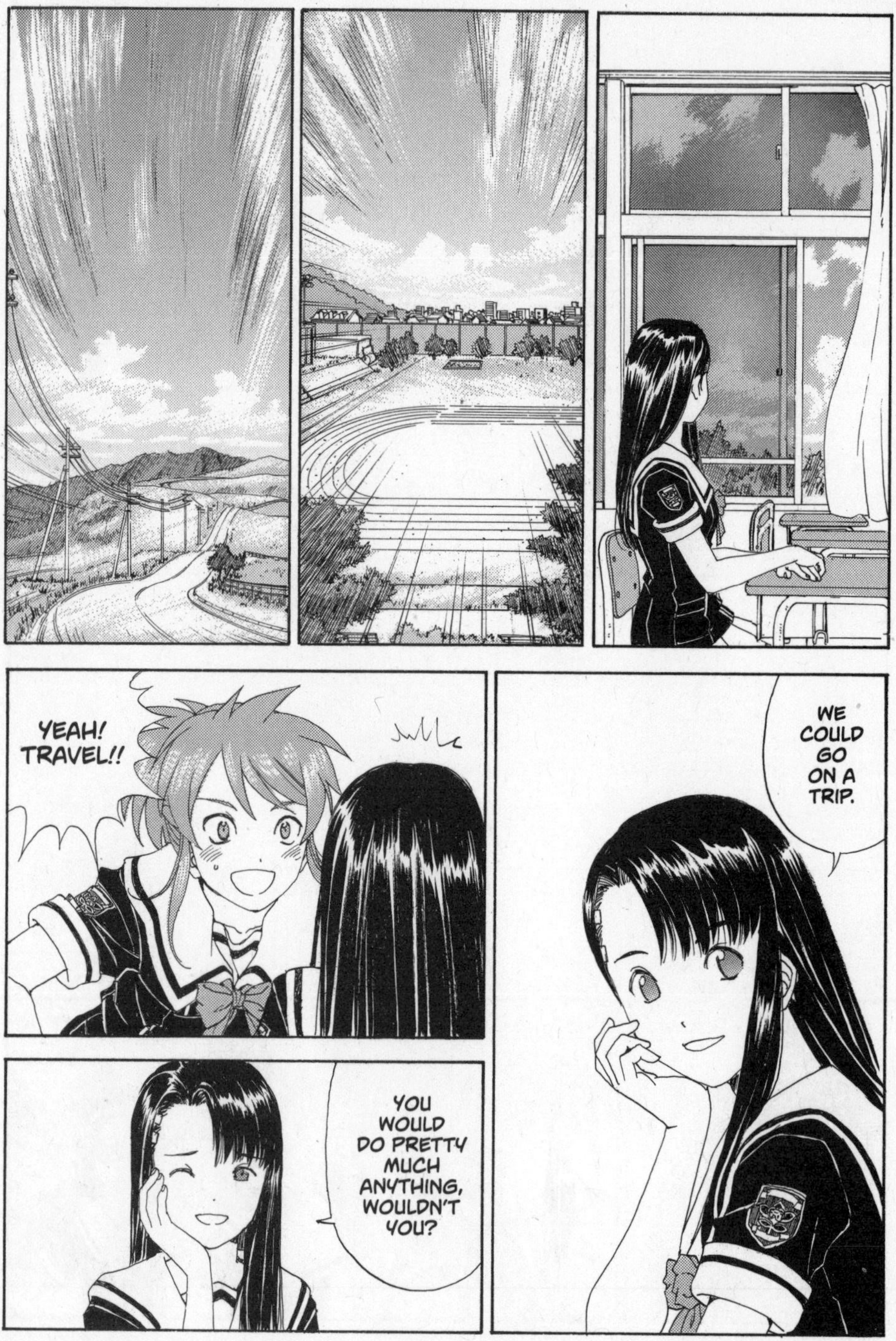
WE COULD GO ON A TRIP.
YEAH! TRAVEL!!
YOU WOULD DO PRETTY MUCH ANYTHING, WOULDN'T YOU?

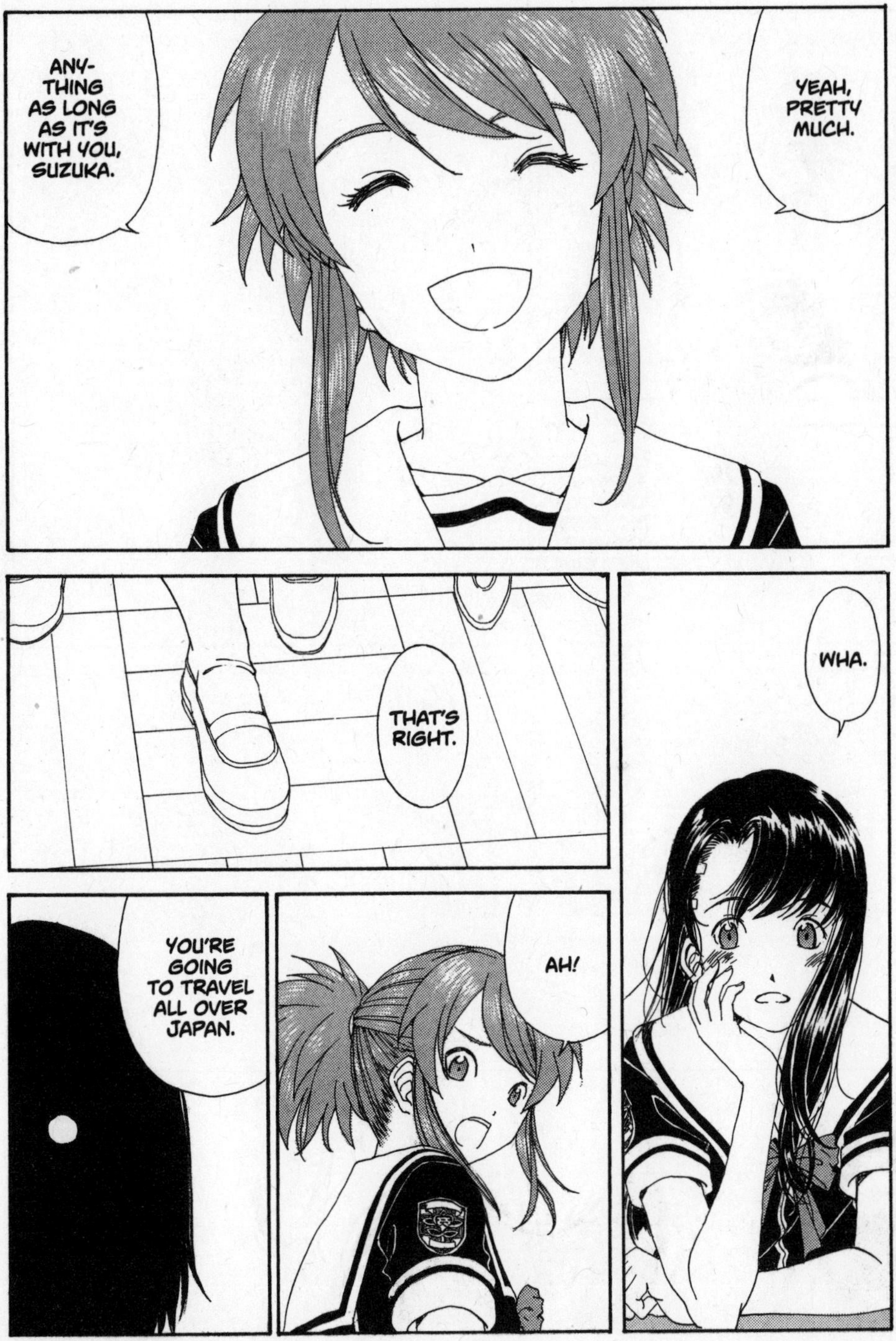
YEAH, PRETTY MUCH.
ANY-THING AS LONG AS IT'S WITH YOU, SUZUKA.
WHA.
THAT'S RIGHT.
AH!
YOU'RE GOING TO TRAVEL ALL OVER JAPAN.

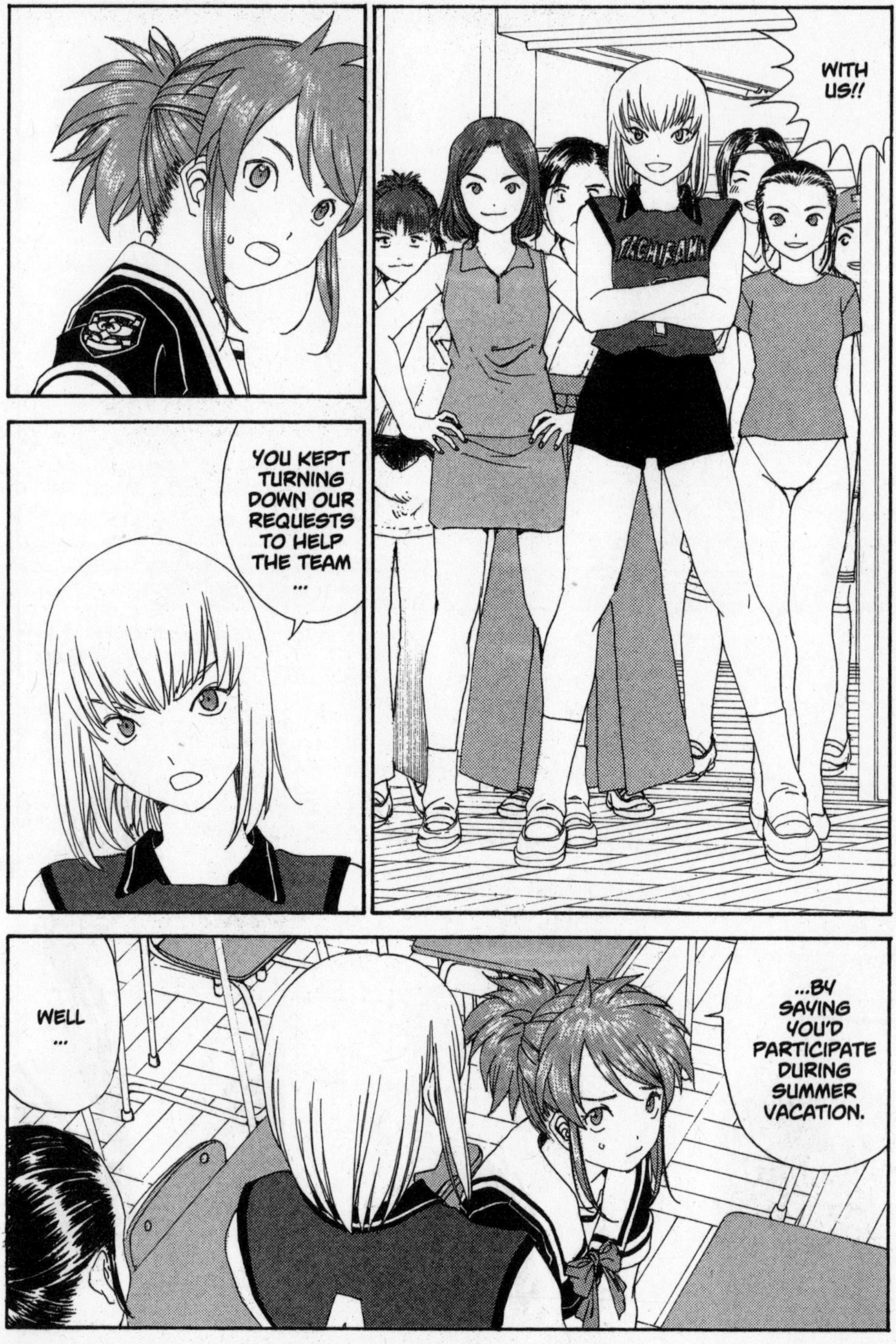
WITH US!!
YOU KEPT TURNING DOWN OUR REQUESTS TO HELP THE TEAM ...
...BY SAYING YOU'D PARTICIPATE DURING SUMMER VACATION.
WELL ...

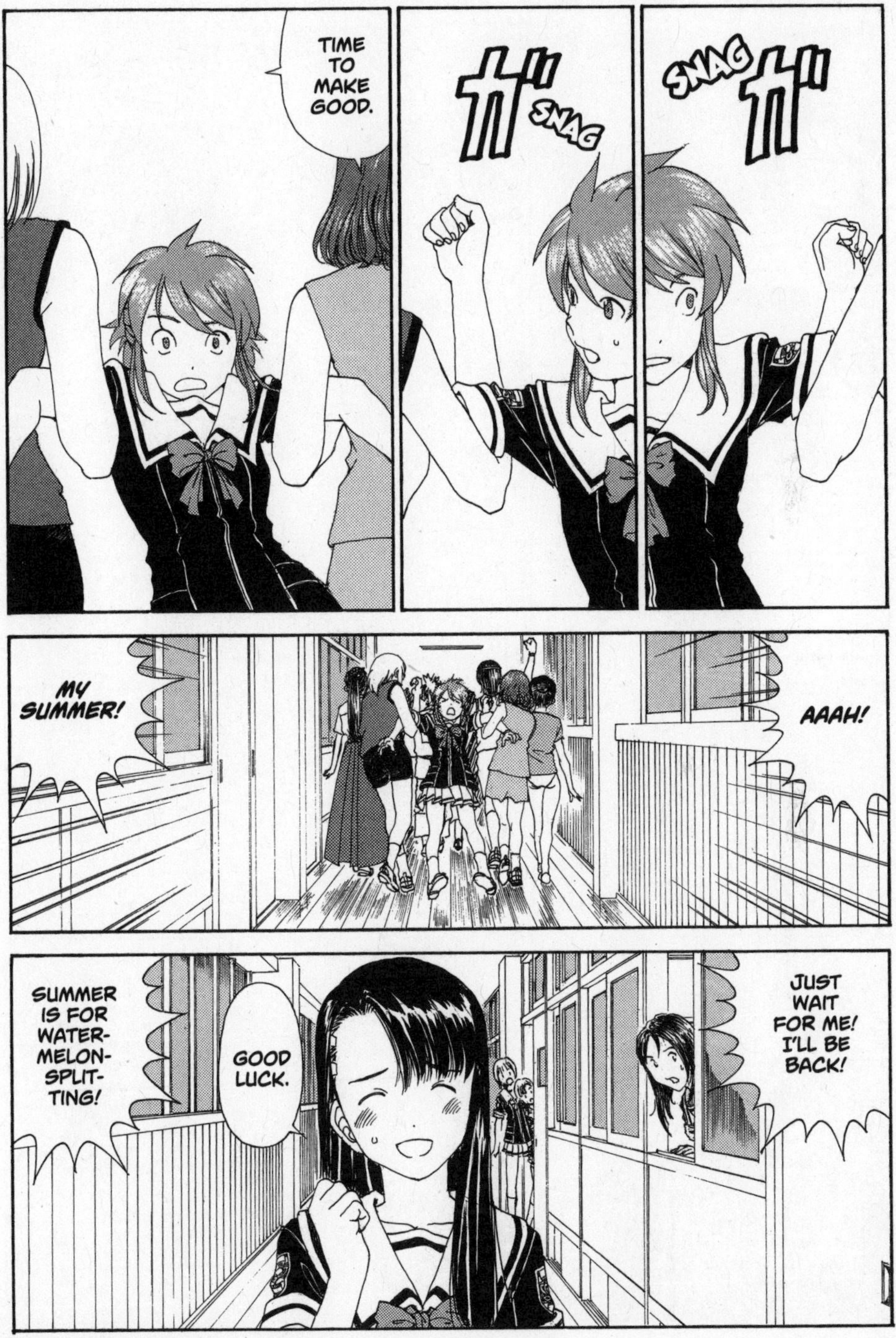
SNAG
ガ
ガ
SNAG
TIME TO MAKE GOOD.
AAAH!
MY SUMMER!
JUST WAIT FOR ME! I'LL BE BACK!
GOOD LUCK.
SUMMER IS FOR WATER-MELON-SPLIT-TING!

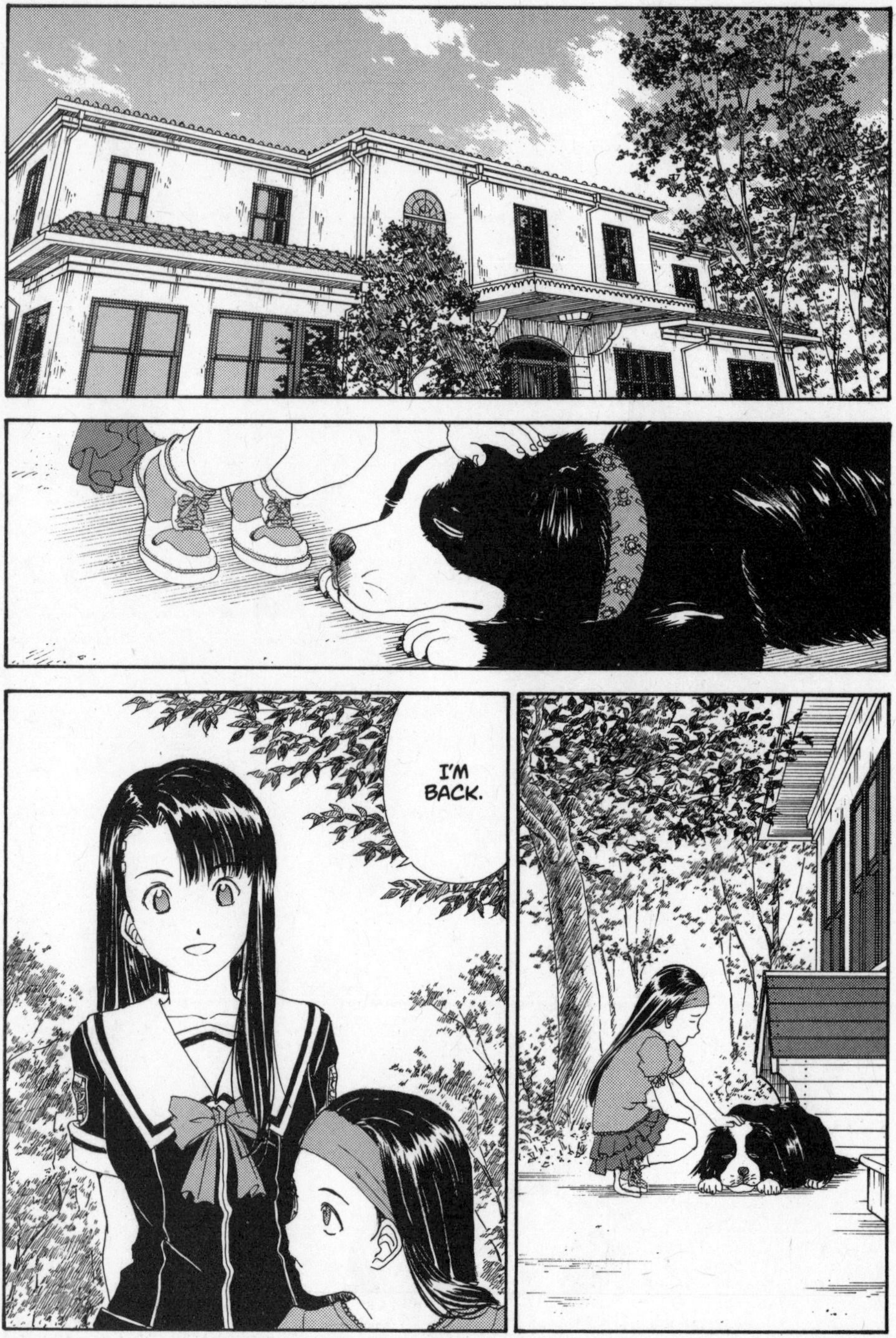
I'M BACK.

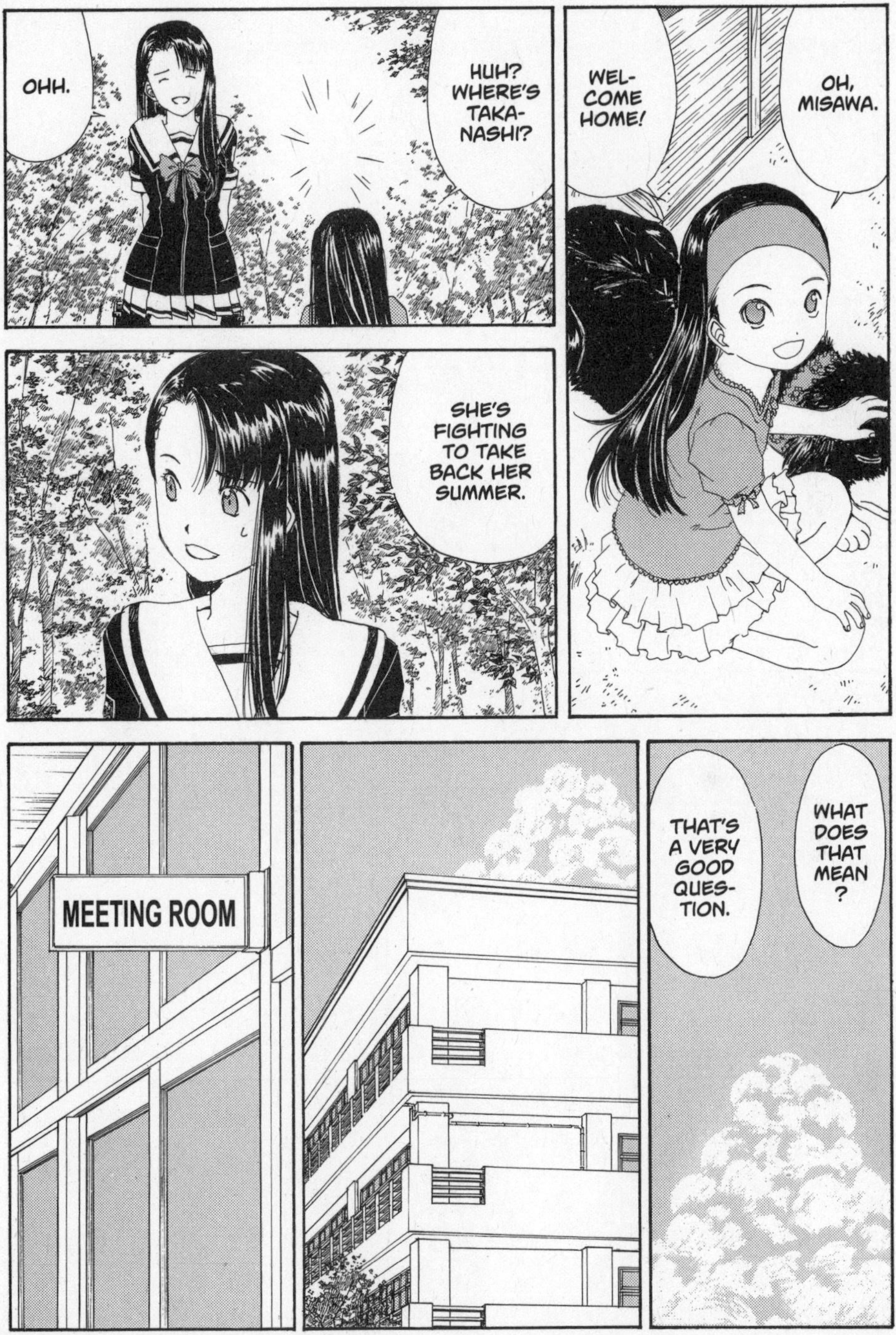
OH, MISAWA.
WEL-COME HOME!
HUH? WHERE'S TAKA-NASHI?
OHH.
SHE'S FIGHTING TO TAKE BACK HER SUMMER.
WHAT DOES THAT MEAN?
THAT'S A VERY GOOD QUES-TION.
MEETING ROOM

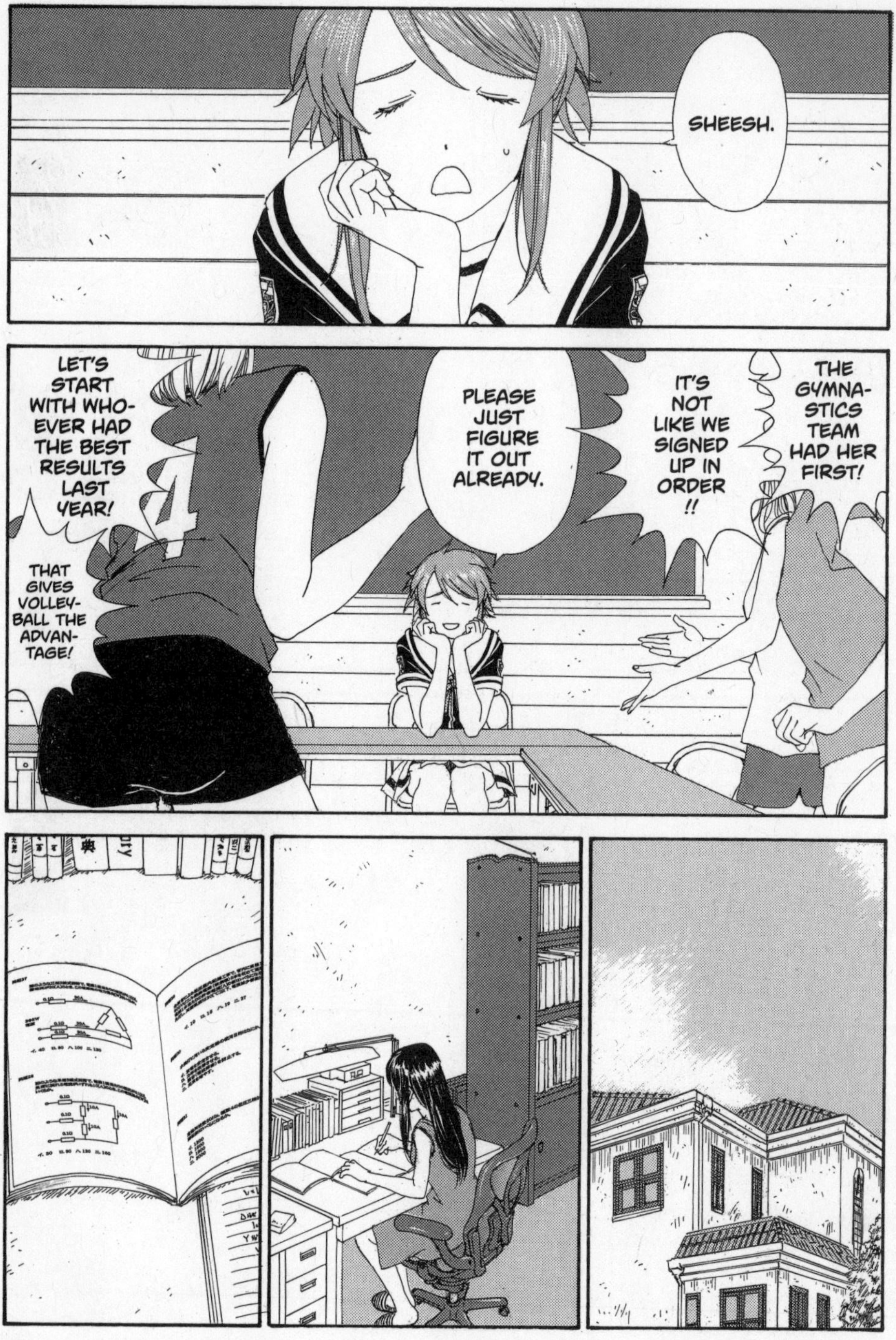
SHEESH.
THE GYMNASTICS TEAM HAD HER FIRST!
IT'S NOT LIKE WE SIGNED UP IN ORDER!!
PLEASE JUST FIGURE IT OUT ALREADY.
LET'S START WITH WHOEVER HAD THE BEST RESULTS LAST YEAR!
THAT GIVES VOLLEYBALL THE ADVANTAGE!

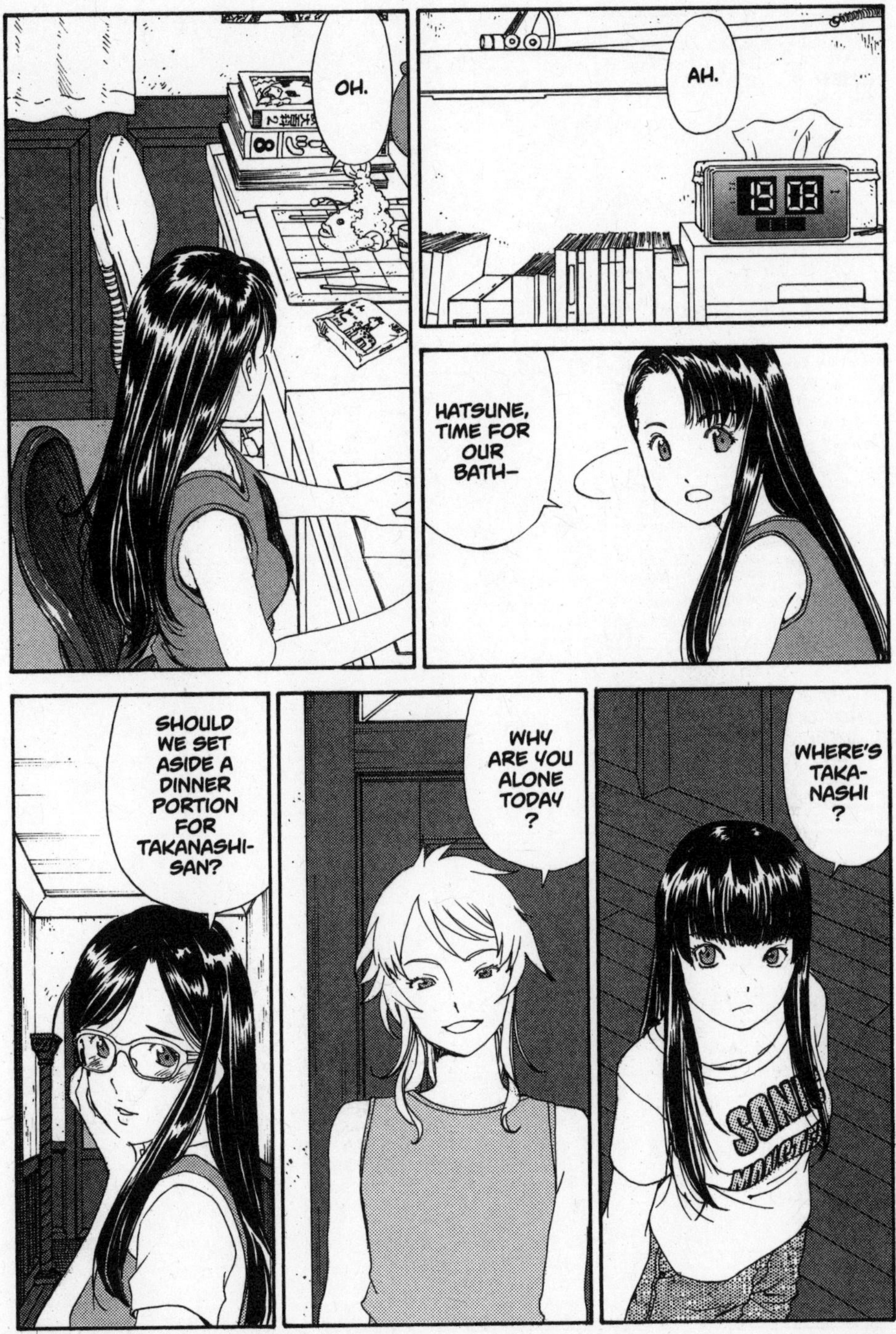
AH.
HATSUNE, TIME FOR OUR BATH-
OH.
WHERE'S TAKA-NASHI?
WHY ARE YOU ALONE TODAY?
SHOULD WE SET ASIDE A DINNER PORTION FOR TAKANASHI-SAN?

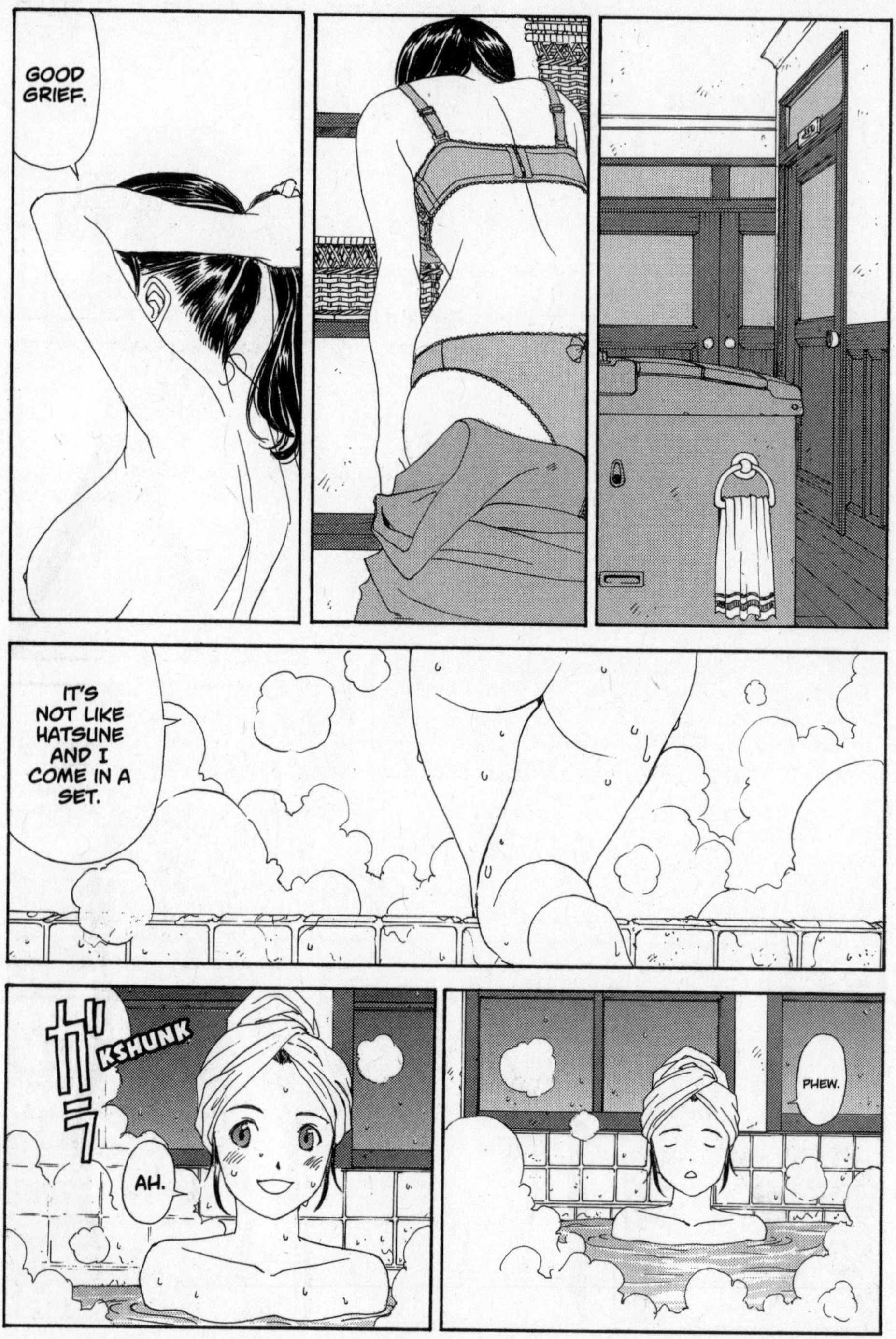
GOOD GRIEF.
IT'S NOT LIKE HATSUNE AND I COME IN A SET.
PHEW.
ガラ
KSHUNK
AH.

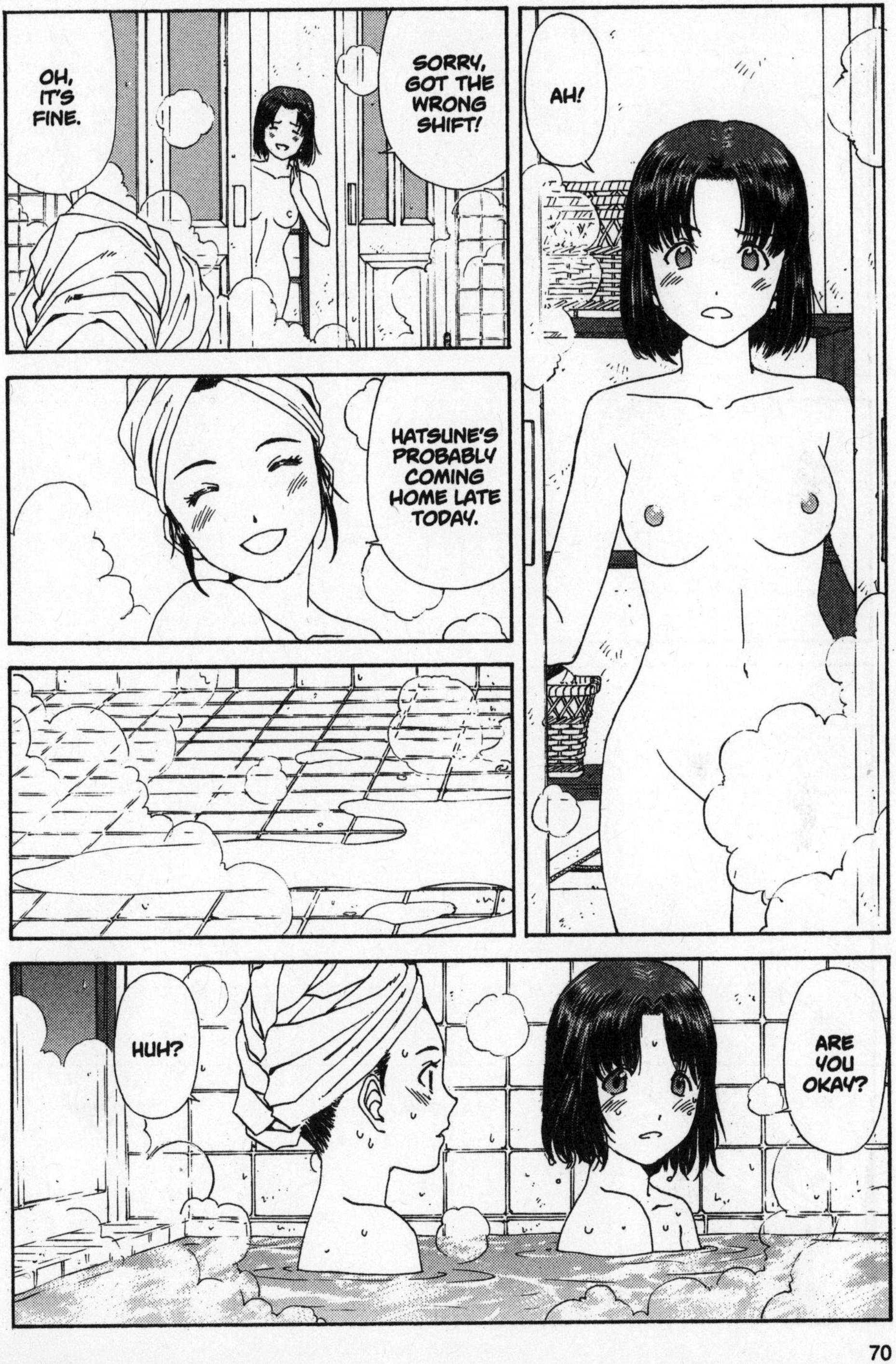
AH!
SORRY, GOT THE WRONG SHIFT!
OH, IT'S FINE.
HATSUNE'S PROBABLY COMING HOME LATE TODAY.
ARE YOU OKAY?
HUH?

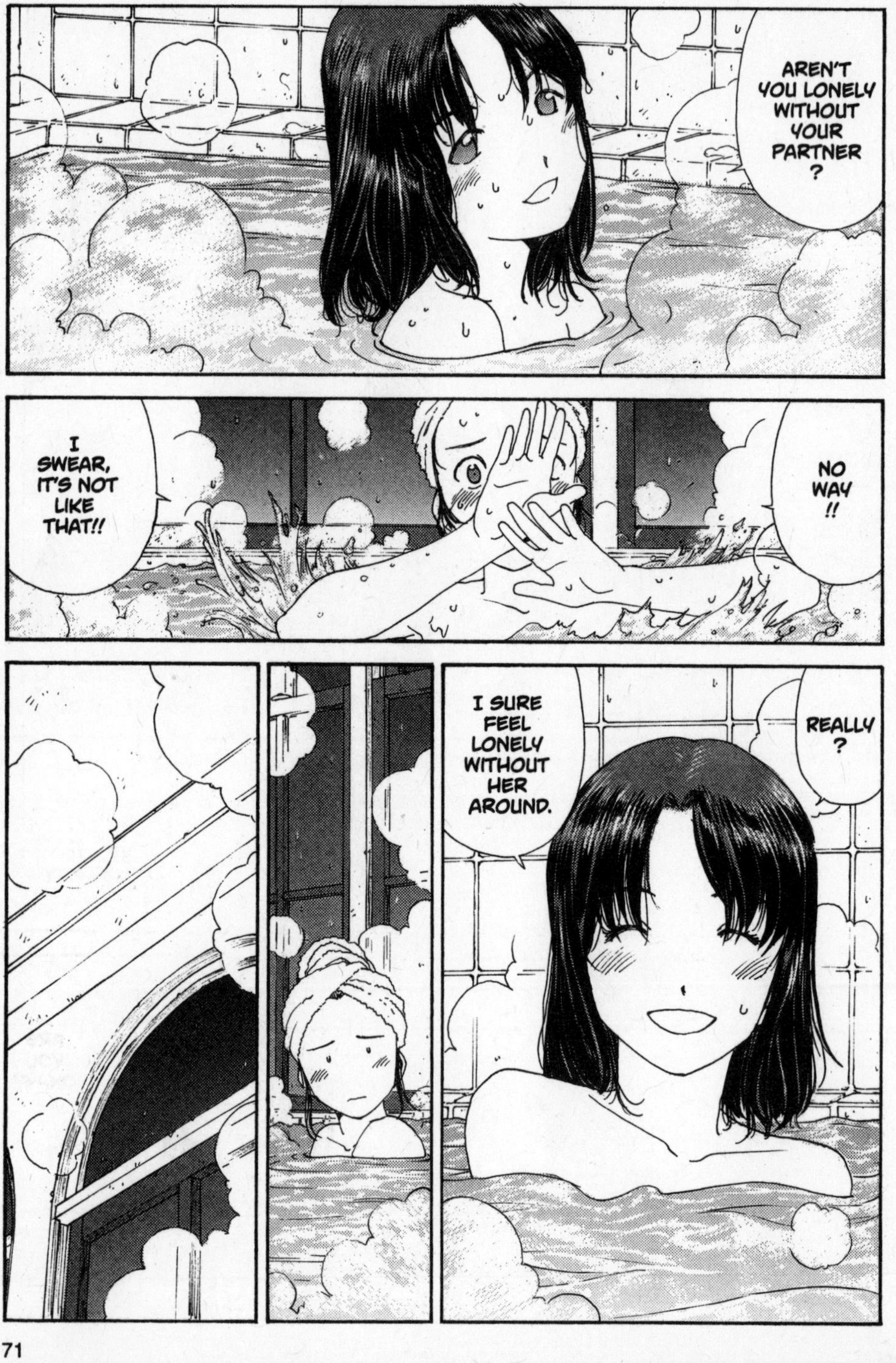
AREN'T YOU LONELY WITHOUT YOUR PARTNER?
NO WAY!!
I SWEAR, IT'S NOT LIKE THAT!!
REALLY?
I SURE FEEL LONELY WITHOUT HER AROUND.

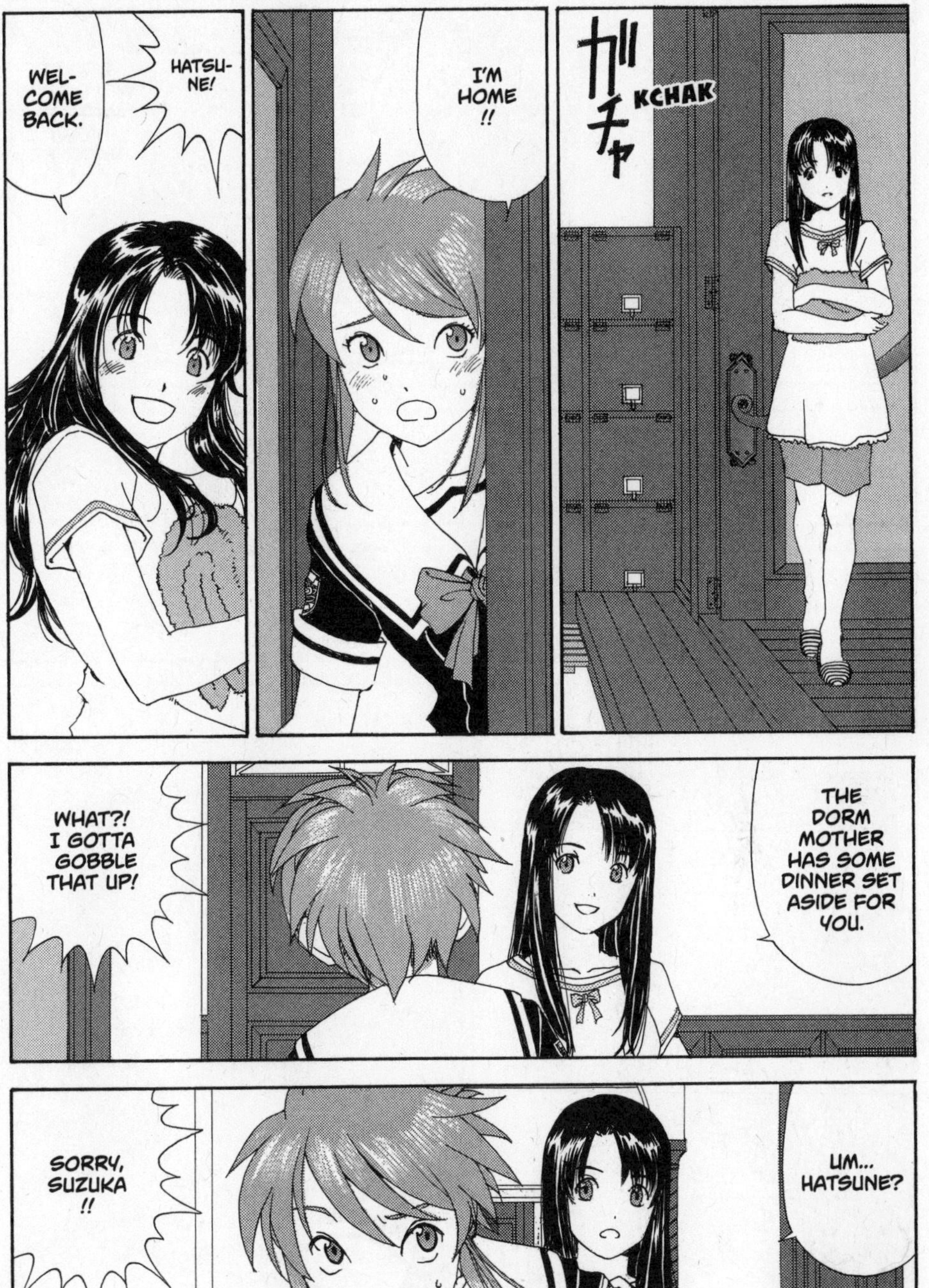
ガチャ
KCHAK
I'M HOME !!
HATSUNE!
WELCOME BACK.
THE DORM MOTHER HAS SOME DINNER SET ASIDE FOR YOU.
WHAT?! I GOTTA GOBBLE THAT UP!
UM... HATSUNE?
SORRY, SUZUKA !!

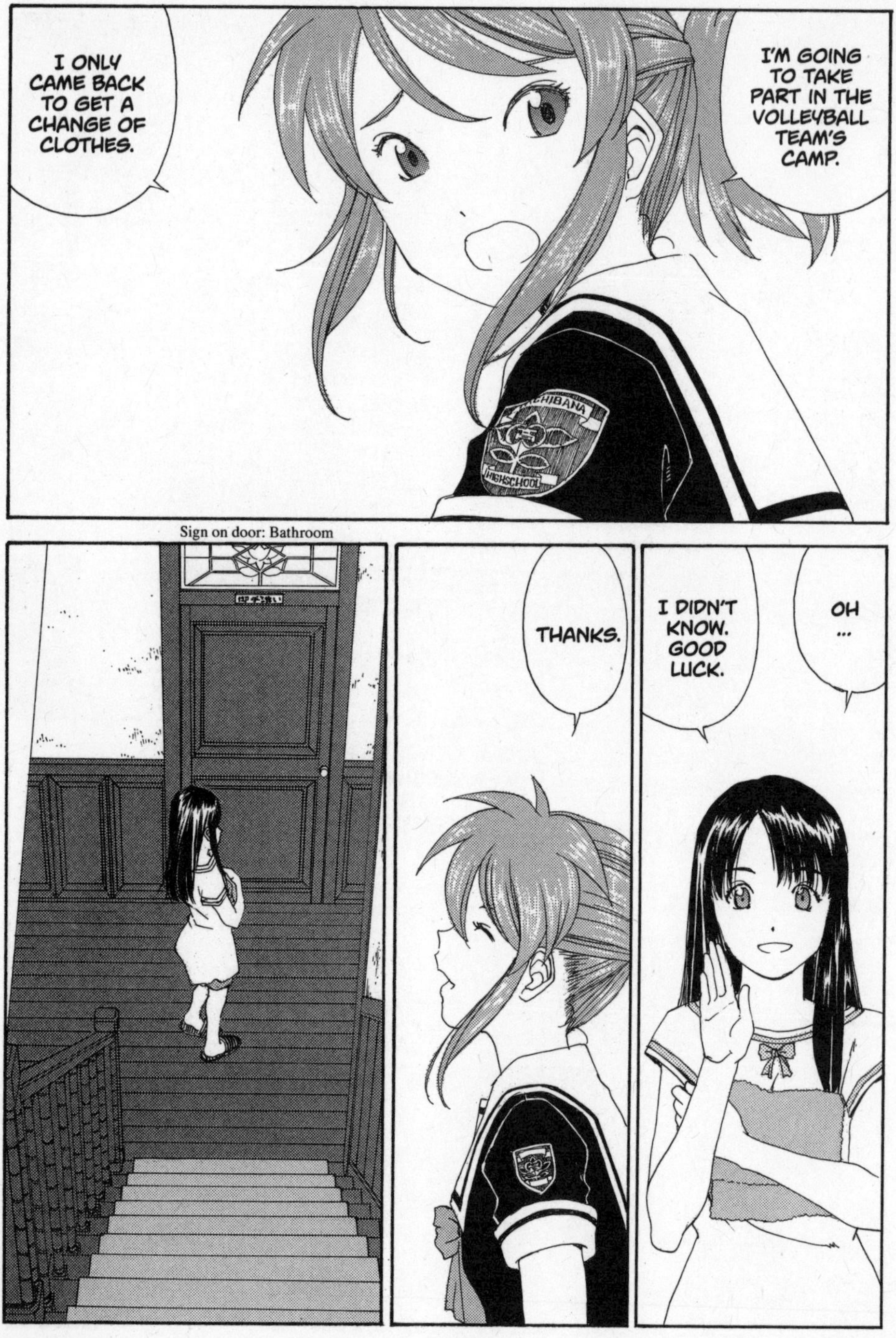
I'M GOING TO TAKE PART IN THE VOLLEYBALL TEAM'S CAMP.
I ONLY CAME BACK TO GET A CHANGE OF CLOTHES.
OH ...
I DIDN'T KNOW. GOOD LUCK.
THANKS.
Sign on door: Bathroom

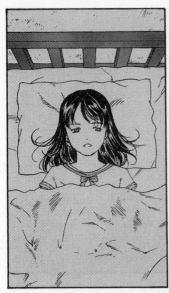

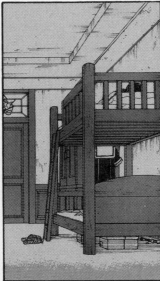

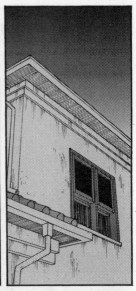

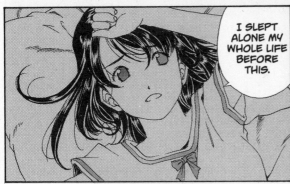

I SLEPT ALONE MY WHOLE LIFE BEFORE THIS.

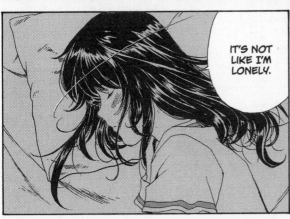

IT'S NOT LIKE I'M LONELY.

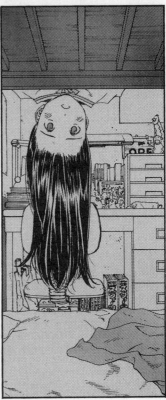

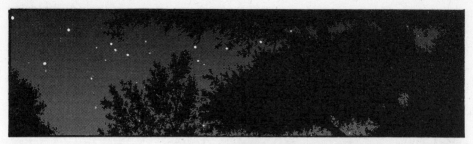

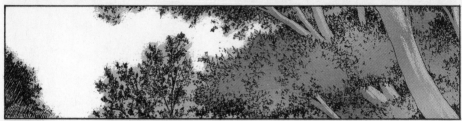

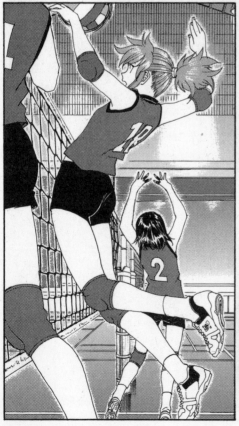

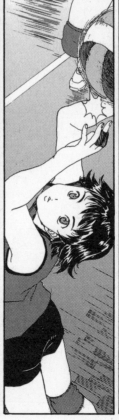

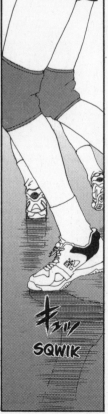

SQWIK

WHAM!
HELL YEAH!
THREE DAYS LATER

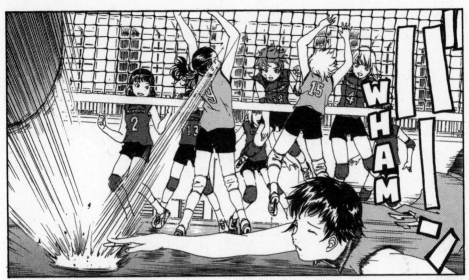

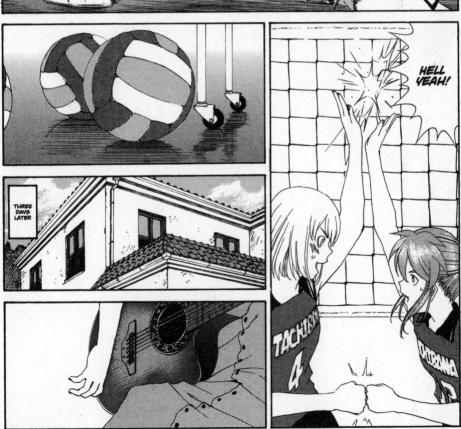

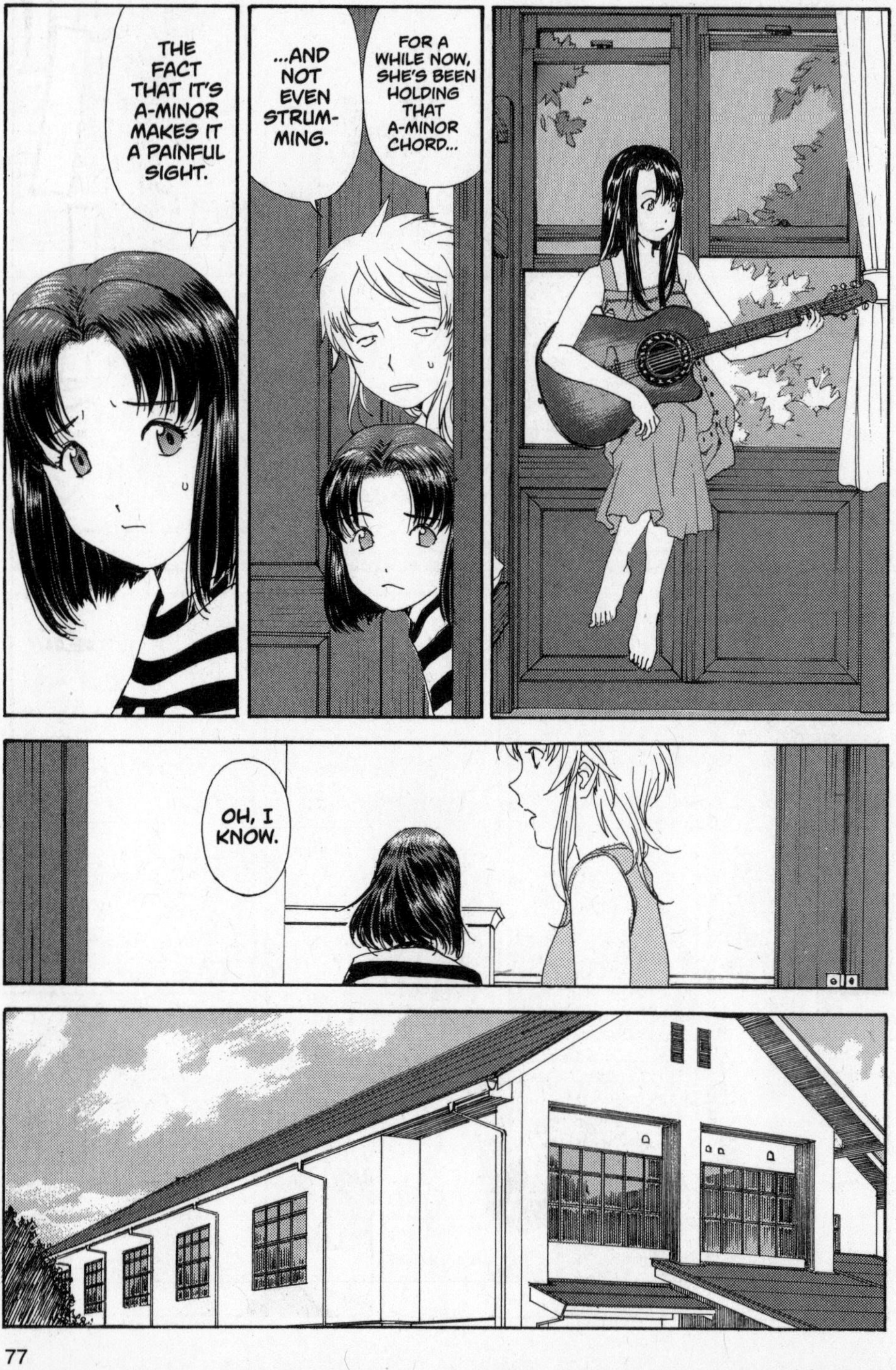
FOR A WHILE NOW, SHE'S BEEN HOLDING THAT A-MINOR CHORD...
...AND NOT EVEN STRUMMING.
THE FACT THAT IT'S A-MINOR MAKES IT A PAINFUL SIGHT.
OH, I KNOW.

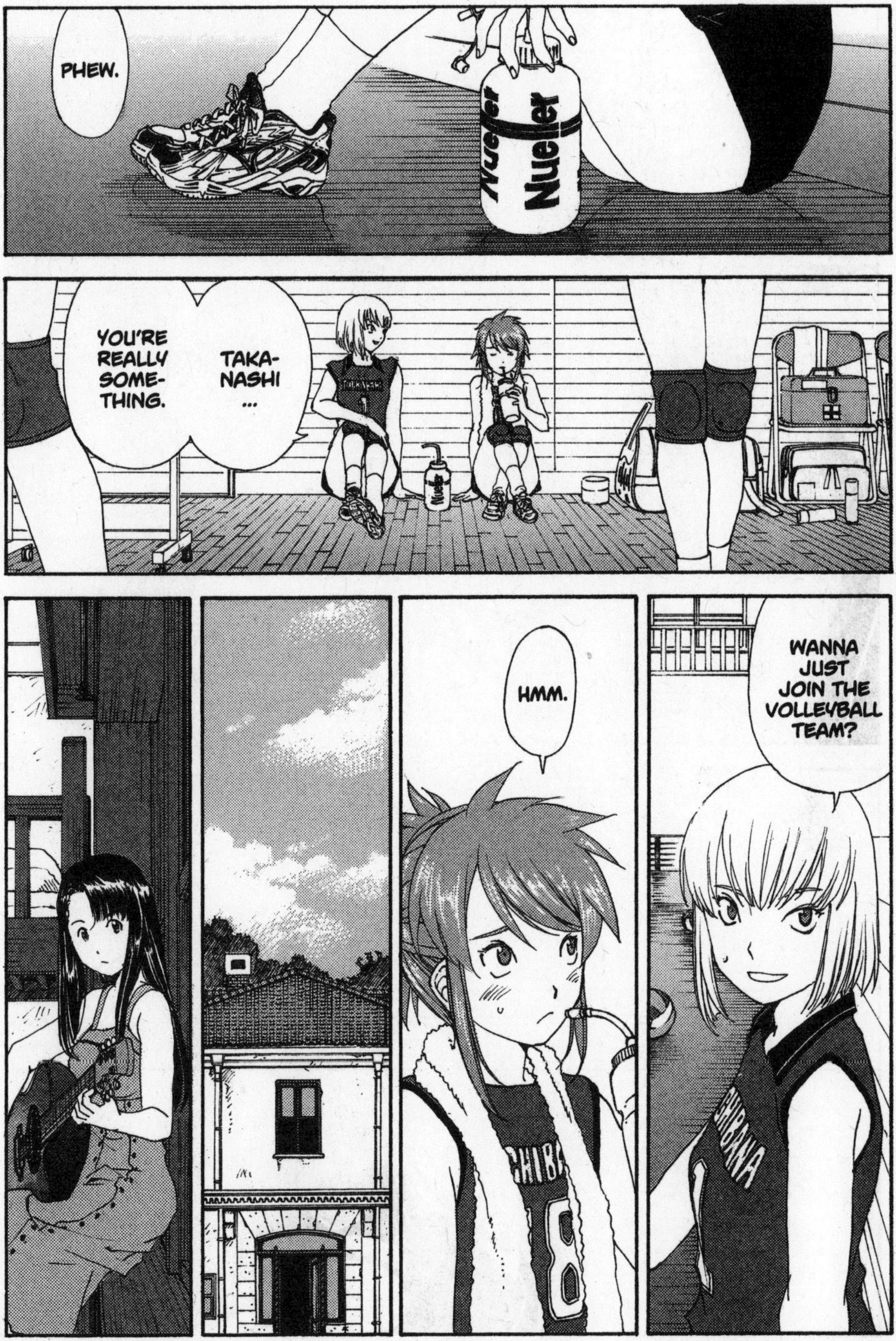
PHEW.
Nueller
TAKA-NASHI ...
YOU'RE REALLY SOME-THING.
WANNA JUST JOIN THE VOLLEYBALL TEAM?
HMM.

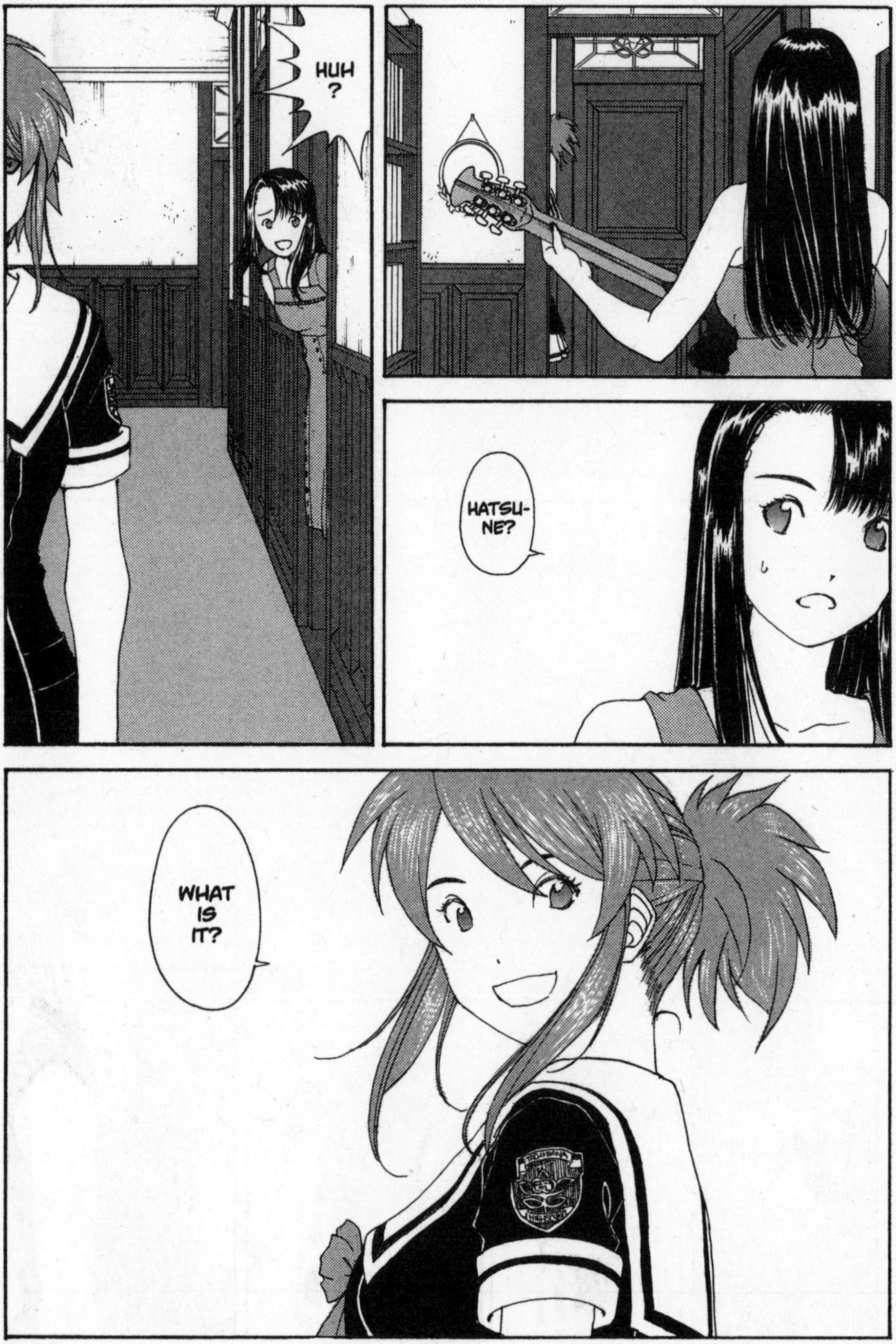
HATSU-NE?
HUH ?
WHAT IS IT?

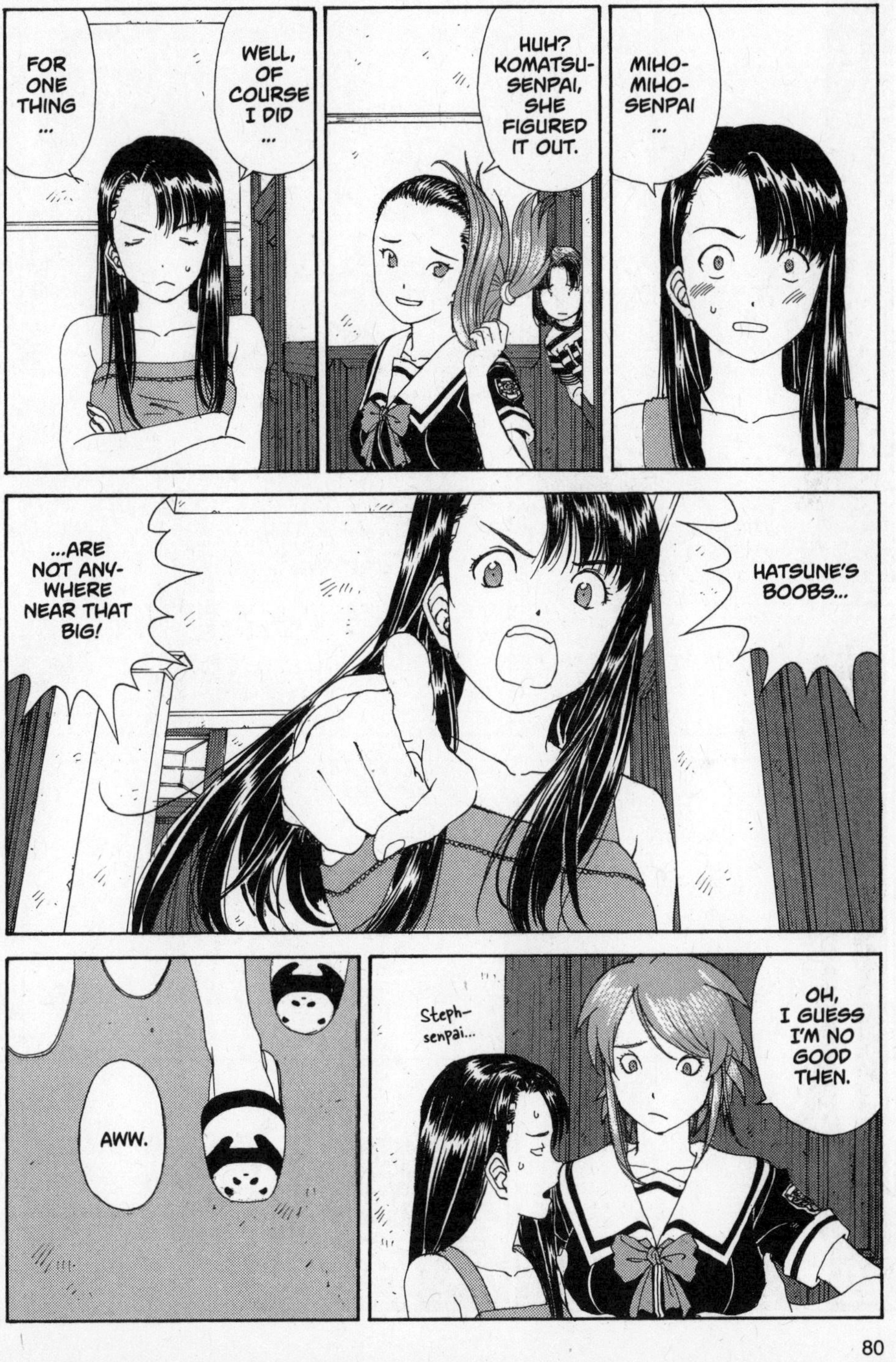
MIHO-MIHO-SENPAI ...
HUH? KOMATSU-SENPAI, SHE FIGURED IT OUT.
WELL, OF COURSE I DID ...
FOR ONE THING ...
HATSUNE'S BOOBS...
...ARE NOT ANY-WHERE NEAR THAT BIG!
OH, I GUESS I'M NO GOOD THEN.
Steph-senpai...
AWW.

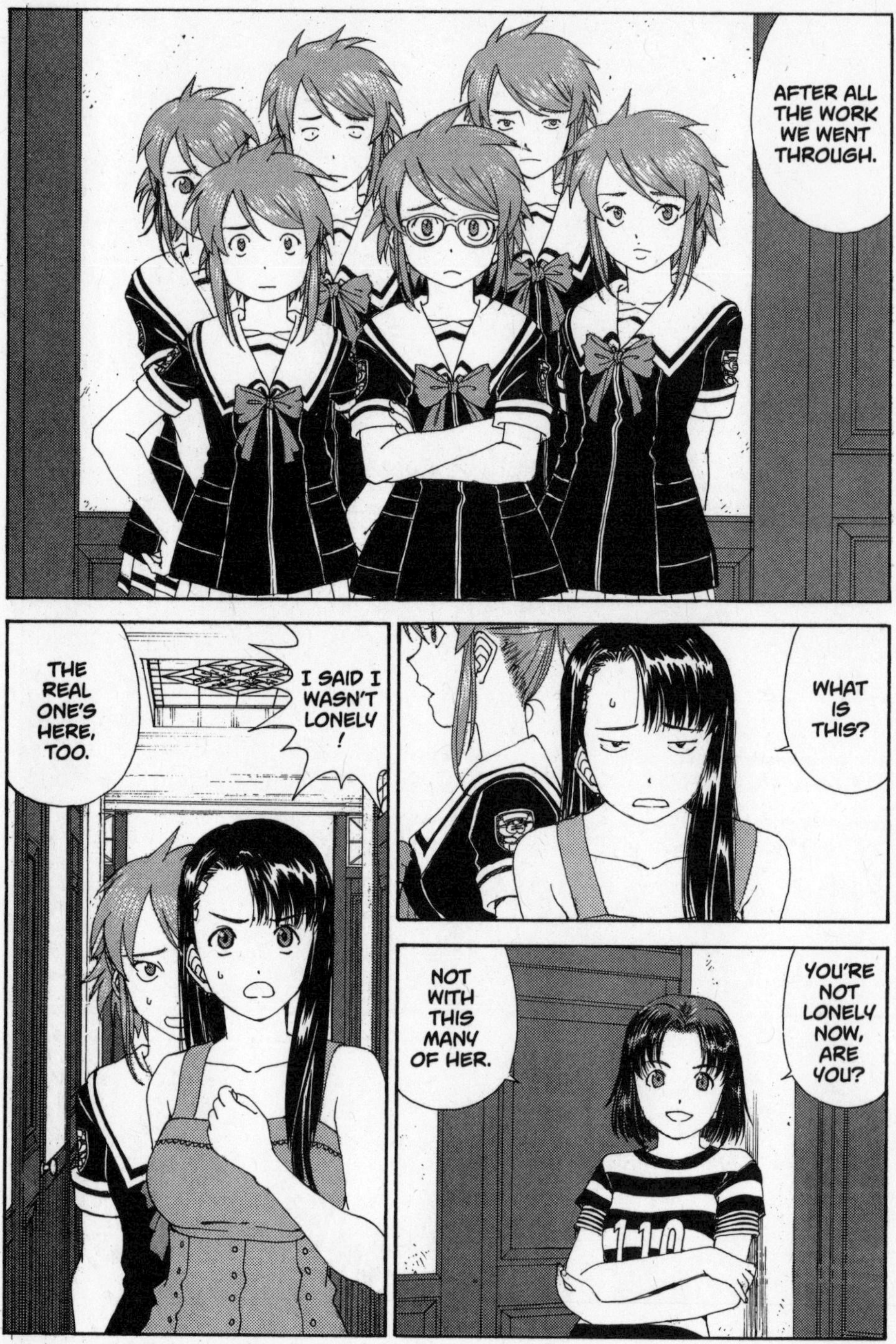
AFTER ALL THE WORK WE WENT THROUGH.
WHAT IS THIS?
YOU'RE NOT LONELY NOW, ARE YOU?
NOT WITH THIS MANY OF HER.
I SAID I WASN'T LONELY!
THE REAL ONE'S HERE, TOO.

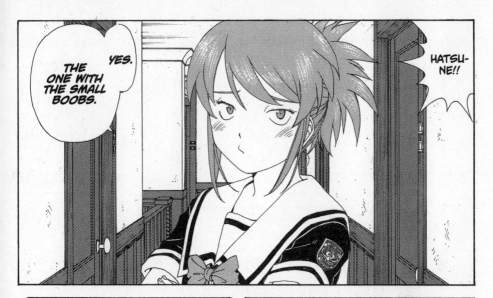

HATSU-NE!!
YES. THE ONE WITH THE SMALL BOOBS.
AAAH! I'M SORRY!
SO TAKA-NASHI WOULDN'T JOIN?
WELL, SHE SAID...
I HAVE THE IMPORTANT ROLE OF DORM SECRE-TARY.
SO WHAT CAN YA DO?

episode.10 / **END**

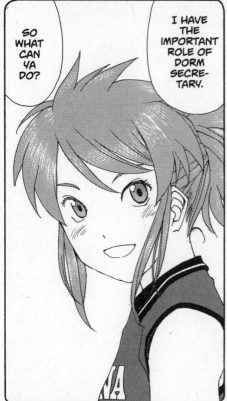

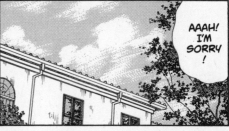

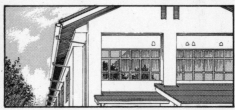

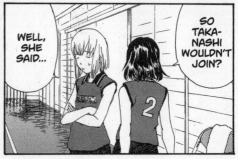

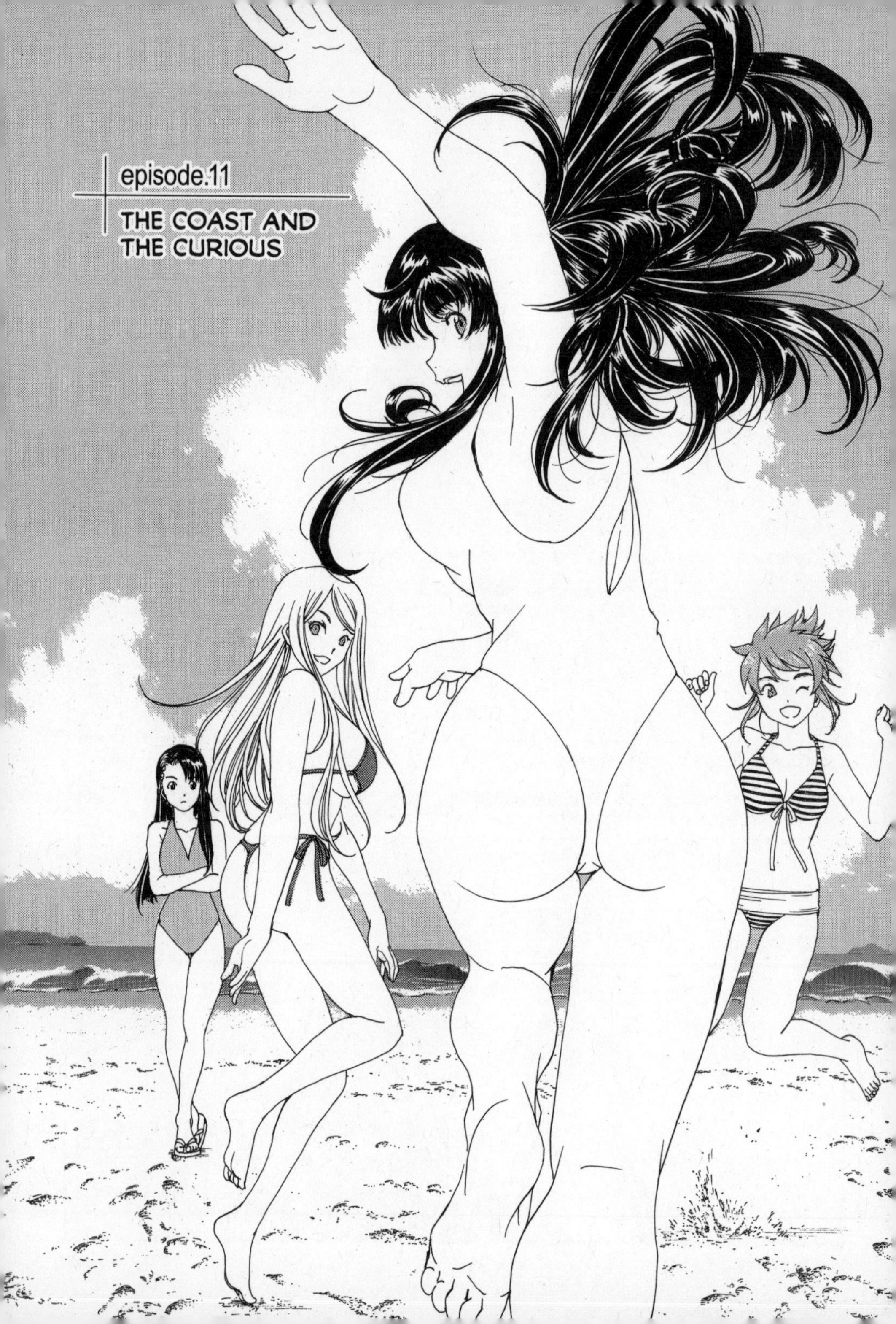
episode.11
THE COAST AND THE CURIOUS

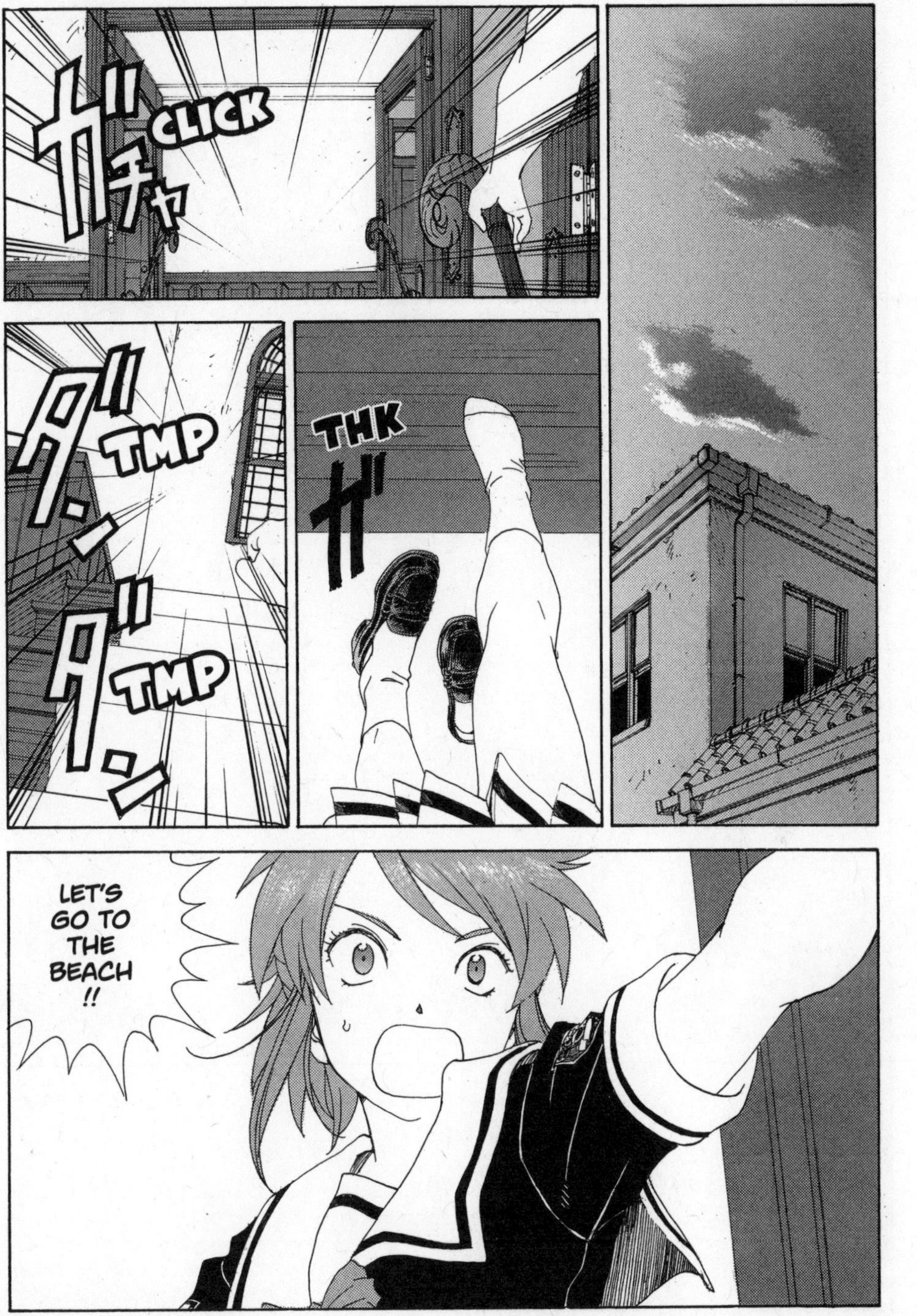
ガチャ
CLICK
ガ
THK
ダーン
TMP
ダーン
TMP
LET'S GO TO THE BEACH!!

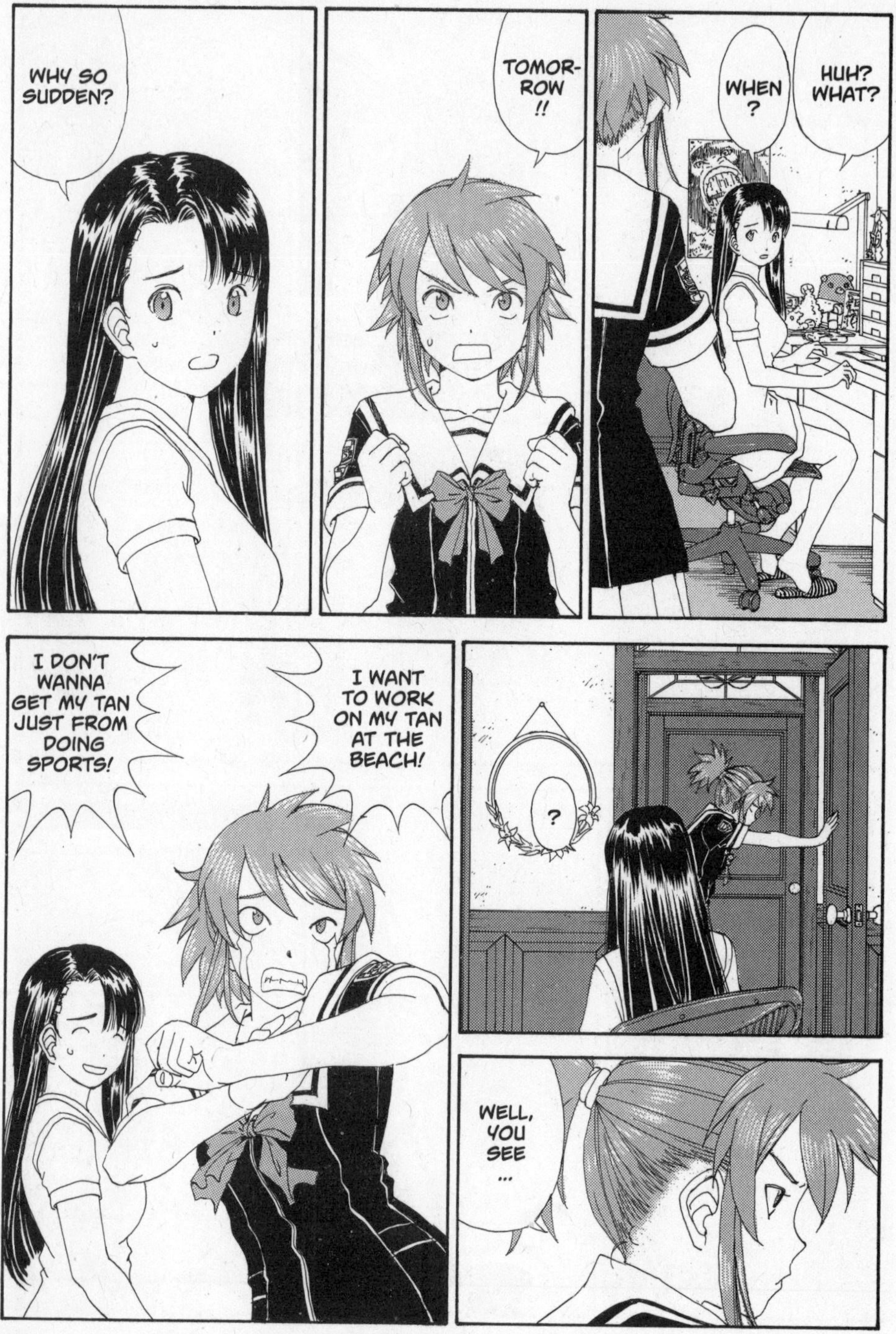
HUH? WHAT?
WHEN ?
TOMOR-ROW !!
WHY SO SUDDEN?
?
WELL, YOU SEE ...
I WANT TO WORK ON MY TAN AT THE BEACH!
I DON'T WANNA GET MY TAN JUST FROM DOING SPORTS!

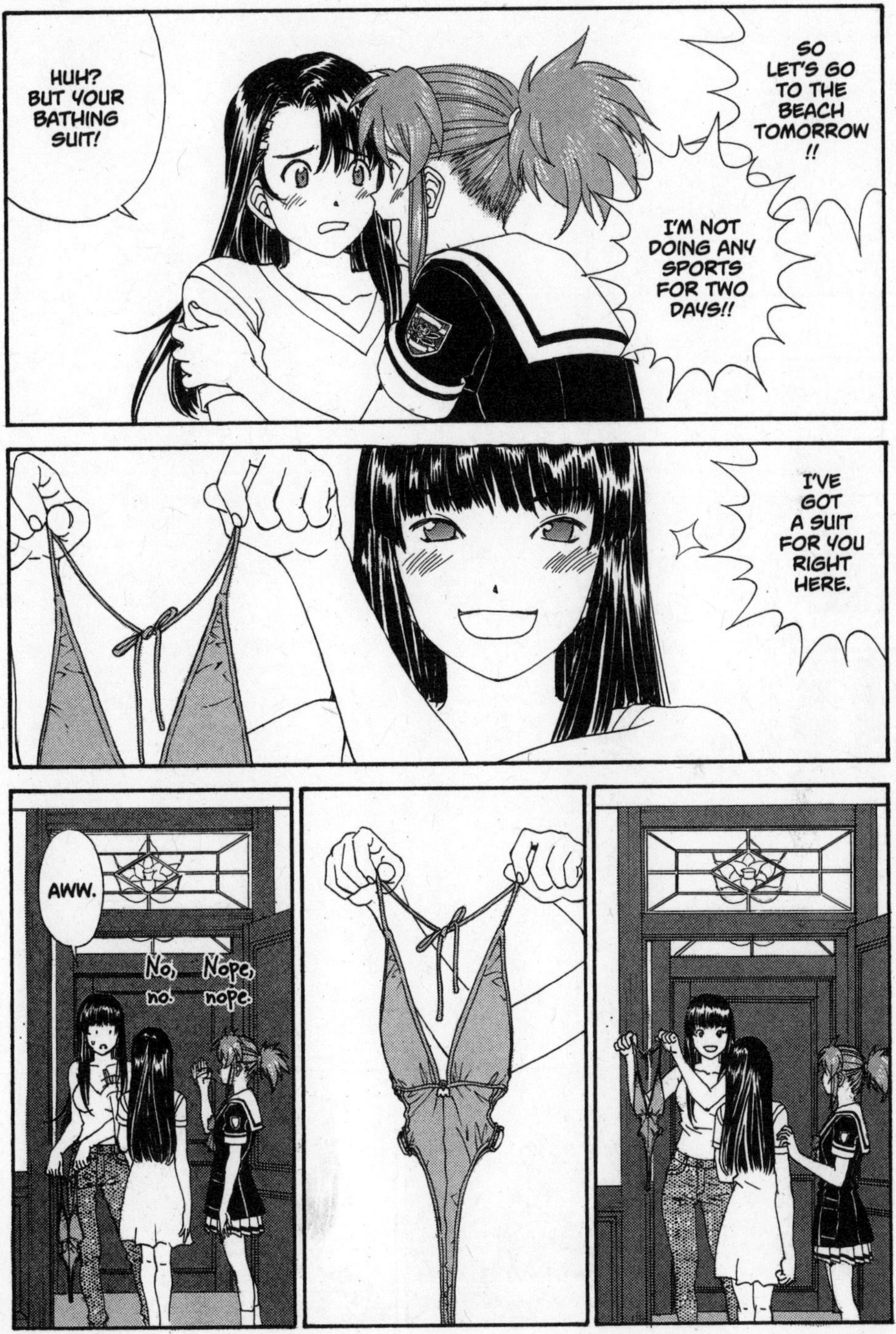
SO LET'S GO TO THE BEACH TOMORROW !!
I'M NOT DOING ANY SPORTS FOR TWO DAYS!!
HUH? BUT YOUR BATHING SUIT!
I'VE GOT A SUIT FOR YOU RIGHT HERE.
AWW.
Nope, nope.
No, no.

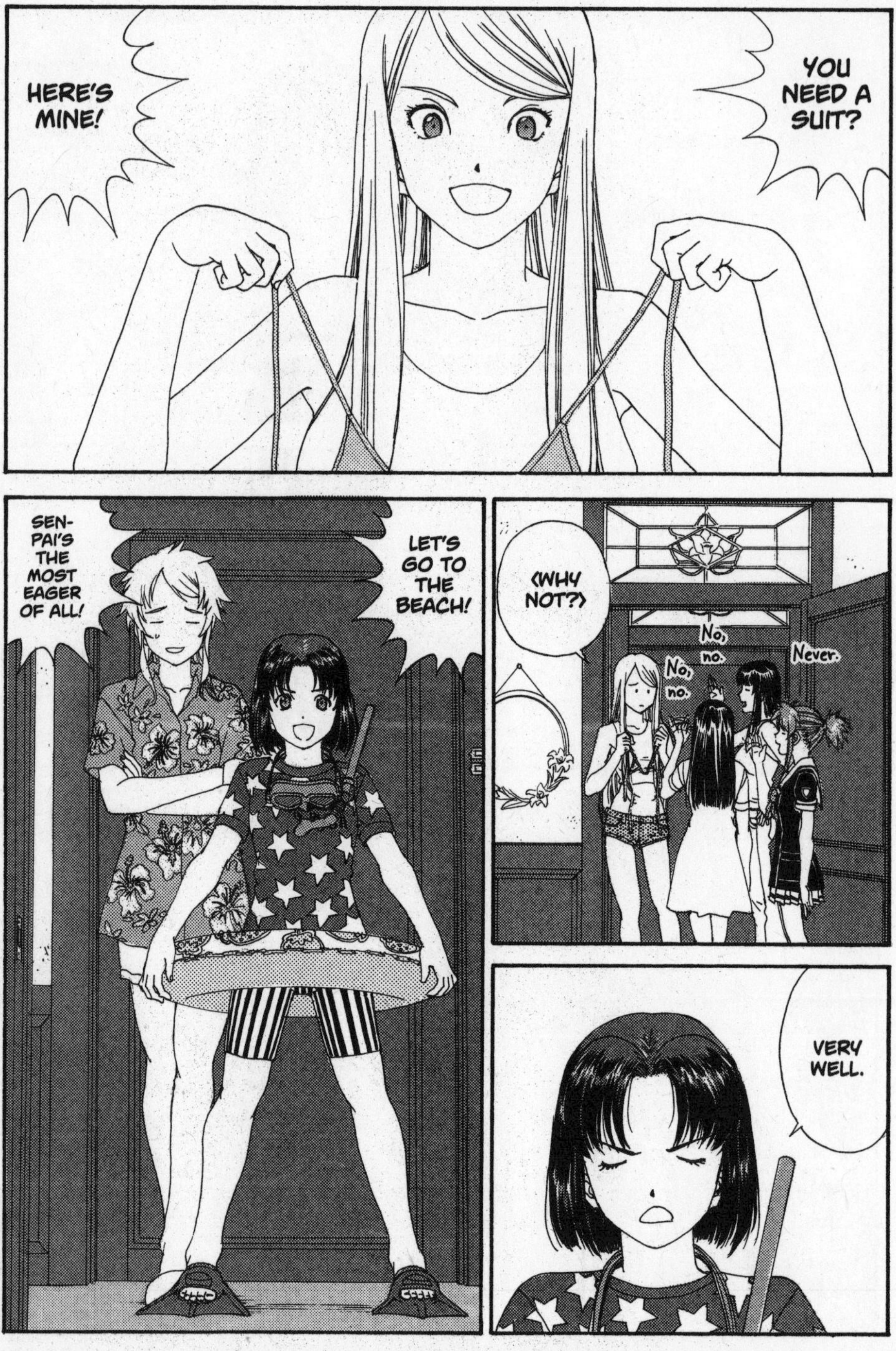
YOU NEED A SUIT?
HERE'S MINE!
‹WHY NOT?›
Never.
No, no.
No, no.
VERY WELL.
LET'S GO TO THE BEACH!
SEN-PAI'S THE MOST EAGER OF ALL!

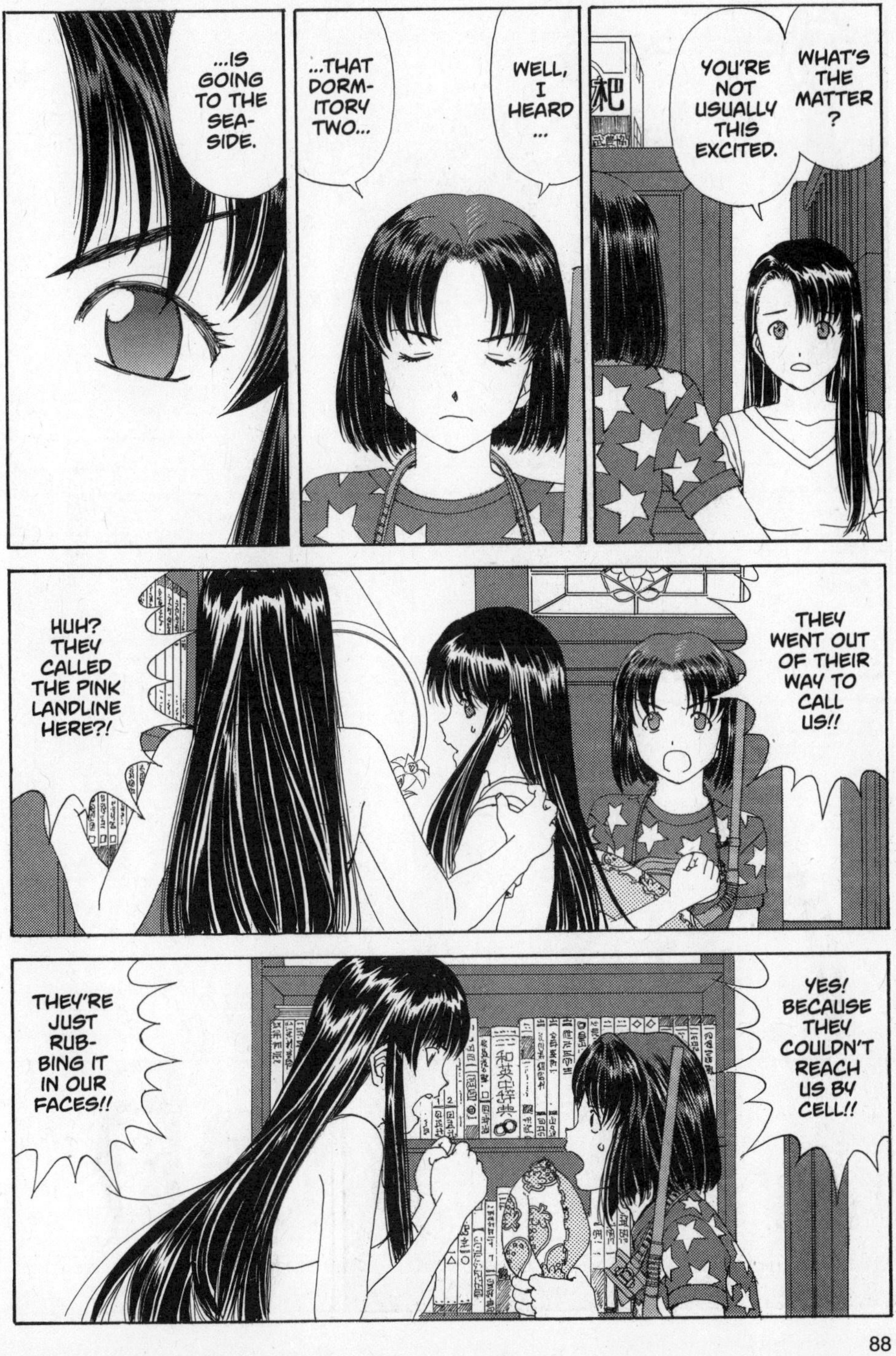
WHAT'S THE MATTER?
YOU'RE NOT USUALLY THIS EXCITED.
WELL, I HEARD...
...THAT DORMITORY TWO...
...IS GOING TO THE SEASIDE.
THEY WENT OUT OF THEIR WAY TO CALL US!!
HUH? THEY CALLED THE PINK LANDLINE HERE?!
YES! BECAUSE THEY COULDN'T REACH US BY CELL!!
THEY'RE JUST RUBBING IT IN OUR FACES!!

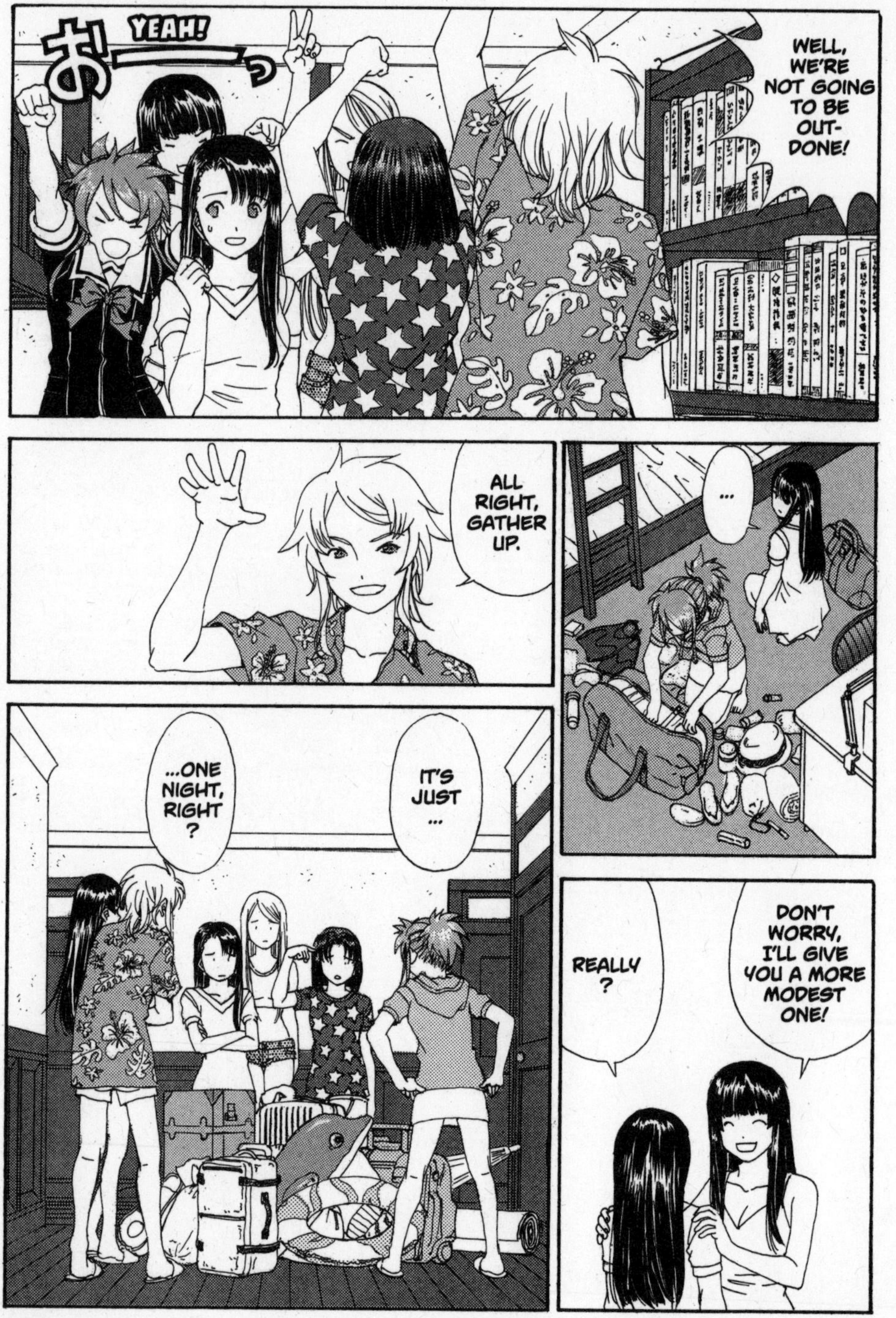
WELL, WE'RE NOT GOING TO BE OUT-DONE!
YEAH!
おーっ
...
ALL RIGHT, GATHER UP.
DON'T WORRY, I'LL GIVE YOU A MORE MODEST ONE!
REALLY?
IT'S JUST ...
...ONE NIGHT, RIGHT?

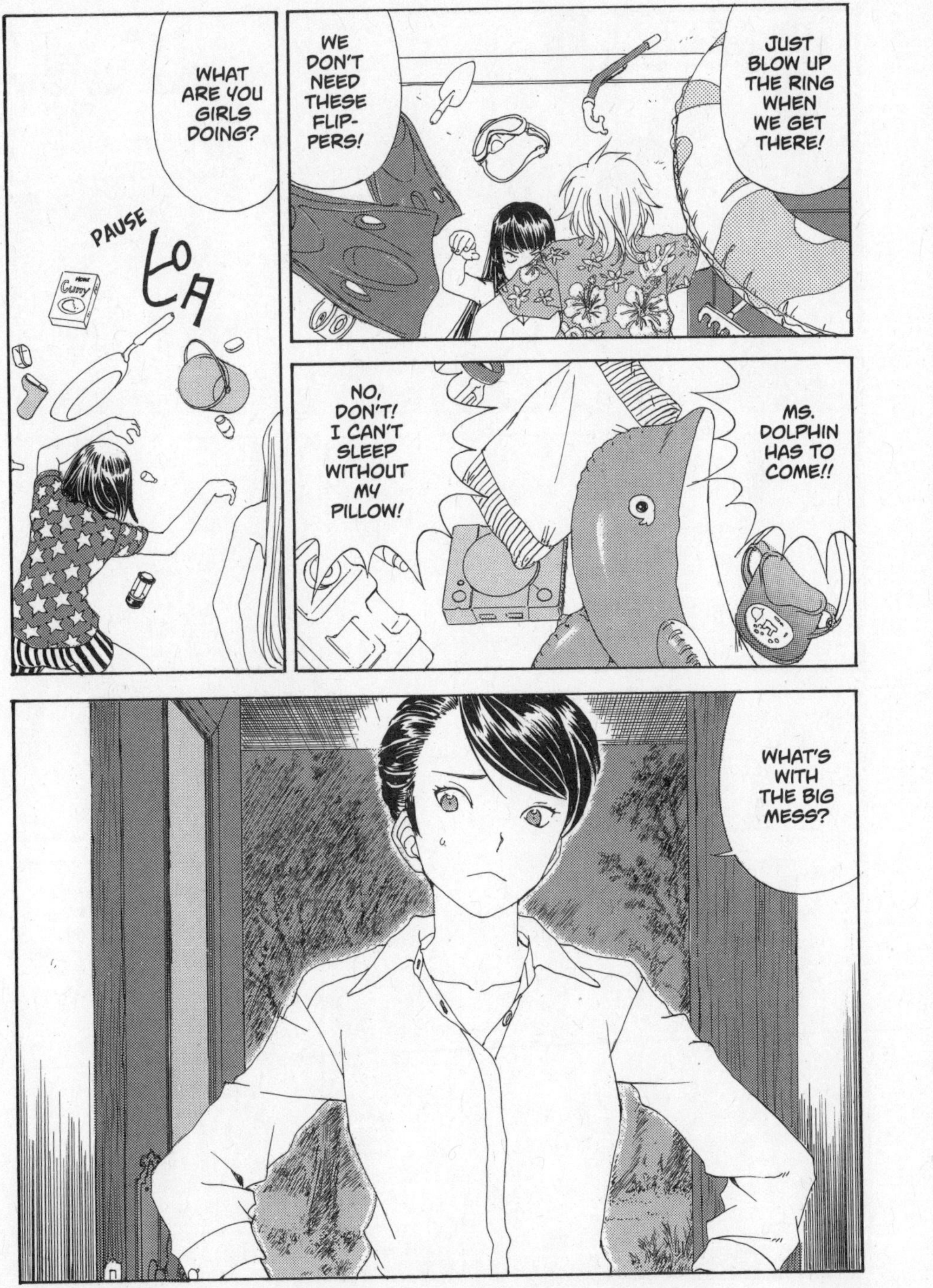
JUST BLOW UP THE RING WHEN WE GET THERE!
WE DON'T NEED THESE FLIP-PERS!
MS. DOLPHIN HAS TO COME!!
NO, DON'T! I CAN'T SLEEP WITHOUT MY PILLOW!
WHAT ARE YOU GIRLS DOING?
PAUSE
WHAT'S WITH THE BIG MESS?

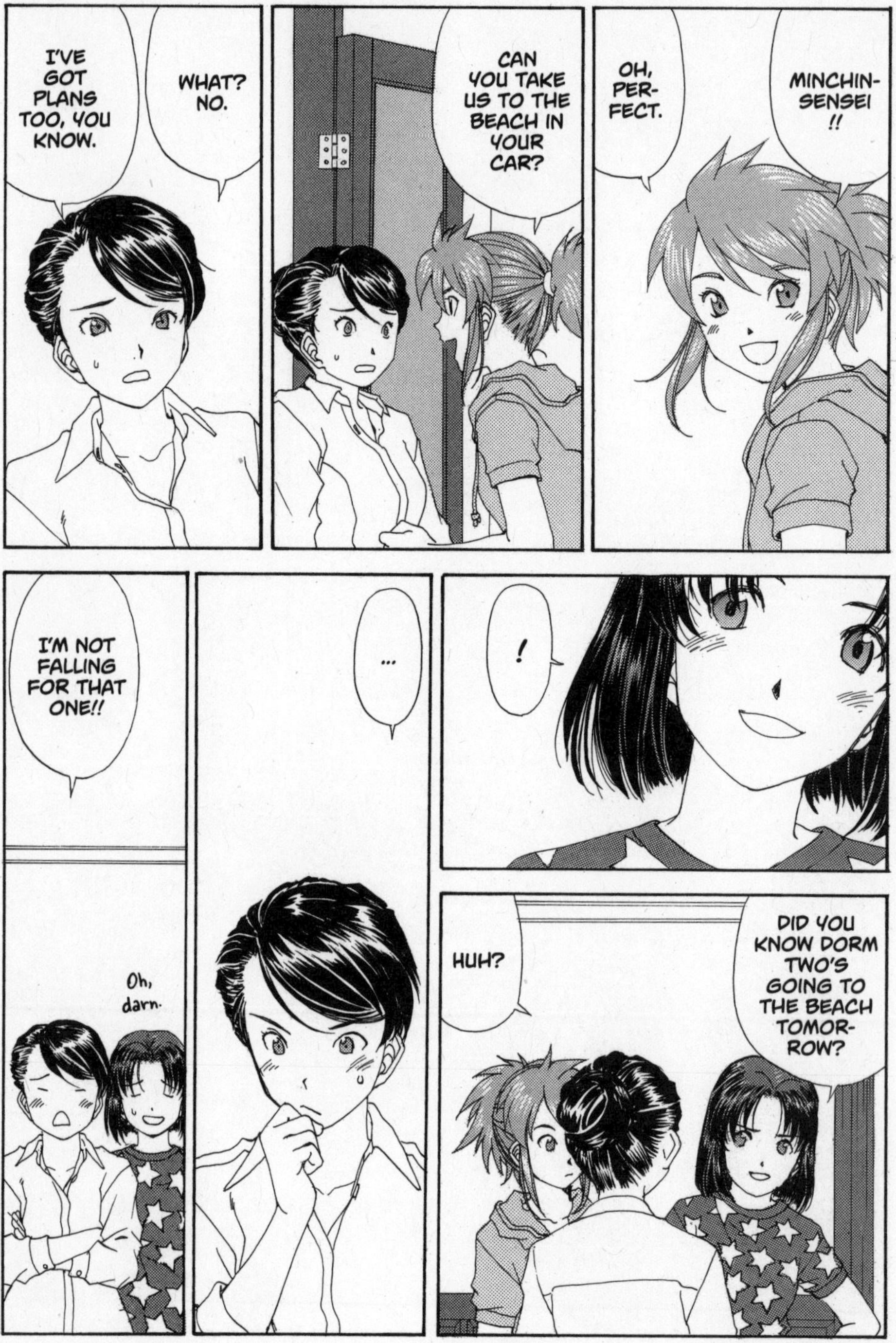
MINCHIN-SENSEI !!
OH, PER-FECT.
CAN YOU TAKE US TO THE BEACH IN YOUR CAR?
WHAT? NO.
I'VE GOT PLANS TOO, YOU KNOW.
!
DID YOU KNOW DORM TWO'S GOING TO THE BEACH TOMOR-ROW?
HUH?
...
I'M NOT FALLING FOR THAT ONE!!
Oh, darn.

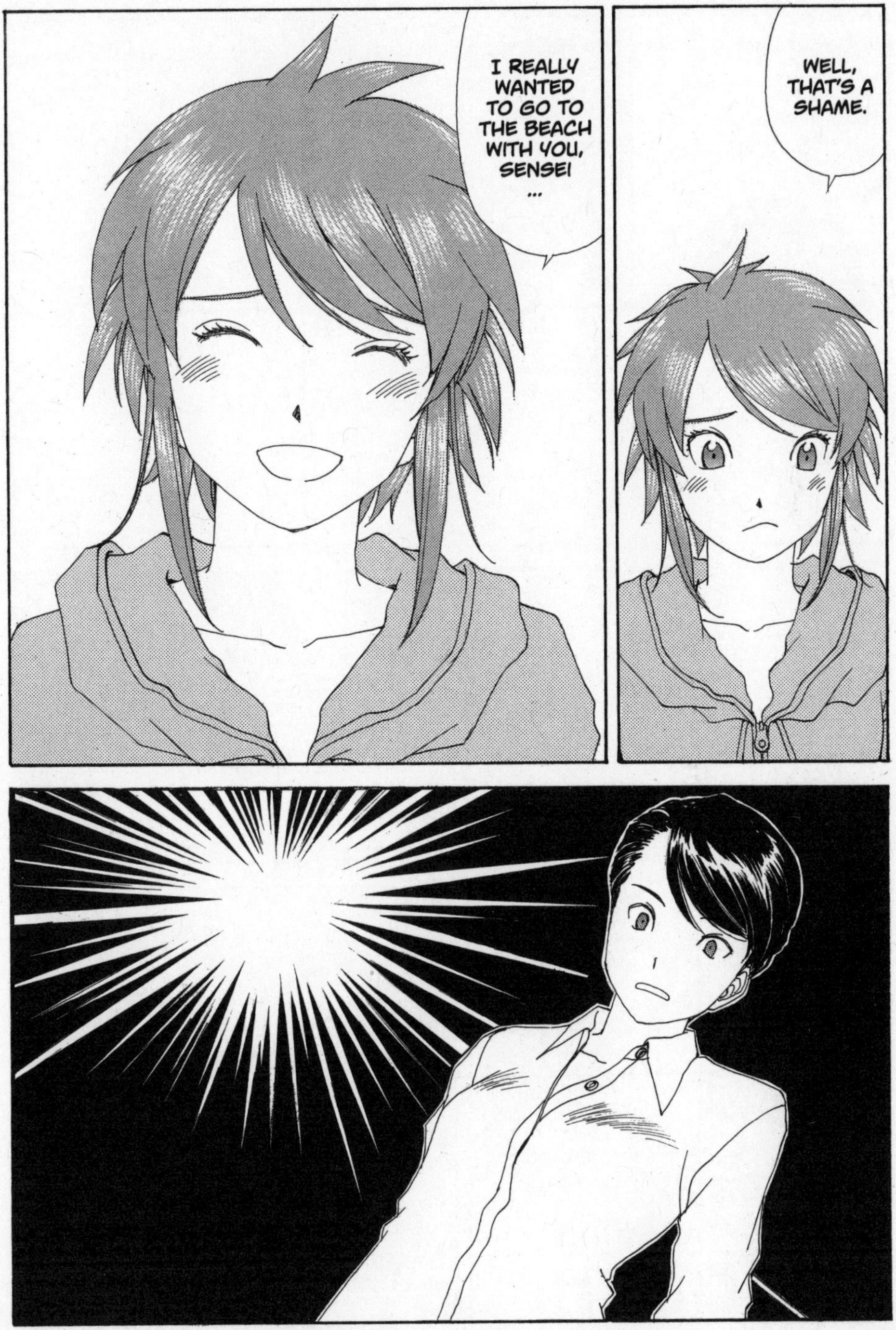
WELL, THAT'S A SHAME.
I REALLY WANTED TO GO TO THE BEACH WITH YOU, SENSEI ...

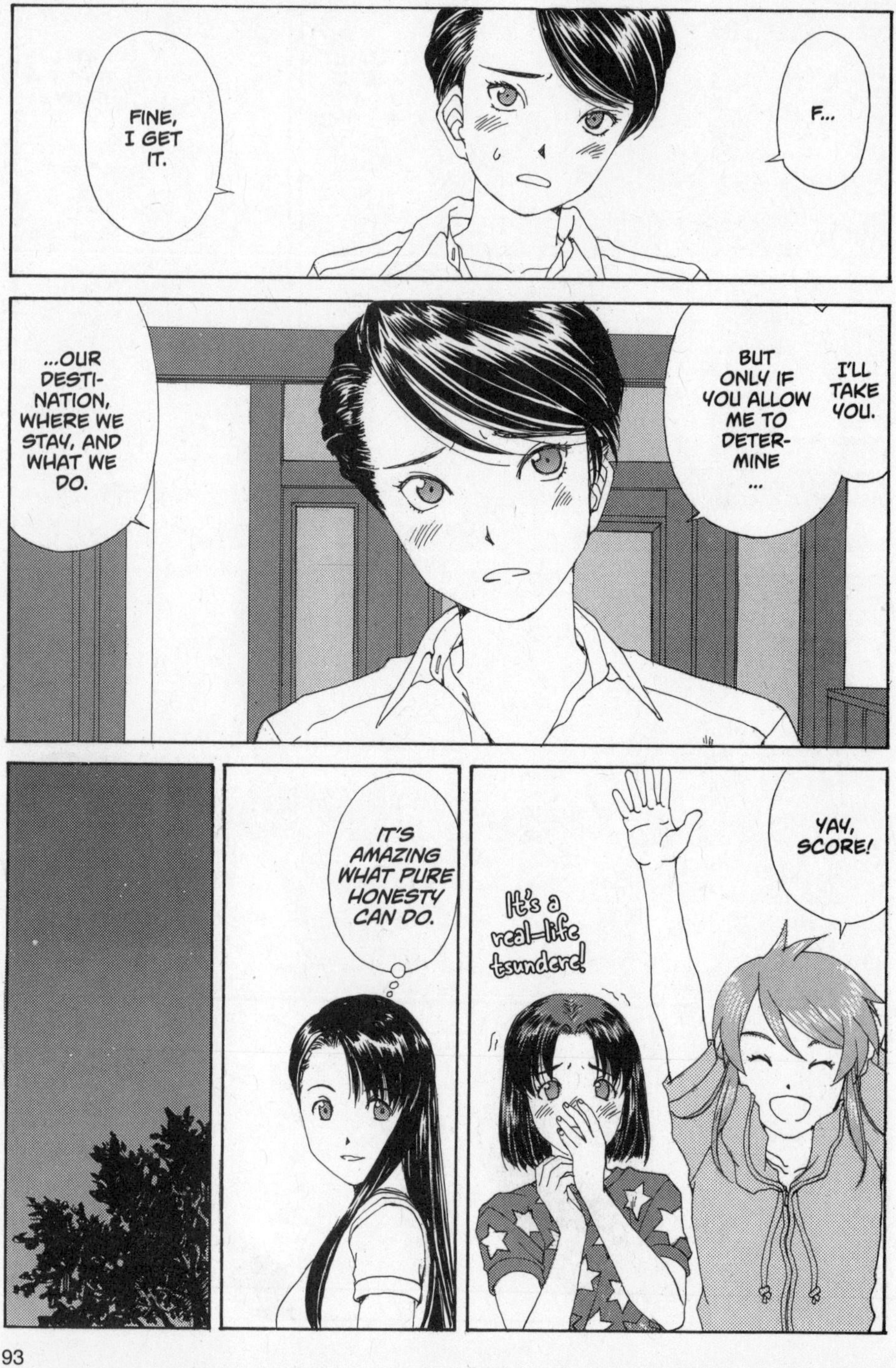
F...
FINE, I GET IT.
I'LL TAKE YOU.
BUT ONLY IF YOU ALLOW ME TO DETERMINE ...
...OUR DESTINATION, WHERE WE STAY, AND WHAT WE DO.
YAY, SCORE!
It's a real-life tsundere!
IT'S AMAZING WHAT PURE HONESTY CAN DO.

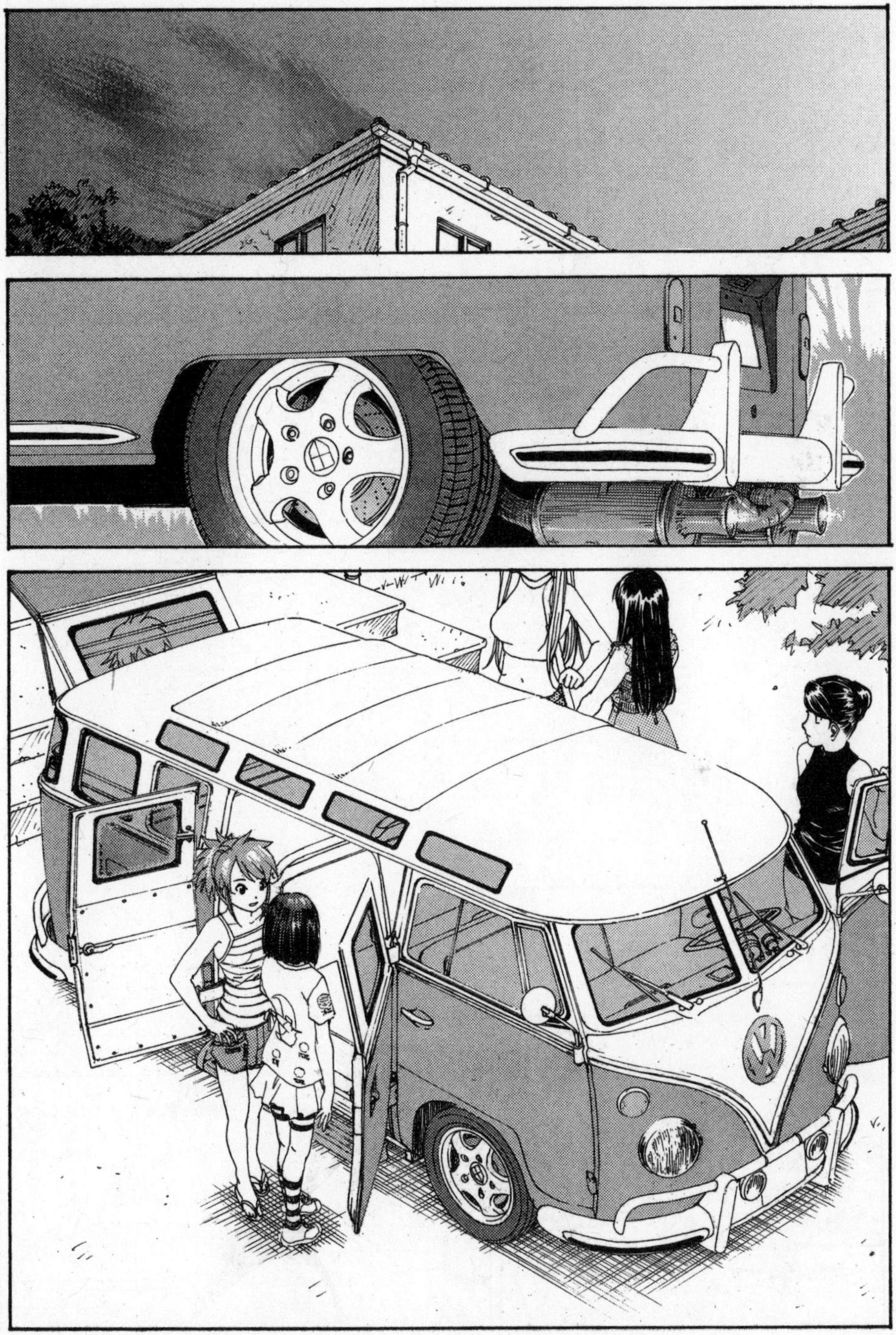

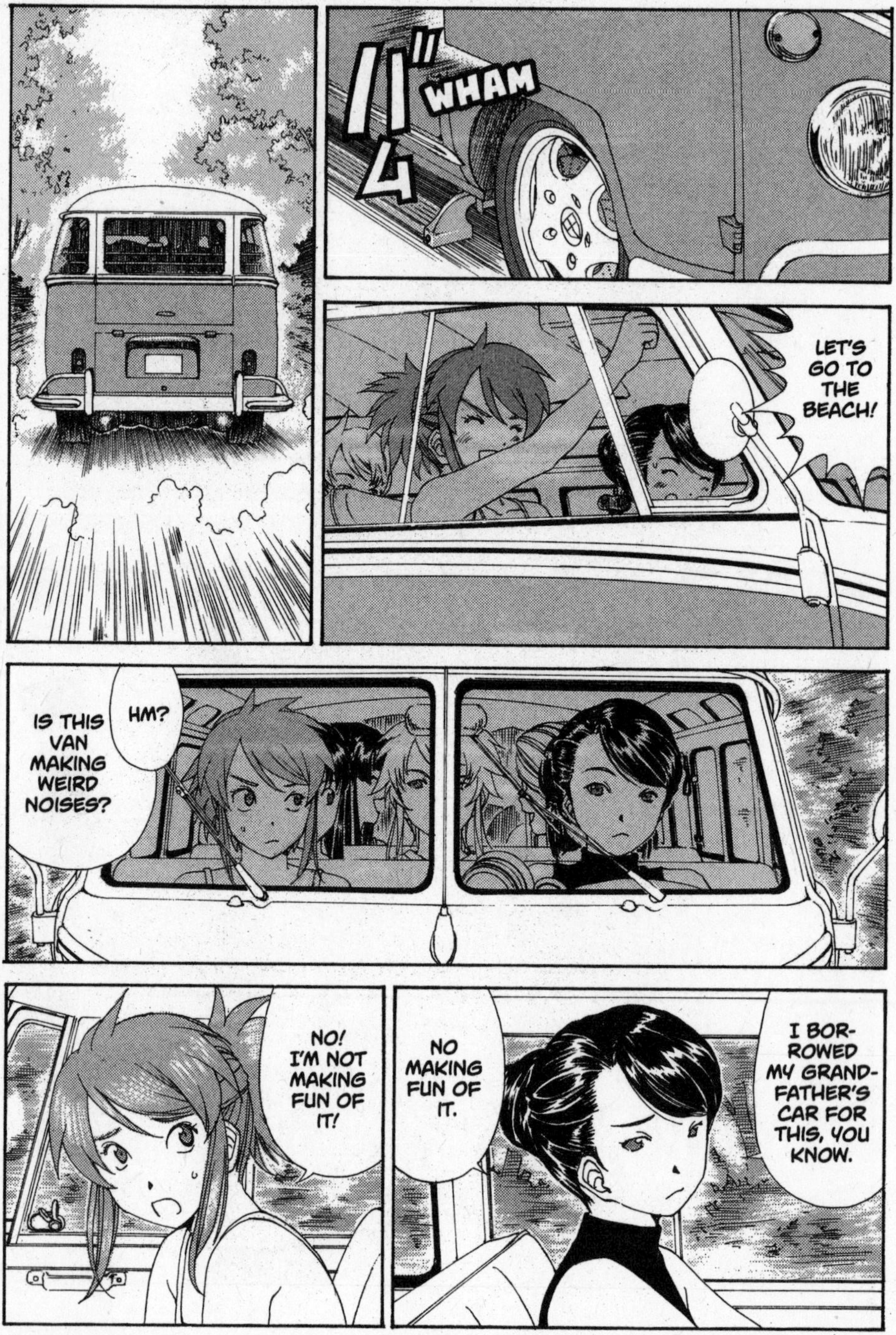
バム
WHAM
LET'S GO TO THE BEACH!
HM?
IS THIS VAN MAKING WEIRD NOISES?
I BOR-ROWED MY GRAND-FATHER'S CAR FOR THIS, YOU KNOW.
NO MAKING FUN OF IT.
NO! I'M NOT MAKING FUN OF IT!

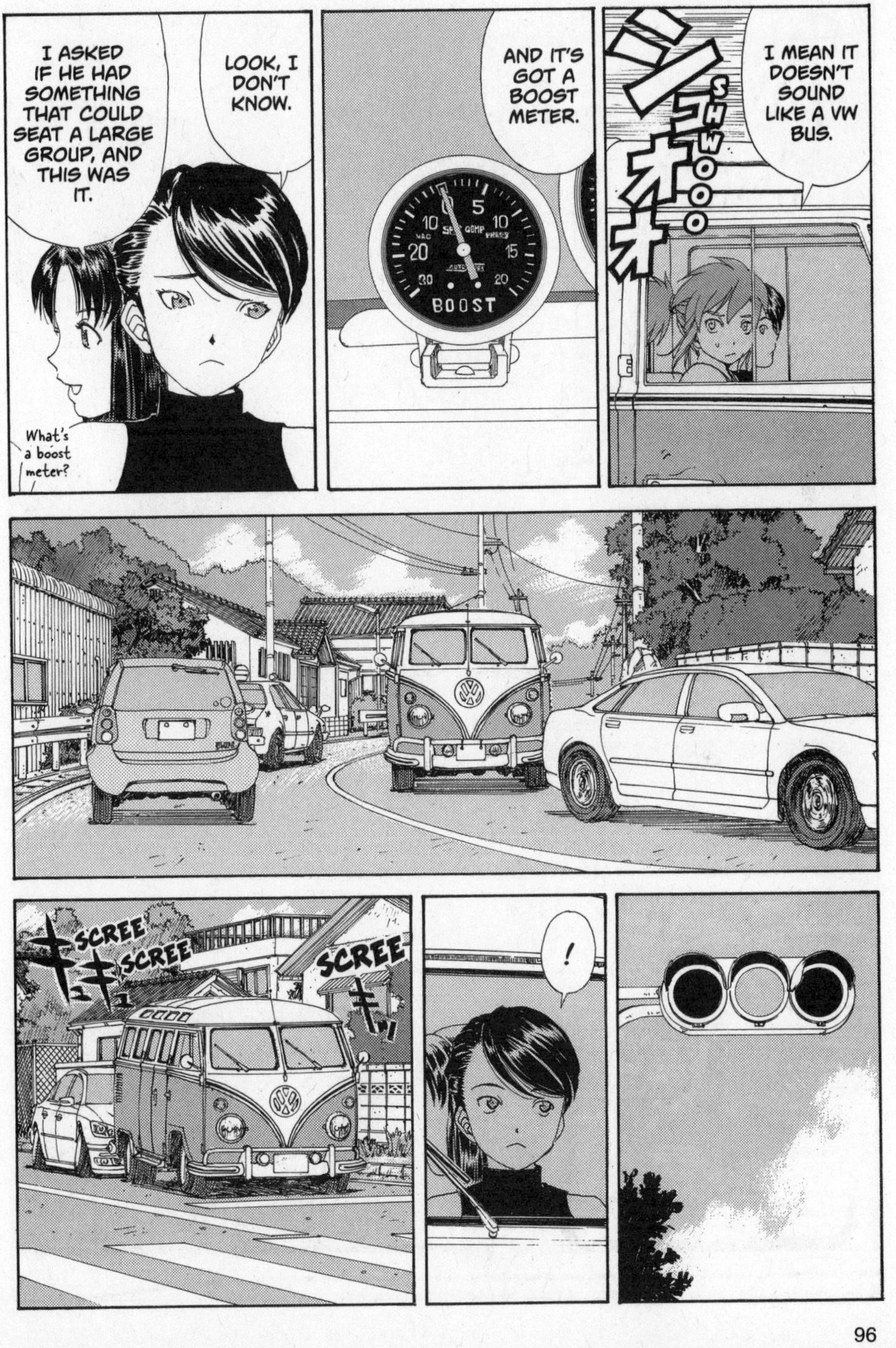
I MEAN IT DOESN'T SOUND LIKE A VW BUS.
SHWOOO
AND IT'S GOT A BOOST METER.
BOOST
LOOK, I DON'T KNOW.
I ASKED IF HE HAD SOMETHING THAT COULD SEAT A LARGE GROUP, AND THIS WAS IT.
What's a boost meter?
!
SCREE
SCREE
SCREE

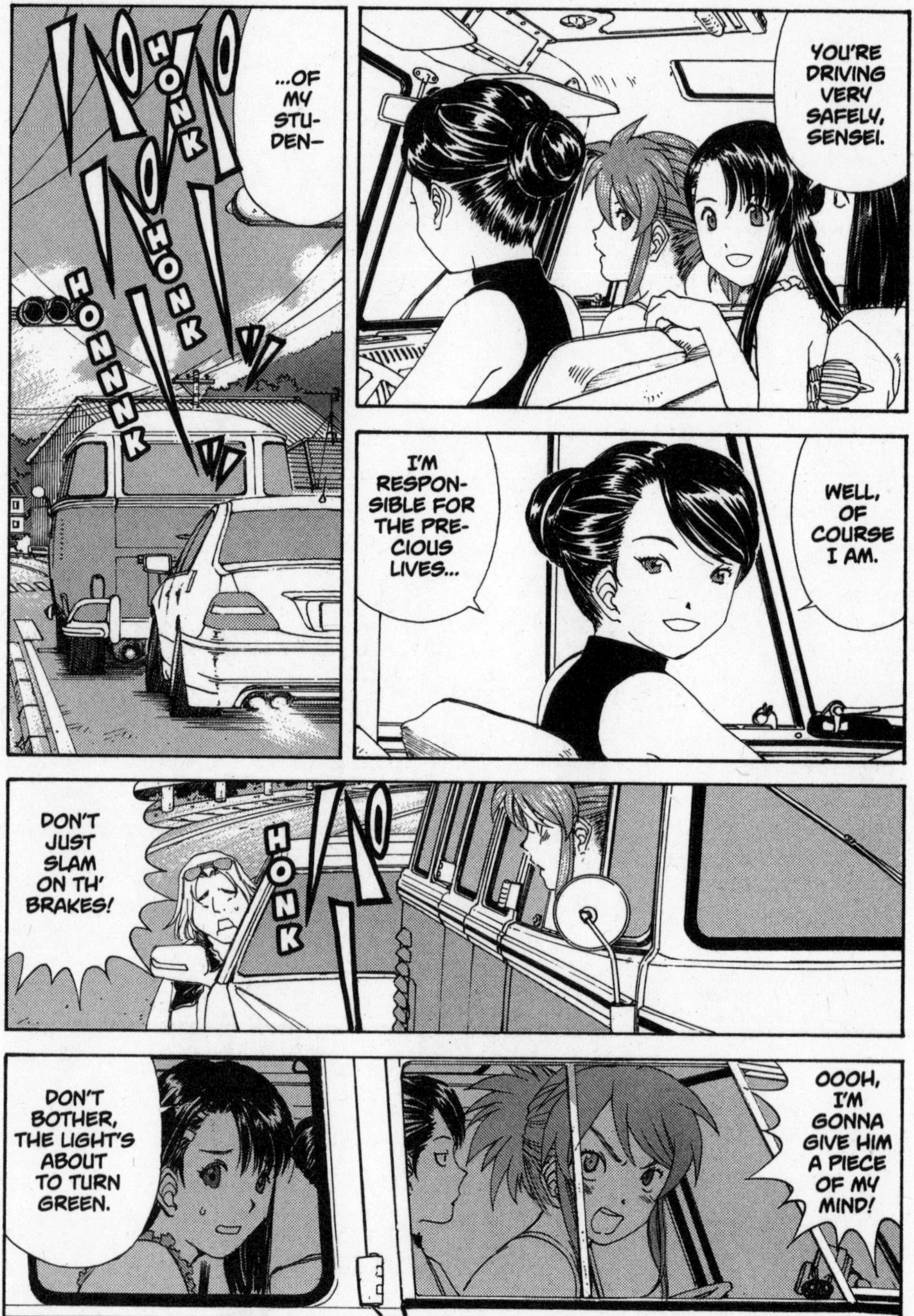
YOU'RE DRIVING VERY SAFELY, SENSEI.
WELL, OF COURSE I AM.
I'M RESPONSIBLE FOR THE PRECIOUS LIVES...
...OF MY STUDEN–
HONK
HONK
HONNNK
HONK
DON'T JUST SLAM ON TH' BRAKES!
OOOH, I'M GONNA GIVE HIM A PIECE OF MY MIND!
DON'T BOTHER, THE LIGHT'S ABOUT TO TURN GREEN.

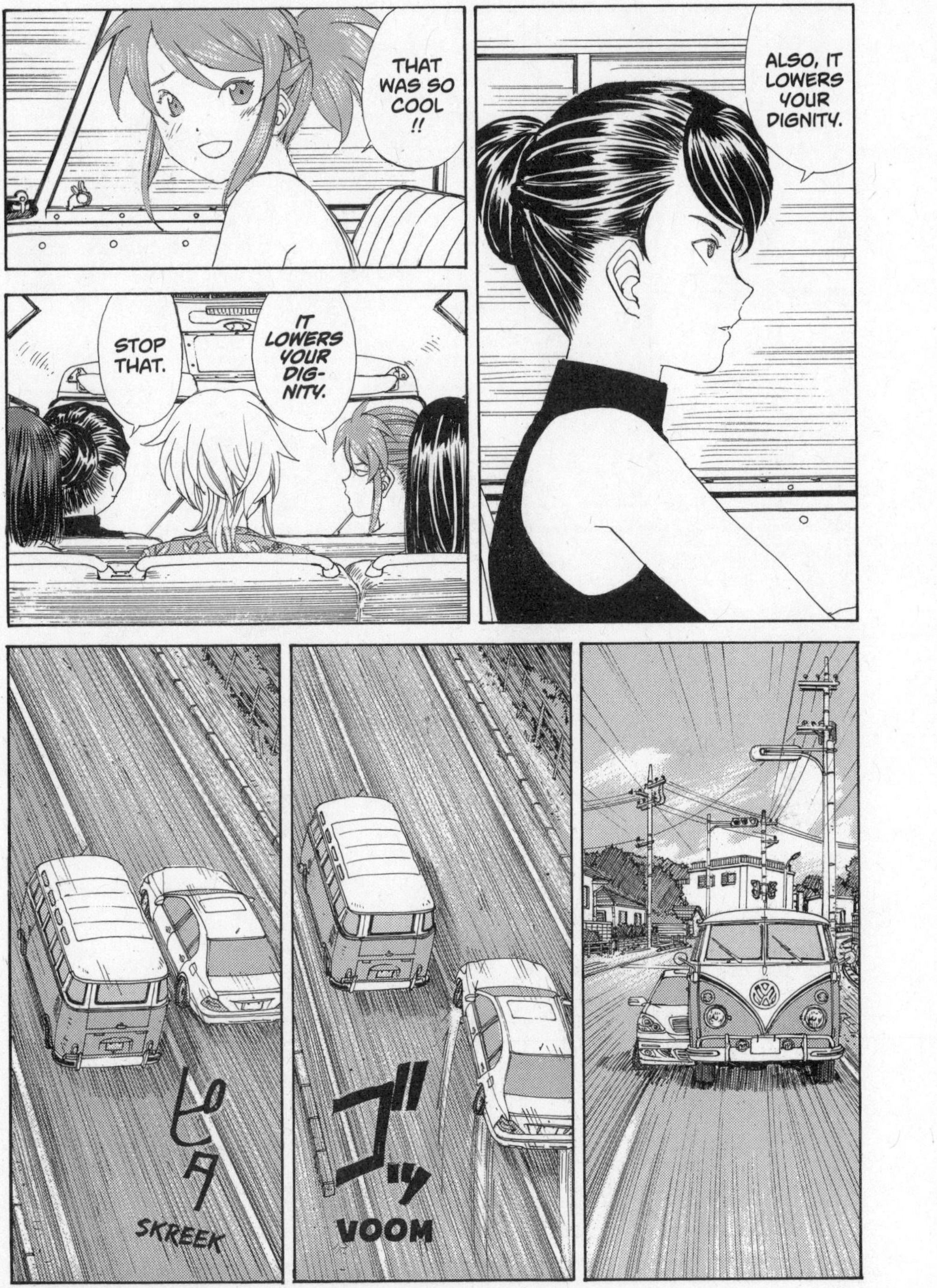
THAT WAS SO COOL !!
STOP THAT.
IT LOWERS YOUR DIG-NITY.
ALSO, IT LOWERS YOUR DIGNITY.
ピタ
SKREEK
ゴッ
VOOM

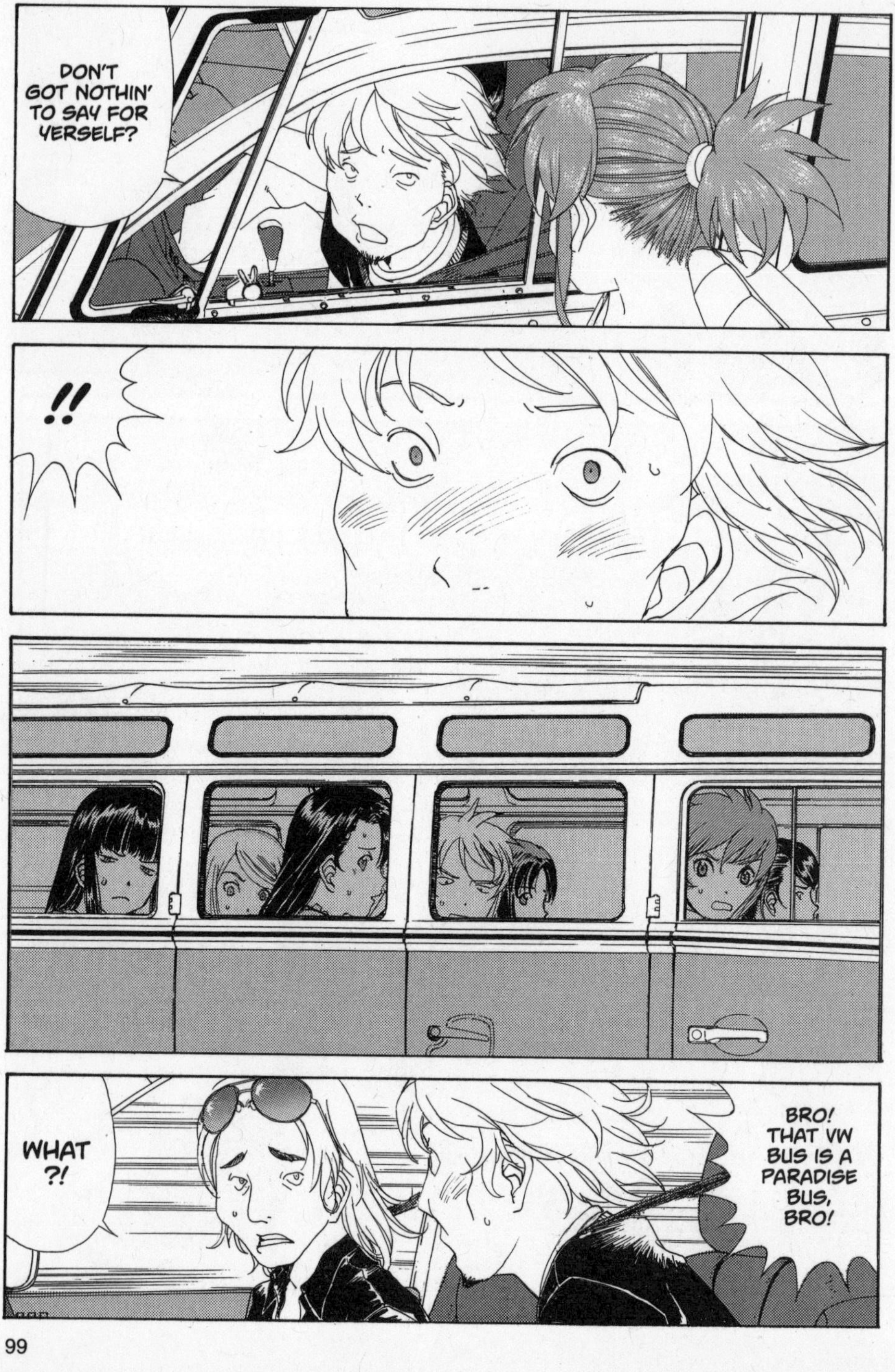
DON'T GOT NOTHIN' TO SAY FOR YERSELF?
!!
BRO! THAT VW BUS IS A PARADISE BUS, BRO!
WHAT ?!

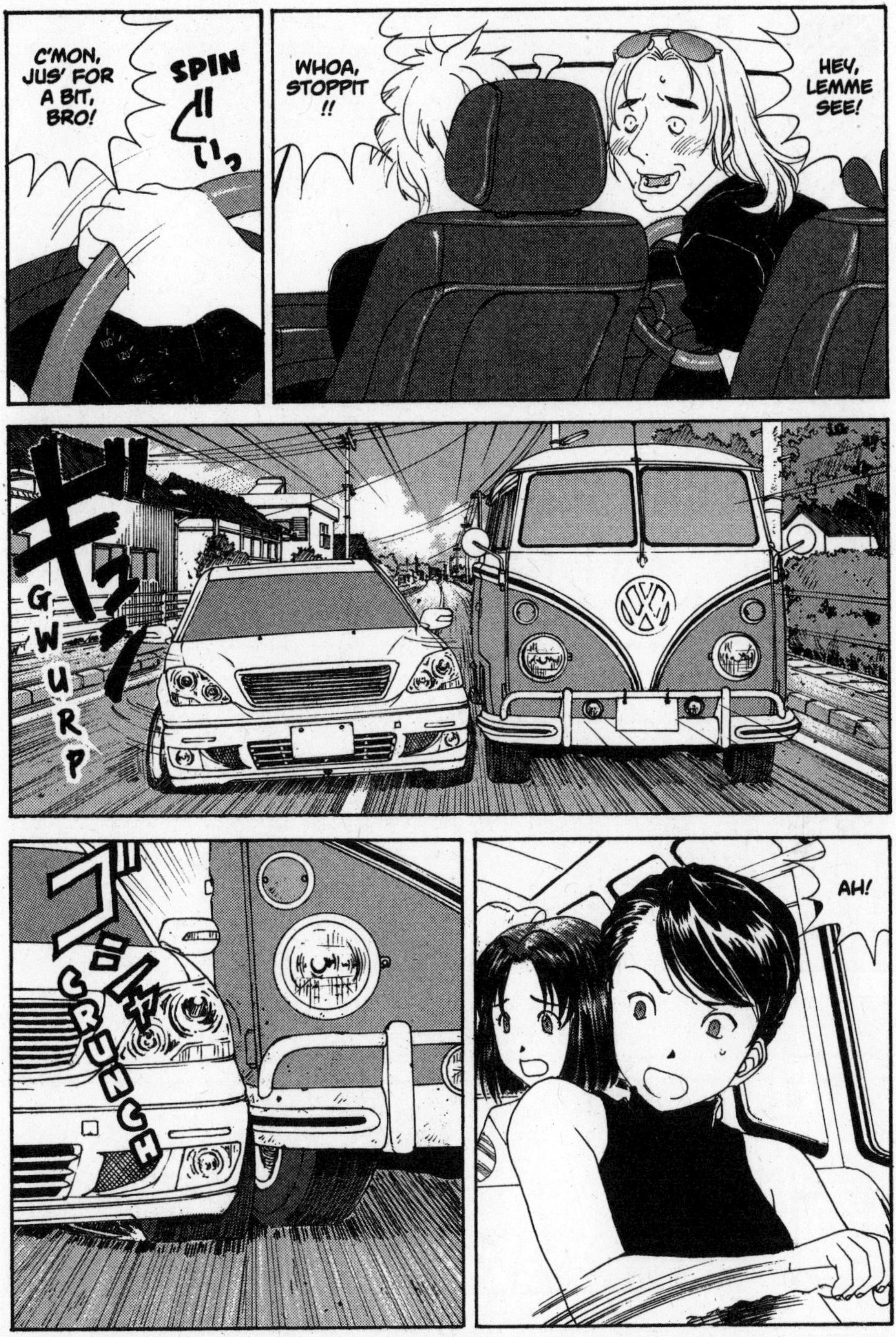
HEY, LEMME SEE!
WHOA, STOPPIT !!
C'MON, JUS' FOR A BIT, BRO!
SPIN
GWURP
AH!
CRUNCH

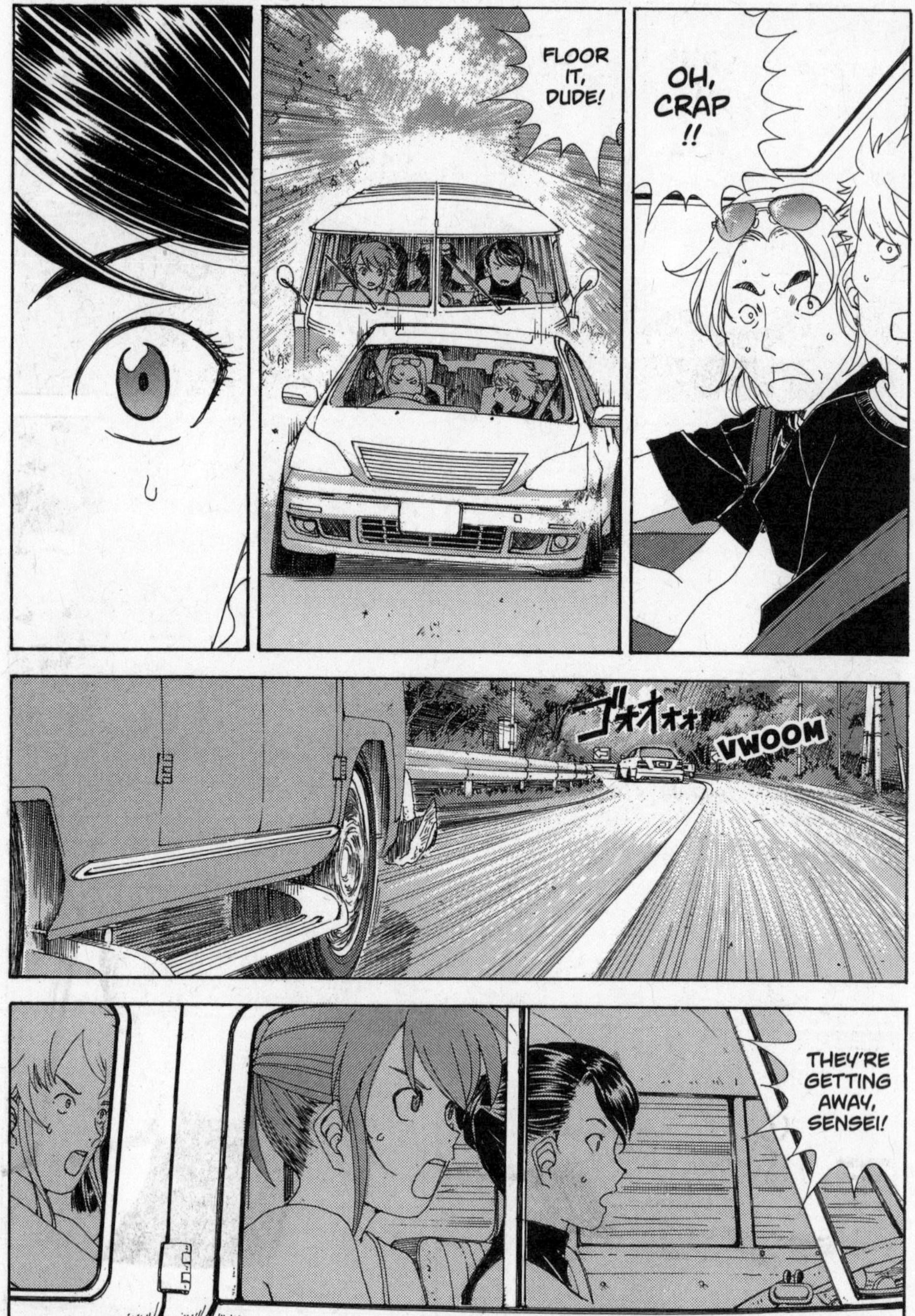
OH, CRAP !!
FLOOR IT, DUDE!
ゴオオォォ
VWOOM
THEY'RE GETTING AWAY, SENSEI!

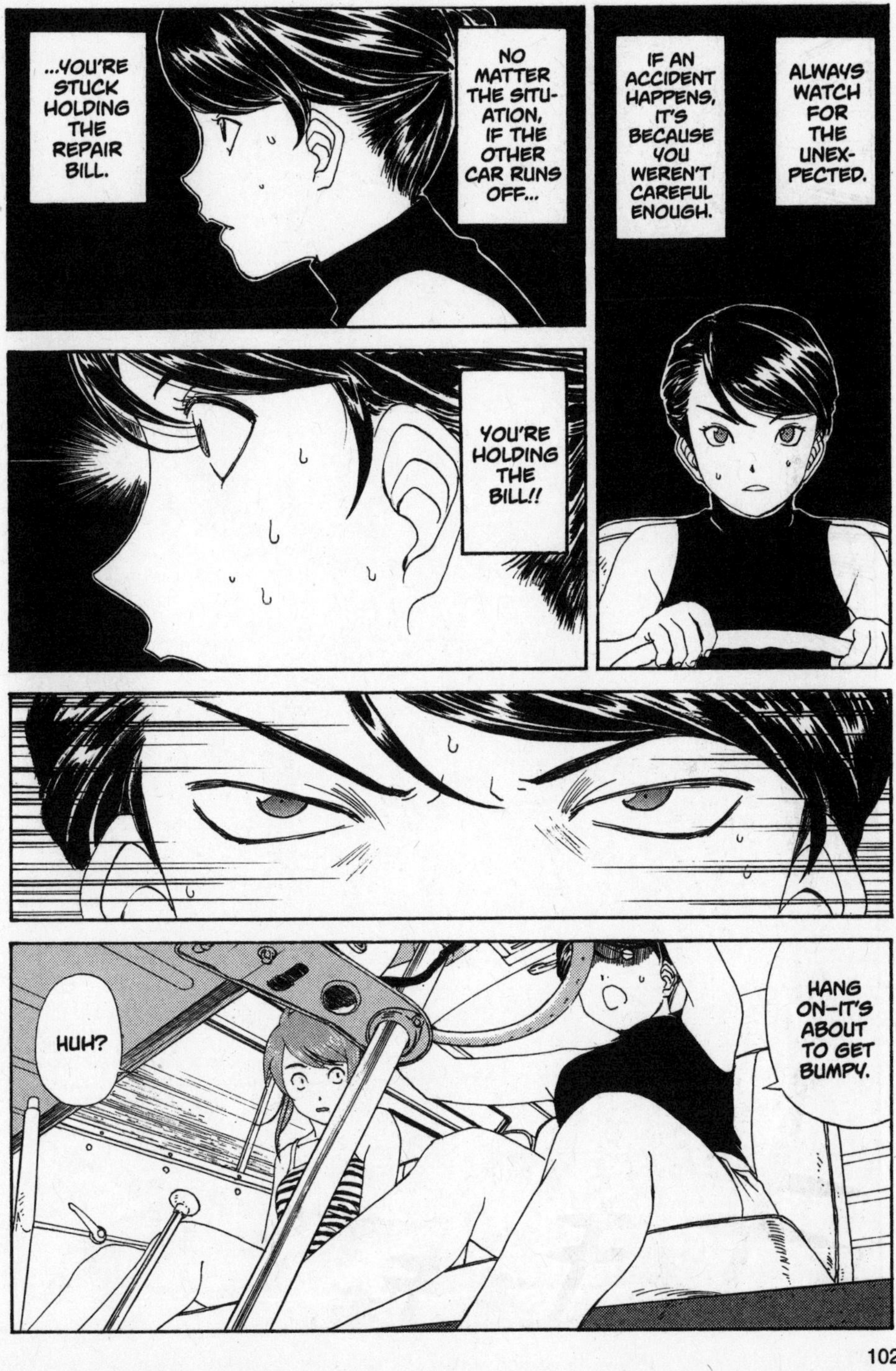
ALWAYS WATCH FOR THE UNEXPECTED.
IF AN ACCIDENT HAPPENS, IT'S BECAUSE YOU WEREN'T CAREFUL ENOUGH.
NO MATTER THE SITUATION, IF THE OTHER CAR RUNS OFF...
...YOU'RE STUCK HOLDING THE REPAIR BILL.
YOU'RE HOLDING THE BILL!!
HANG ON—IT'S ABOUT TO GET BUMPY.
HUH?

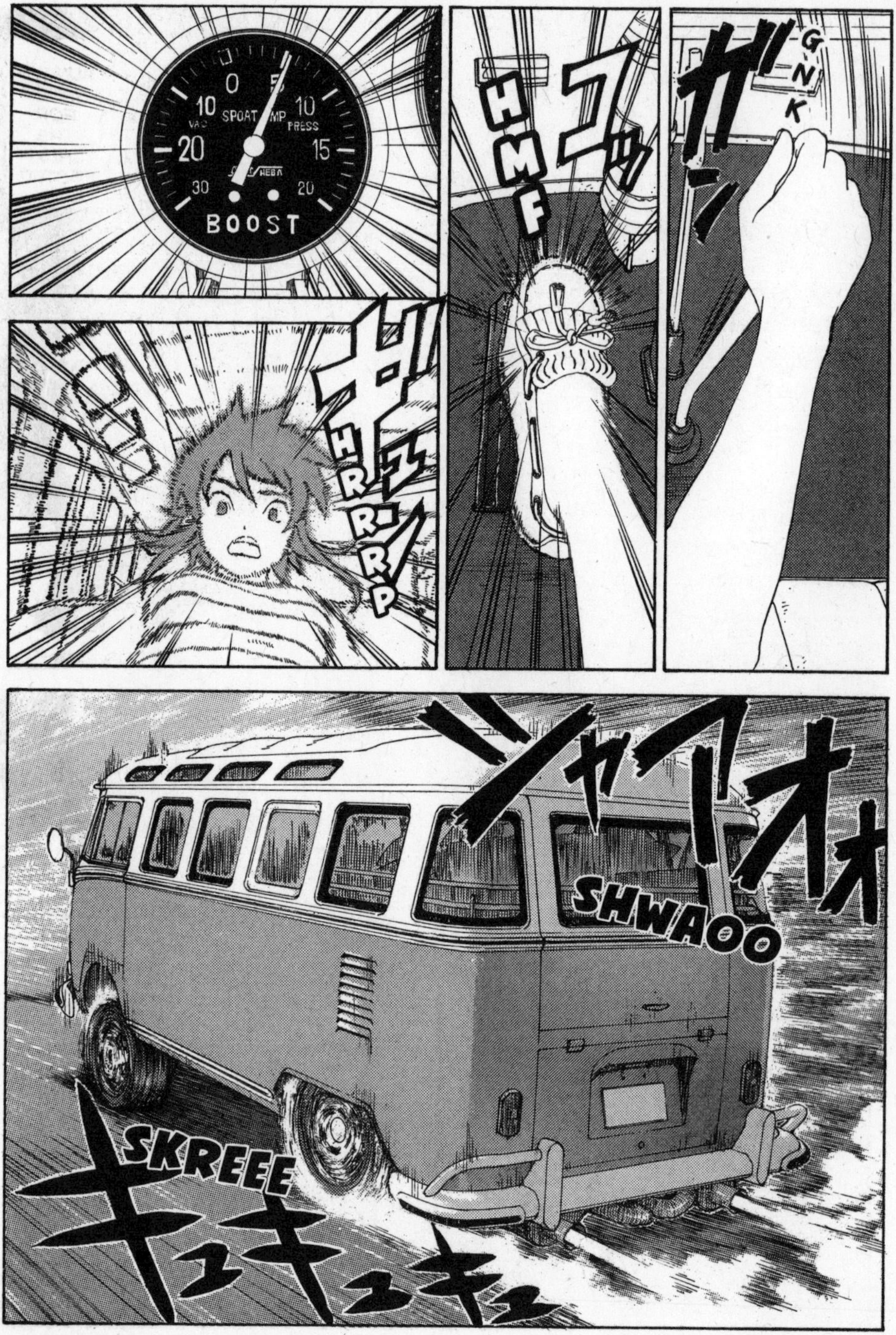
GNK
HMF
BOOST
HRR-R-RP
SHWAOO
SKREEE

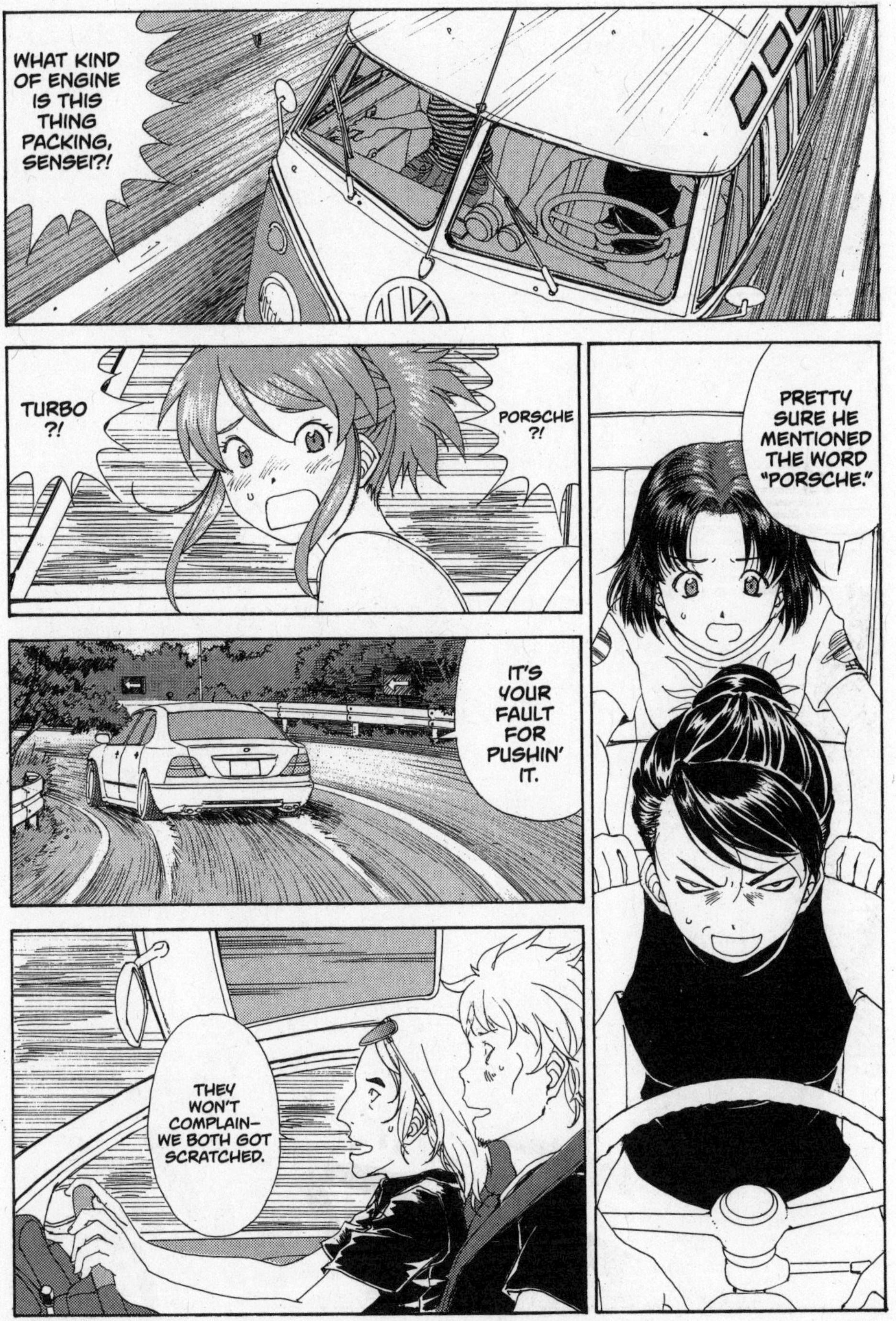
WHAT KIND OF ENGINE IS THIS THING PACKING, SENSEI?!
PRETTY SURE HE MENTIONED THE WORD "PORSCHE."
PORSCHE ?!
TURBO ?!
IT'S YOUR FAULT FOR PUSHIN' IT.
THEY WON'T COMPLAIN— WE BOTH GOT SCRATCHED.

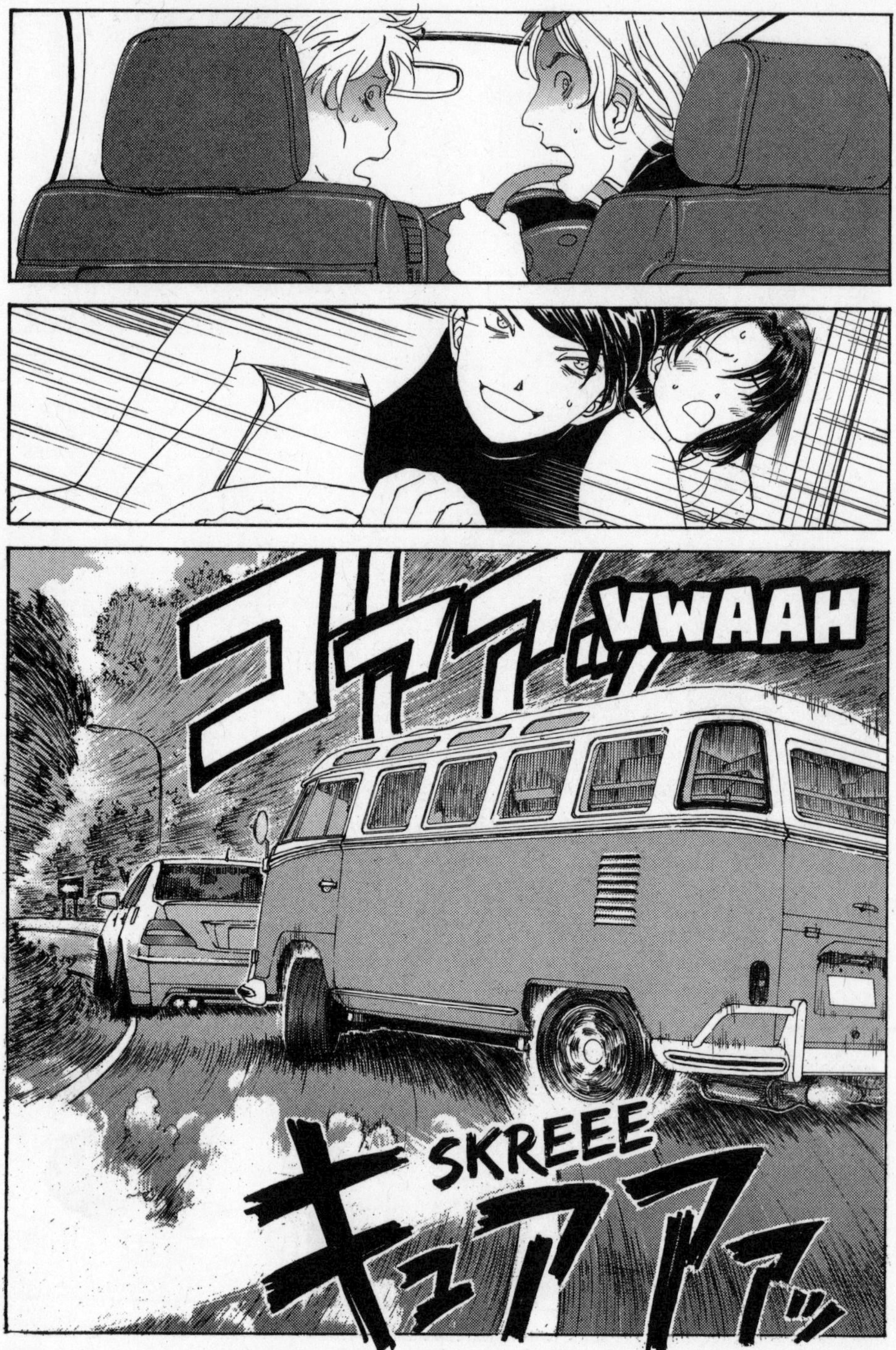
ゴァァッ
VWAAH
SKREEE
キュアアッ

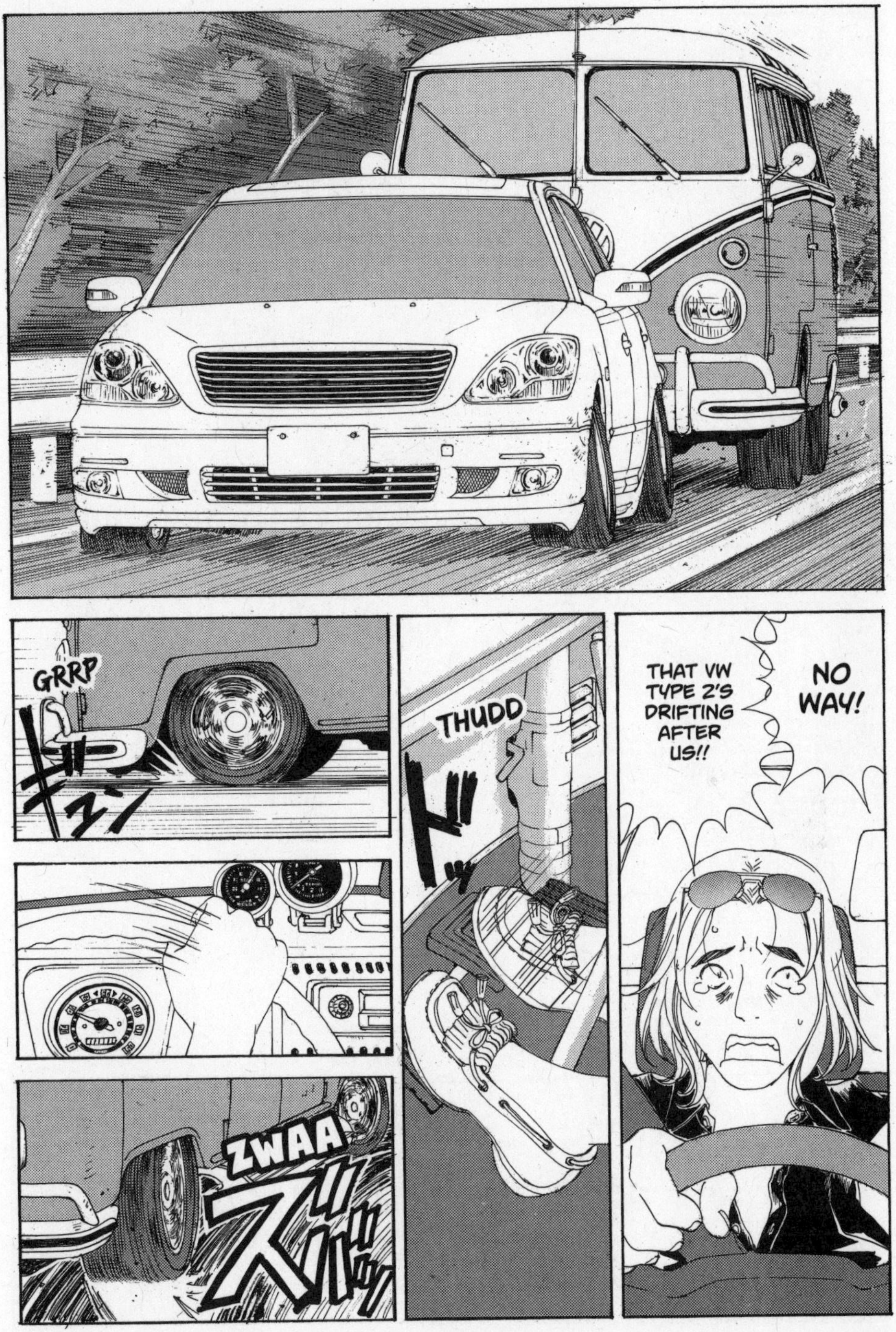
NO WAY!
THAT VW TYPE 2'S DRIFTING AFTER US!!
THUDD
GRRP
ZWAA

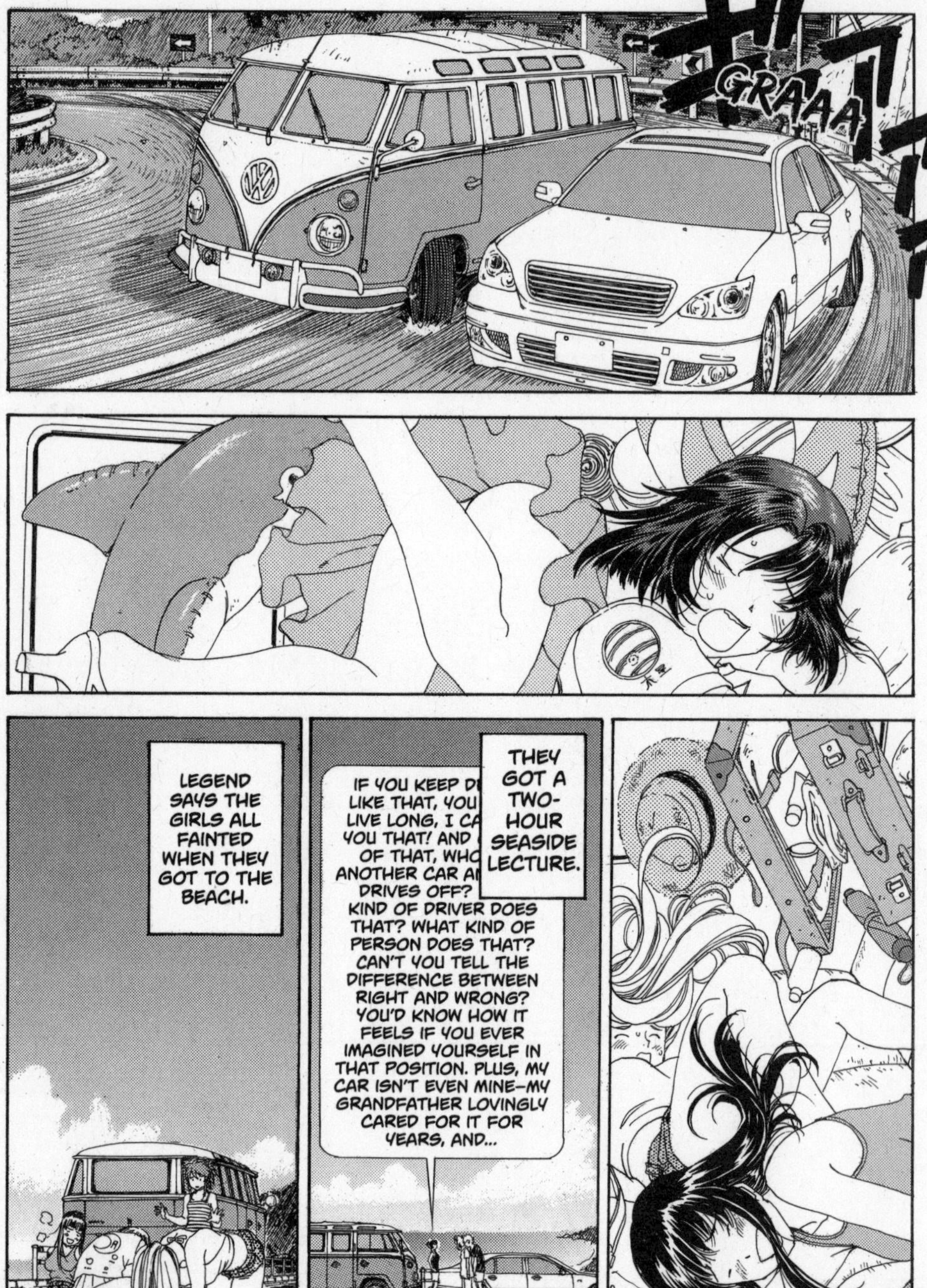
GRAAA
THEY GOT A TWO-HOUR SEASIDE LECTURE.
IF YOU KEEP DR LIKE THAT, YOU LIVE LONG, I CA YOU THAT! AND OF THAT, WHO ANOTHER CAR AN DRIVES OFF? KIND OF DRIVER DOES THAT? WHAT KIND OF PERSON DOES THAT? CAN'T YOU TELL THE DIFFERENCE BETWEEN RIGHT AND WRONG? YOU'D KNOW HOW IT FEELS IF YOU EVER IMAGINED YOURSELF IN THAT POSITION. PLUS, MY CAR ISN'T EVEN MINE—MY GRANDFATHER LOVINGLY CARED FOR IT FOR YEARS, AND...
LEGEND SAYS THE GIRLS ALL FAINTED WHEN THEY GOT TO THE BEACH.

episode.11 / **END**

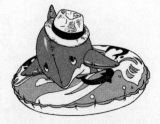

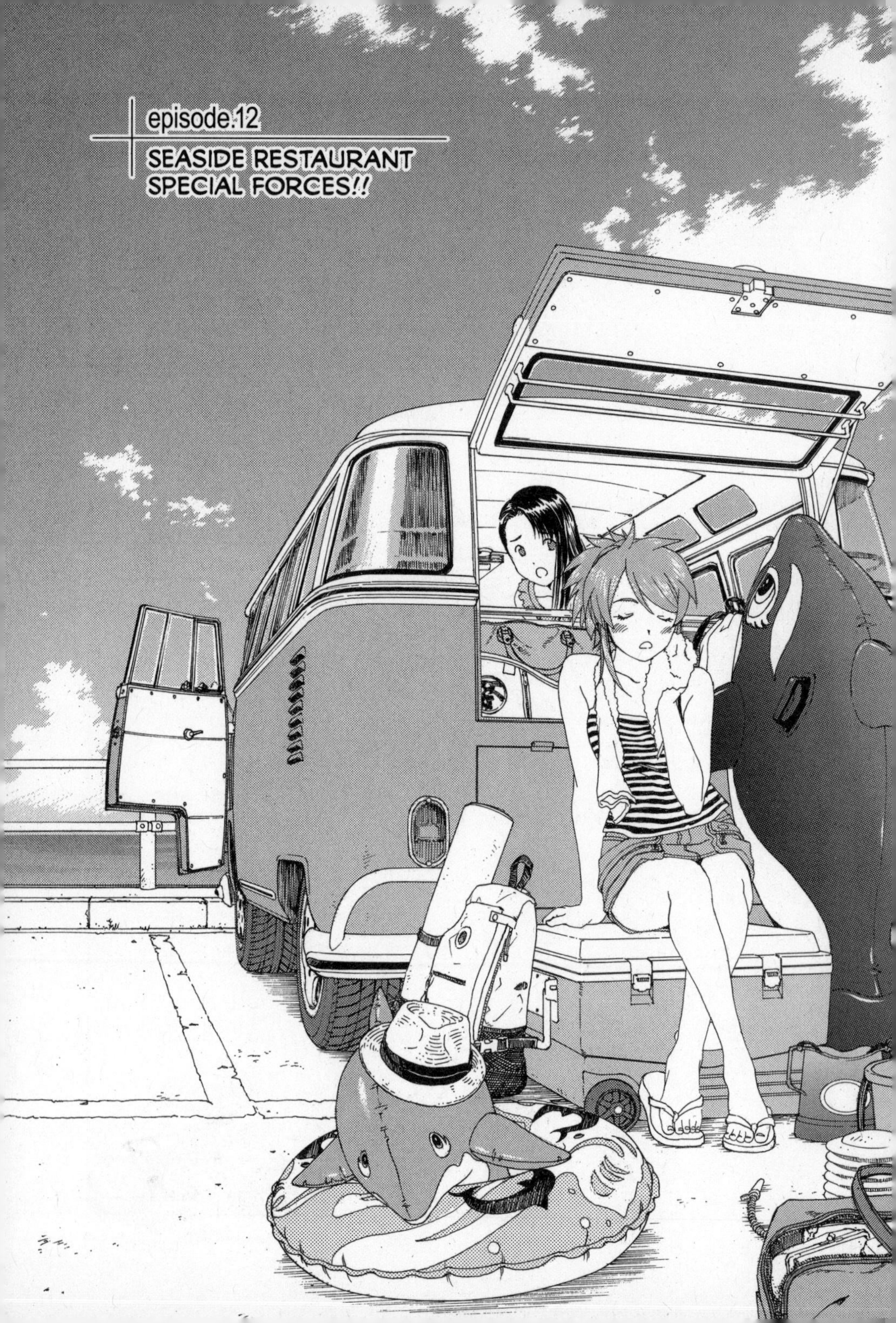
episode.12
SEASIDE RESTAURANT
SPECIAL FORCES!!

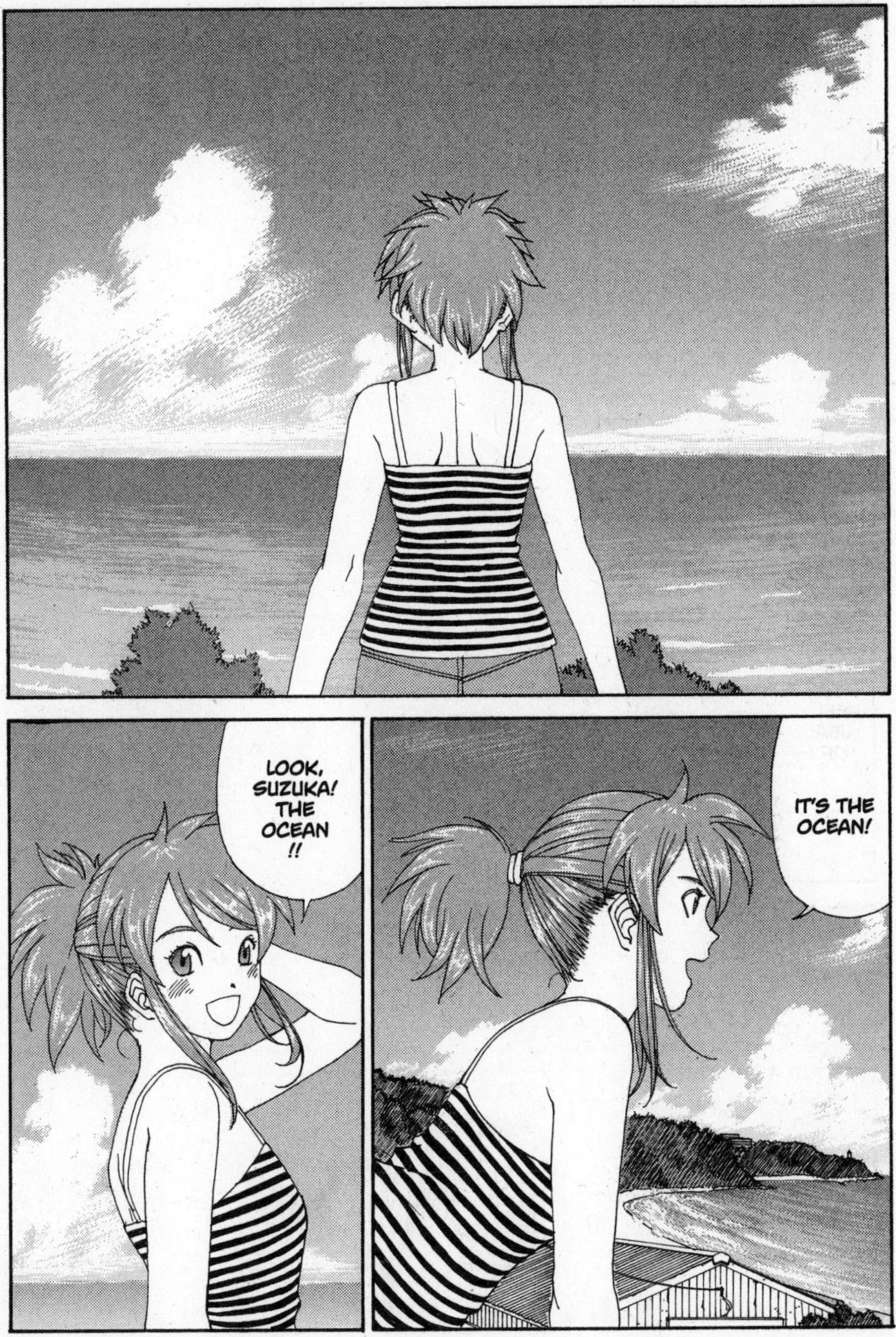
IT'S THE OCEAN!
LOOK, SUZUKA! THE OCEAN !!

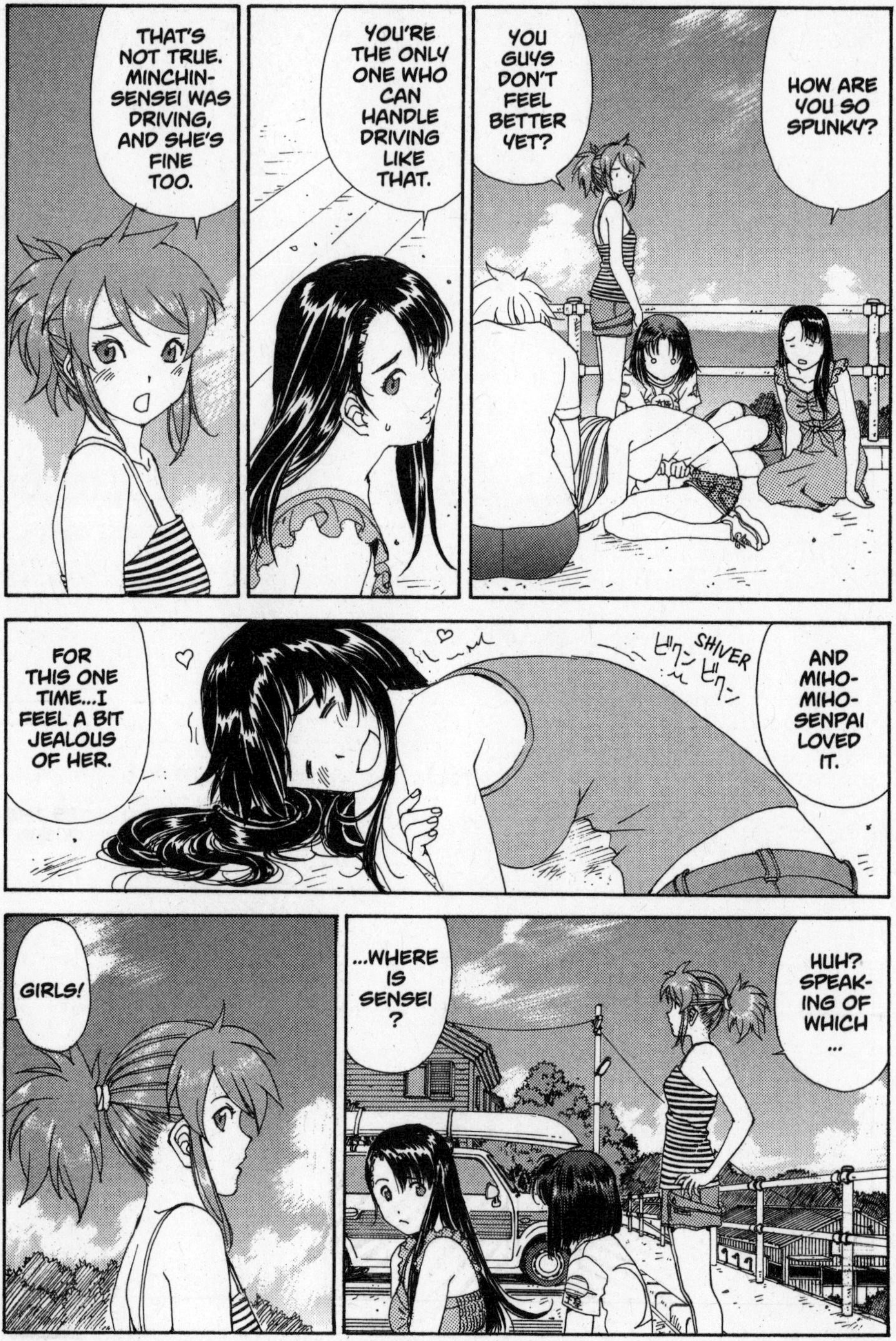
HOW ARE YOU SO SPUNKY?
YOU GUYS DON'T FEEL BETTER YET?
YOU'RE THE ONLY ONE WHO CAN HANDLE DRIVING LIKE THAT.
THAT'S NOT TRUE. MINCHIN-SENSEI WAS DRIVING, AND SHE'S FINE TOO.
AND MIHO-MIHO-SENPAI LOVED IT.
SHIVER
ビクン ビクン
FOR THIS ONE TIME...I FEEL A BIT JEALOUS OF HER.
HUH? SPEAK-ING OF WHICH ...
...WHERE IS SENSEI ?
GIRLS!

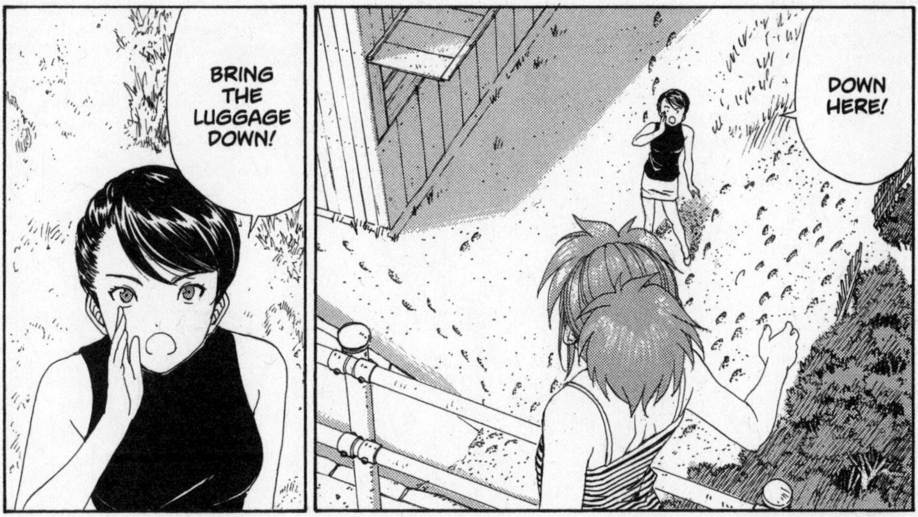
DOWN HERE!
BRING THE LUGGAGE DOWN!

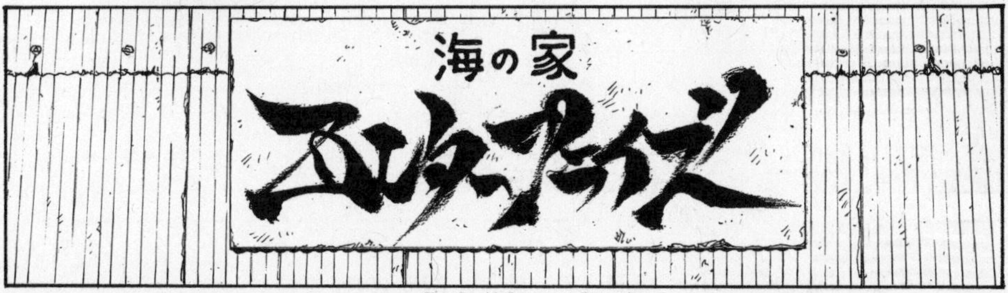
海の家

Sign: Seaside Restaurant: Enterprise

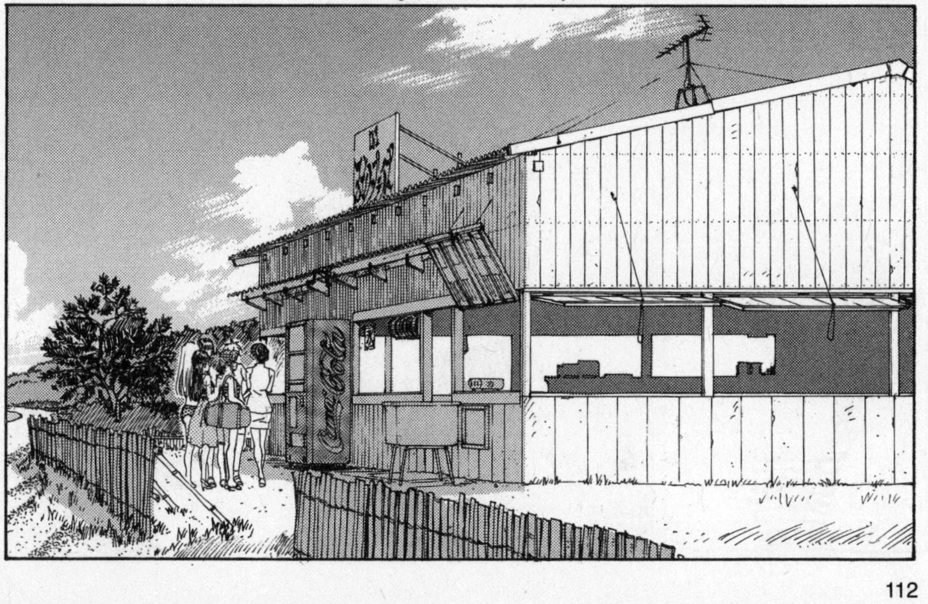

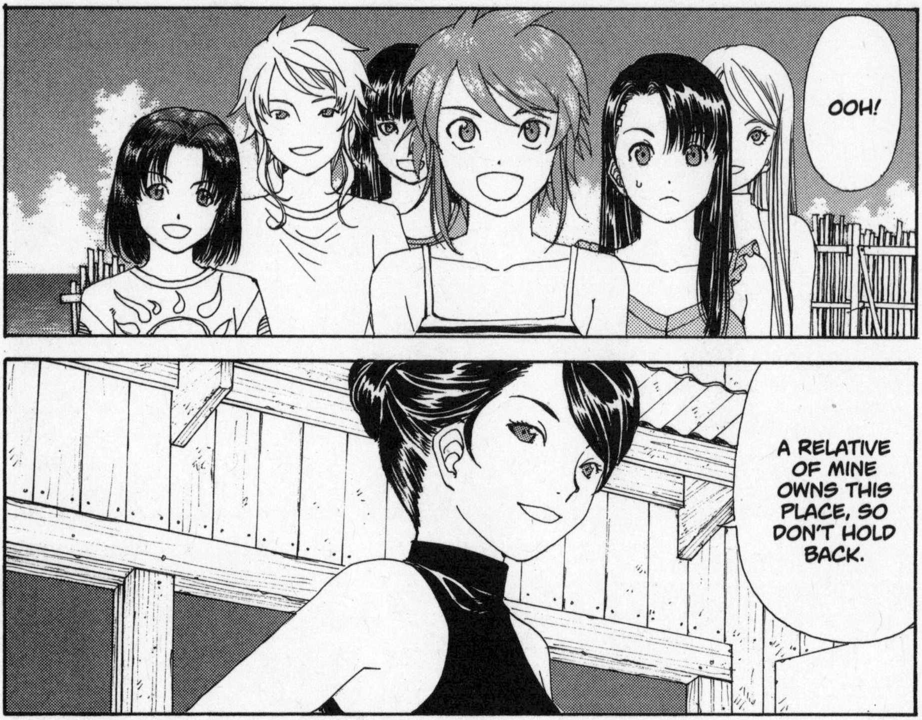
OOH!
A RELATIVE OF MINE OWNS THIS PLACE, SO DON'T HOLD BACK.

Signs: (L) Oden, (R) Toilet

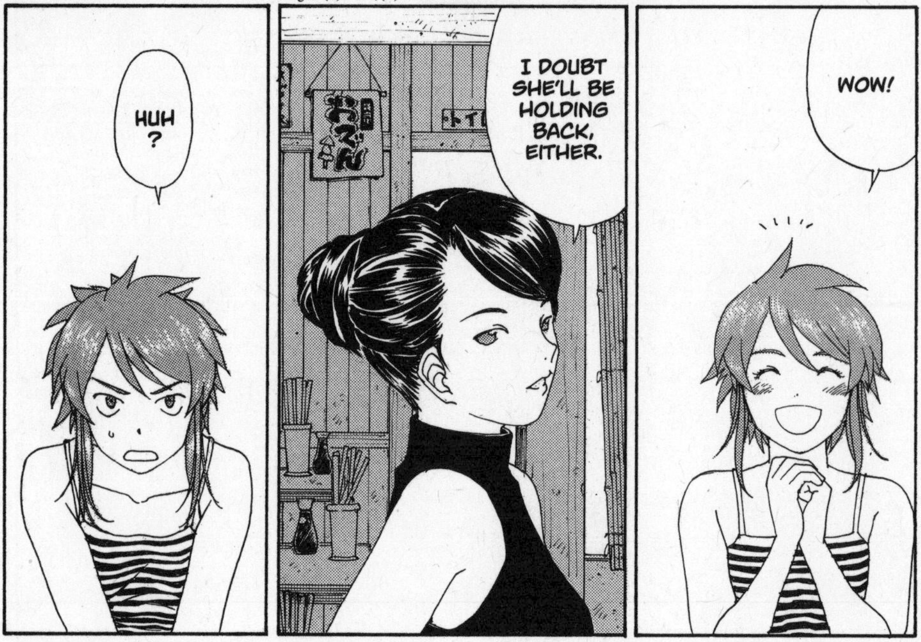
WOW!
I DOUBT SHE'LL BE HOLDING BACK, EITHER.
HUH?

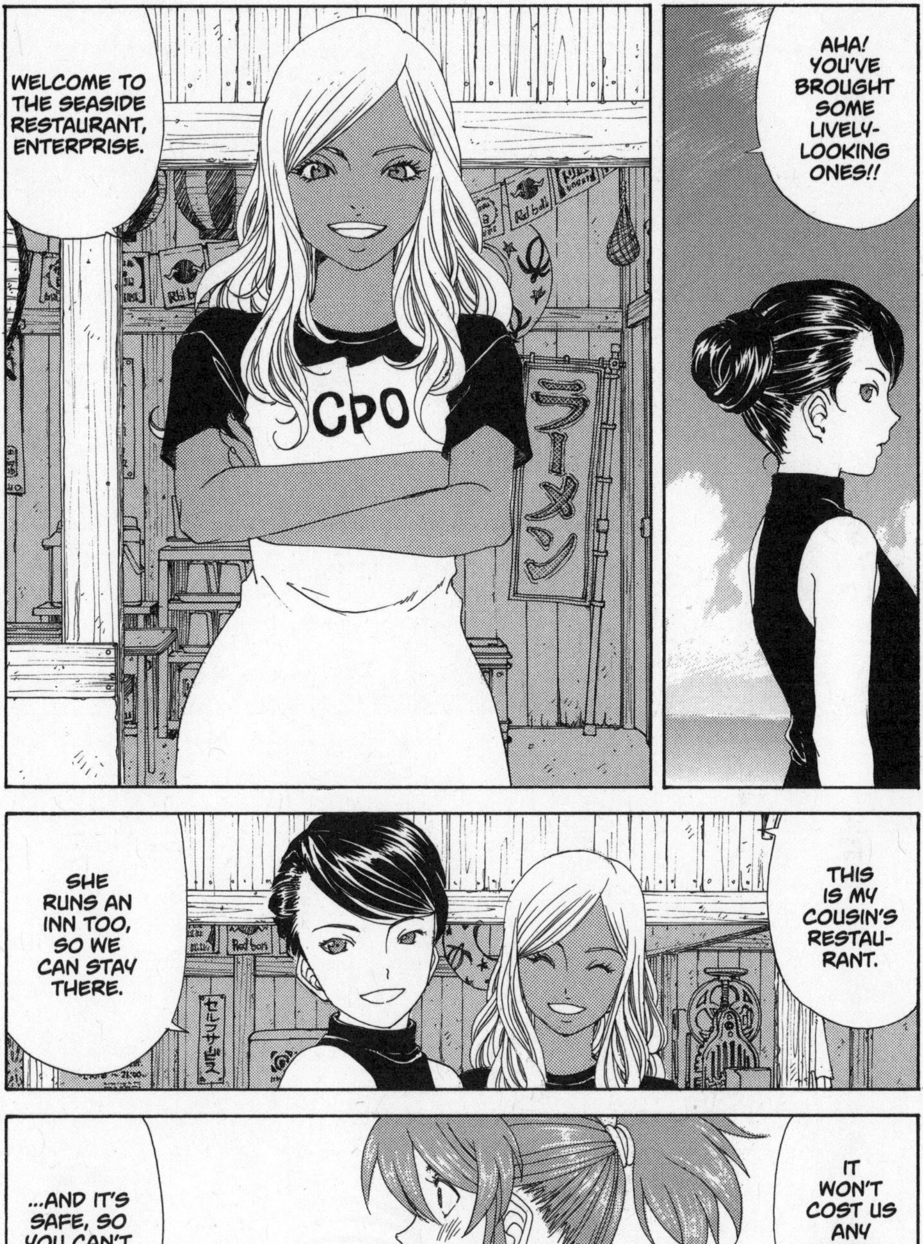
AHA! YOU'VE BROUGHT SOME LIVELY-LOOKING ONES!!
WELCOME TO THE SEASIDE RESTAURANT, ENTERPRISE.
CPO
ラーメン
THIS IS MY COUSIN'S RESTAU-RANT.
SHE RUNS AN INN TOO, SO WE CAN STAY THERE.
セルフサービス
IT WON'T COST US ANY MONEY...
...AND IT'S SAFE, SO YOU CAN'T COMPLAIN.

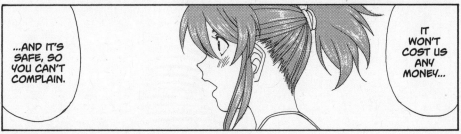

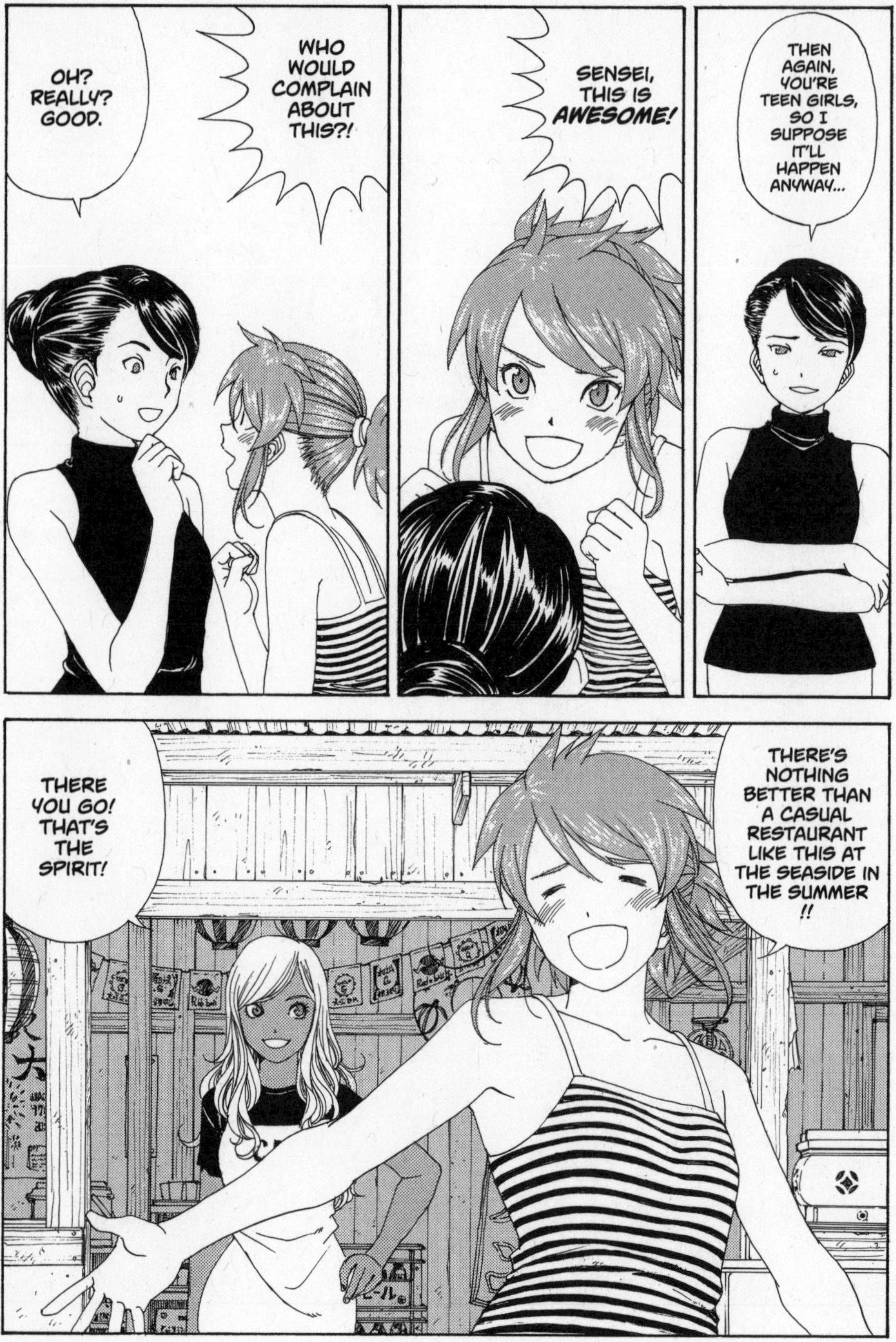
THEN AGAIN, YOU'RE TEEN GIRLS, SO I SUPPOSE IT'LL HAPPEN ANYWAY...
SENSEI, THIS IS AWESOME!
WHO WOULD COMPLAIN ABOUT THIS?!
OH? REALLY? GOOD.
THERE'S NOTHING BETTER THAN A CASUAL RESTAURANT LIKE THIS AT THE SEASIDE IN THE SUMMER !!
THERE YOU GO! THAT'S THE SPIRIT!

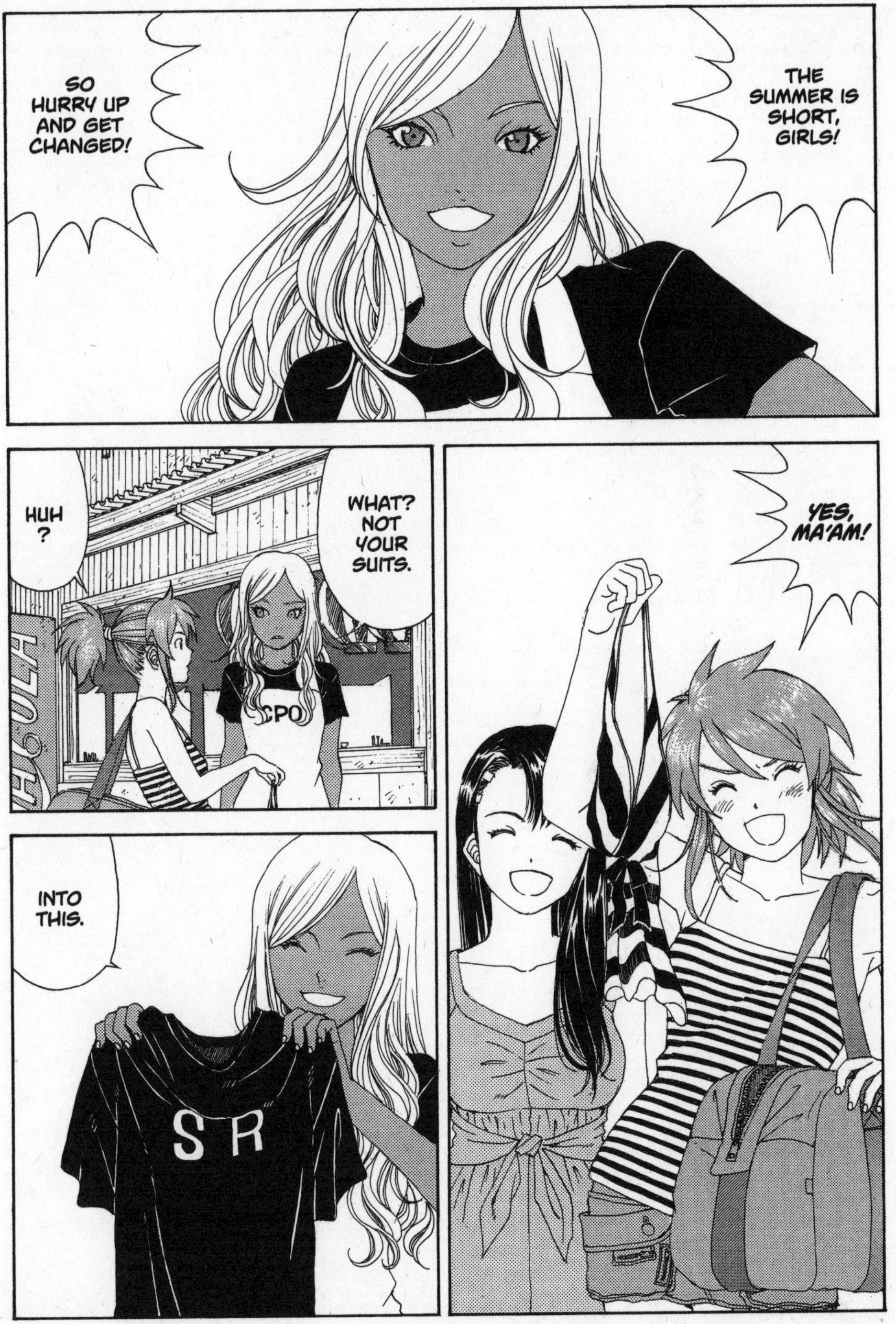
THE SUMMER IS SHORT, GIRLS!
SO HURRY UP AND GET CHANGED!
YES, MA'AM!
WHAT? NOT YOUR SUITS.
HUH ?
CPO
INTO THIS.
SR

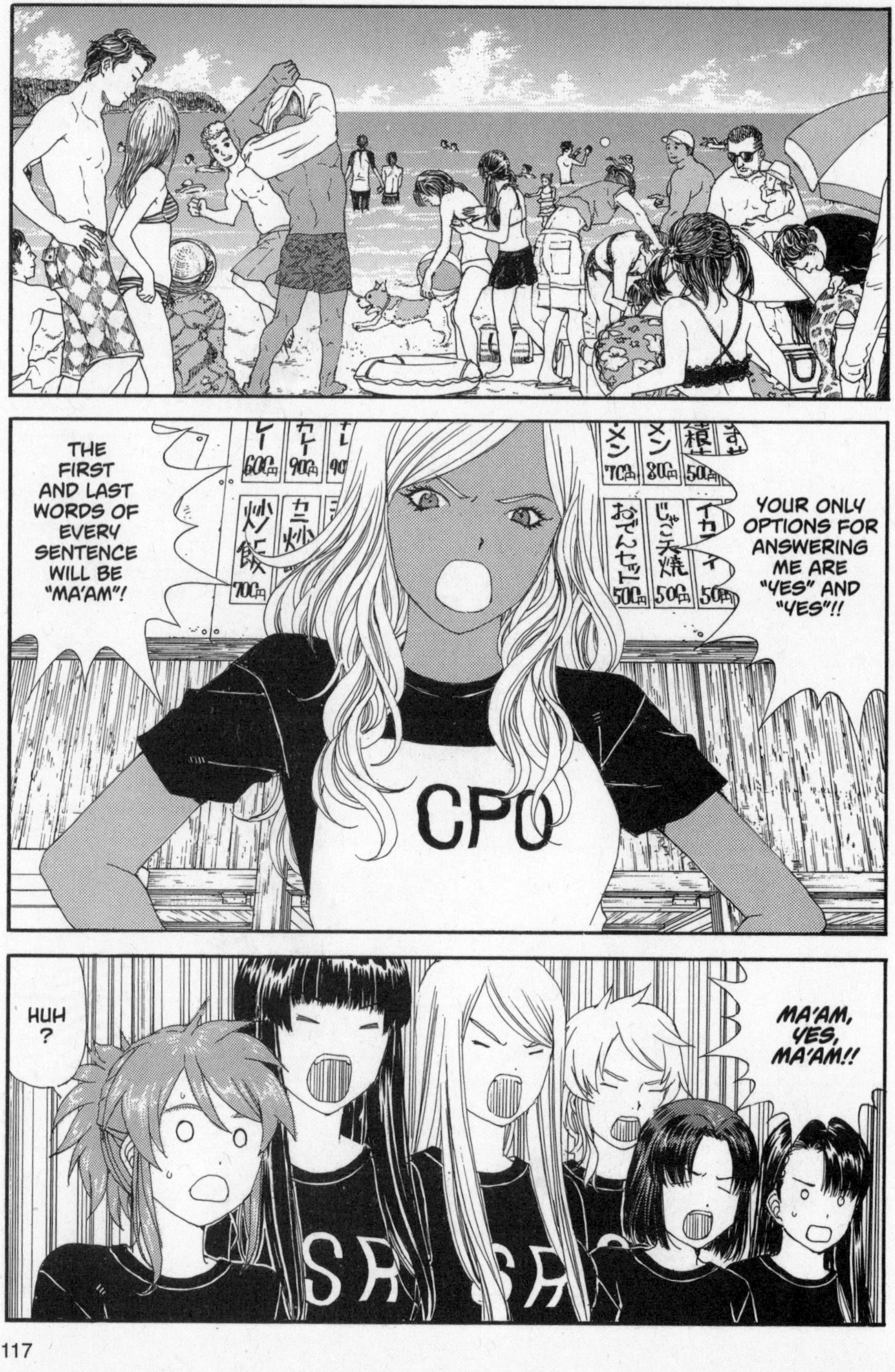
YOUR ONLY OPTIONS FOR ANSWERING ME ARE "YES" AND "YES"!!
THE FIRST AND LAST WORDS OF EVERY SENTENCE WILL BE "MA'AM"!
CPO
MA'AM, YES, MA'AM!!
HUH?

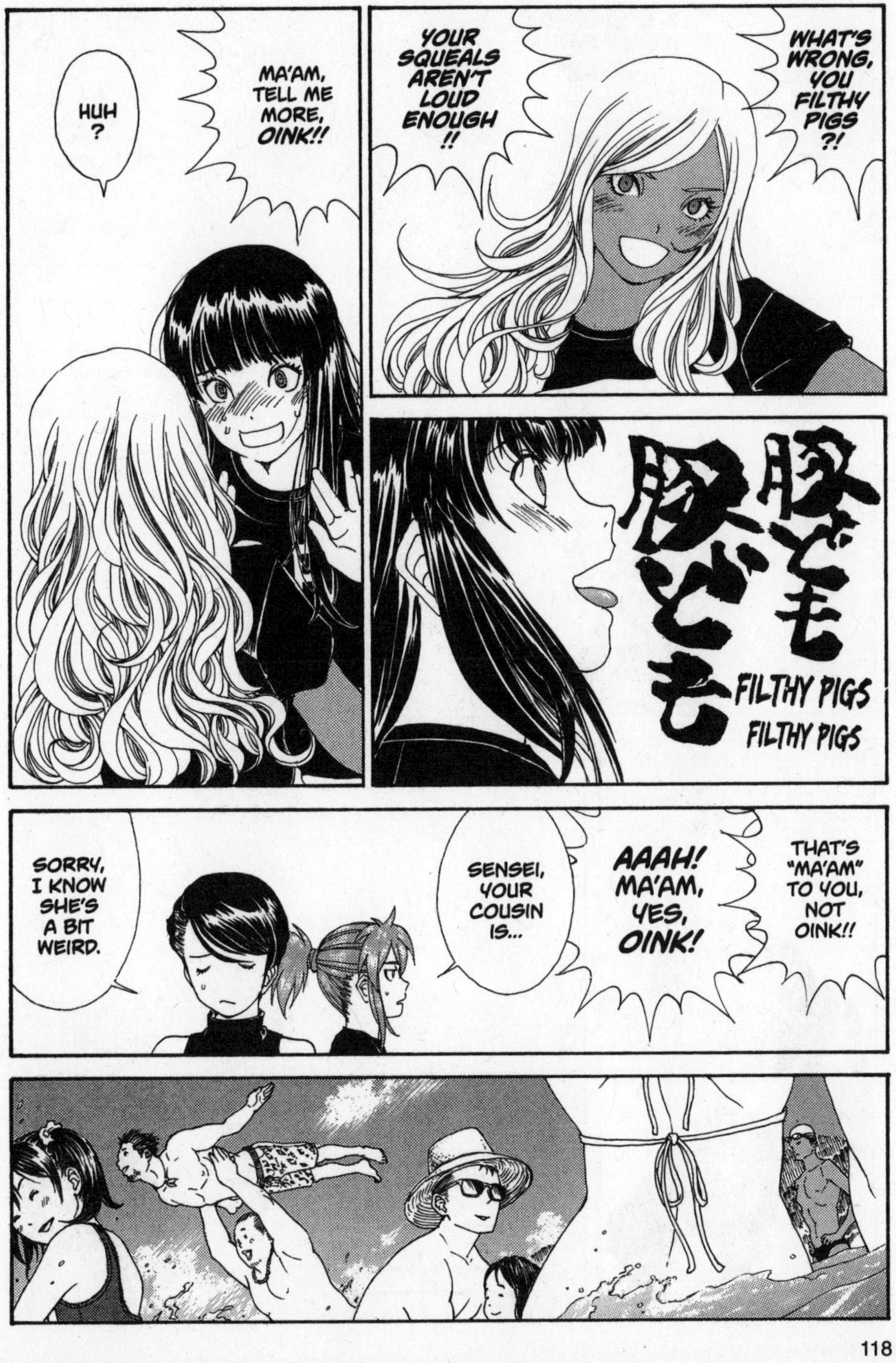
WHAT'S WRONG, YOU FILTHY PIGS?!
YOUR SQUEALS AREN'T LOUD ENOUGH!!
豚ども
豚ども
FILTHY PIGS
FILTHY PIGS
MA'AM, TELL ME MORE, OINK!!
HUH?
THAT'S "MA'AM" TO YOU, NOT OINK!!
AAAH! MA'AM, YES, OINK!
SENSEI, YOUR COUSIN IS...
SORRY, I KNOW SHE'S A BIT WEIRD.

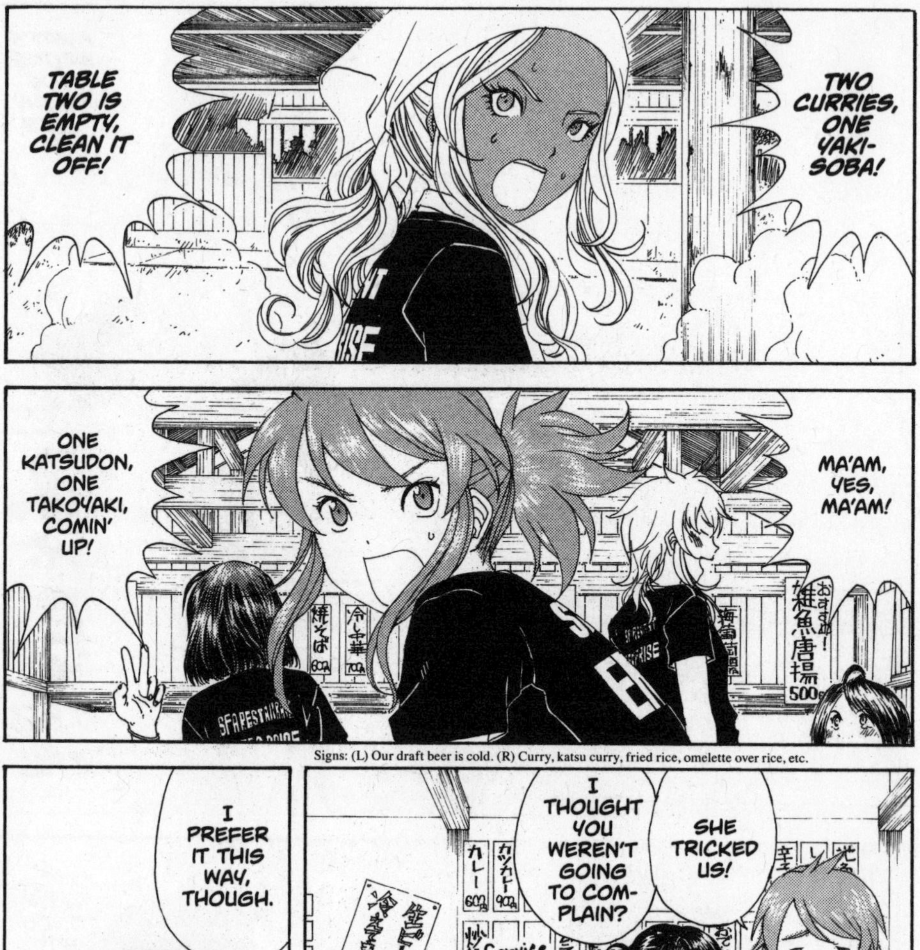
TWO CURRIES, ONE YAKI-SOBA!
TABLE TWO IS EMPTY, CLEAN IT OFF!
MA'AM, YES, MA'AM!
ONE KATSUDON, ONE TAKOYAKI, COMIN' UP!

Signs: (L) Our draft beer is cold. (R) Curry, katsu curry, fried rice, omelette over rice, etc.

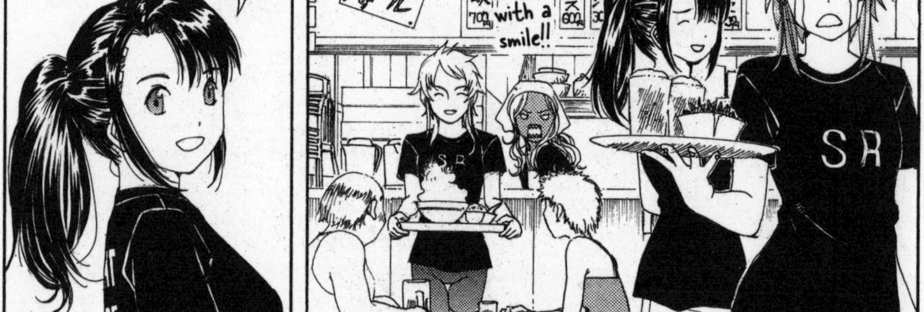
SHE TRICKED US!
I THOUGHT YOU WEREN'T GOING TO COMPLAIN?
Service with a smile!!
I PREFER IT THIS WAY, THOUGH.

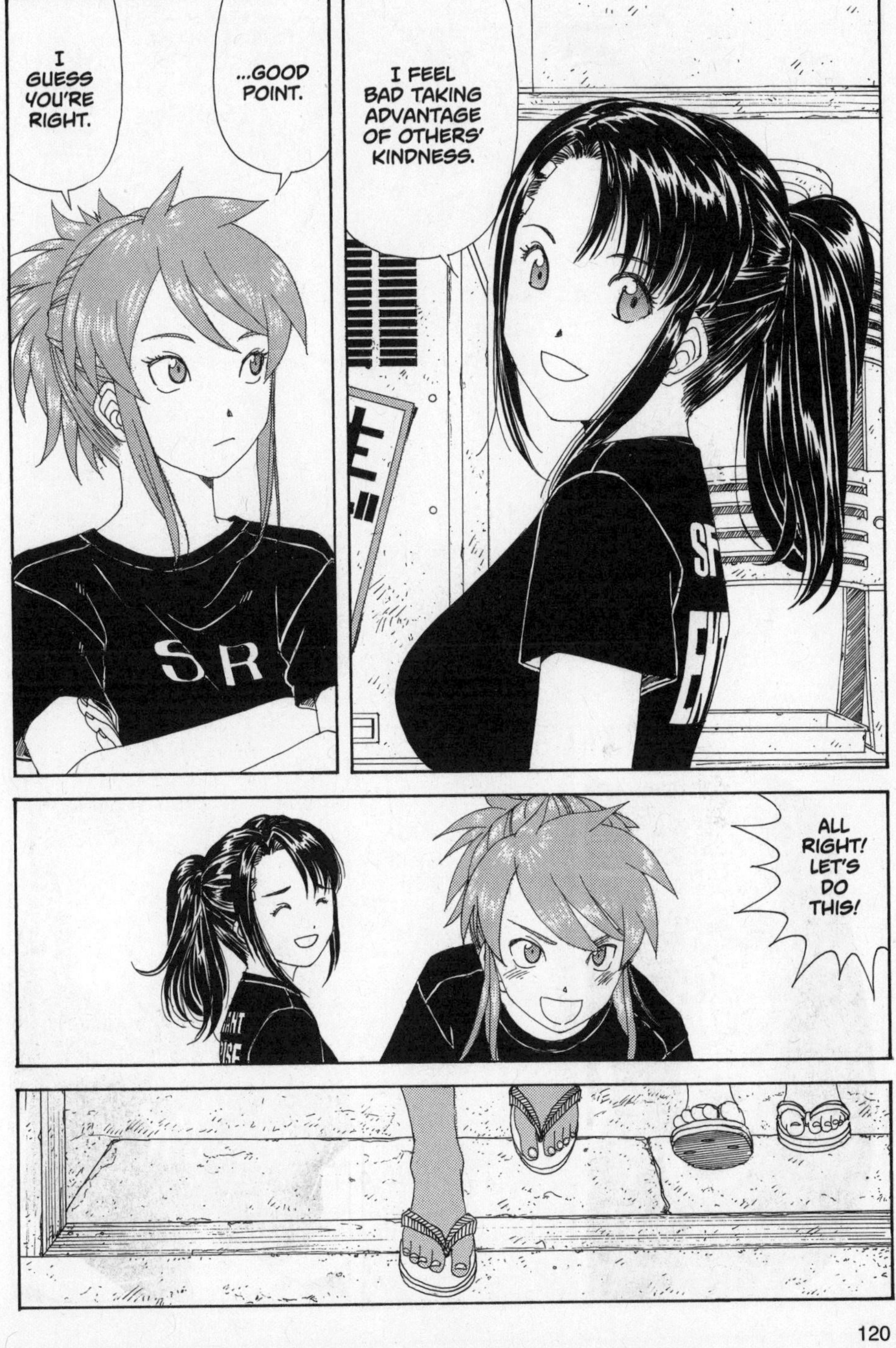
I FEEL BAD TAKING ADVANTAGE OF OTHERS' KINDNESS.
...GOOD POINT.
I GUESS YOU'RE RIGHT.
ALL RIGHT! LET'S DO THIS!

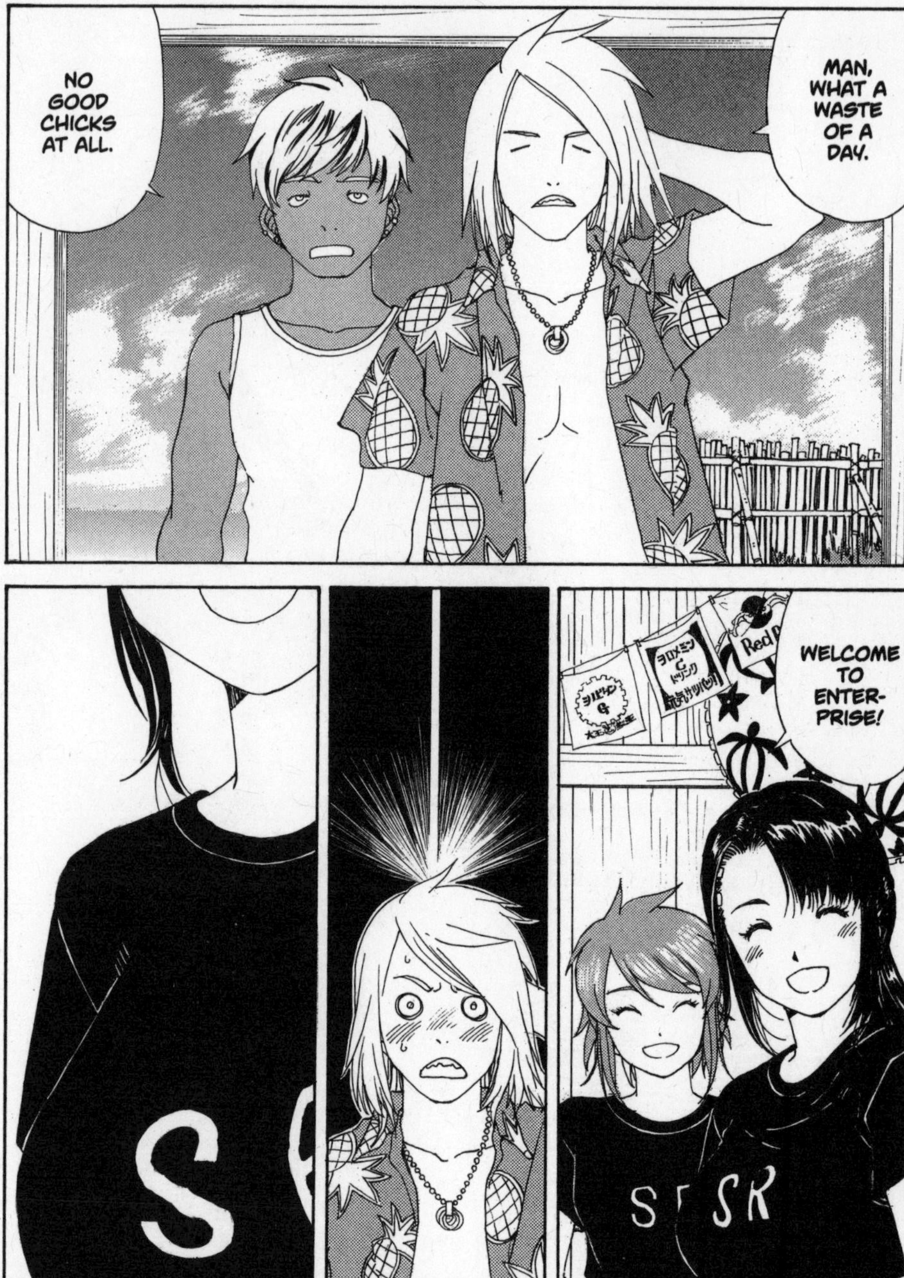
MAN, WHAT A WASTE OF A DAY.
NO GOOD CHICKS AT ALL.
WELCOME TO ENTER-PRISE!

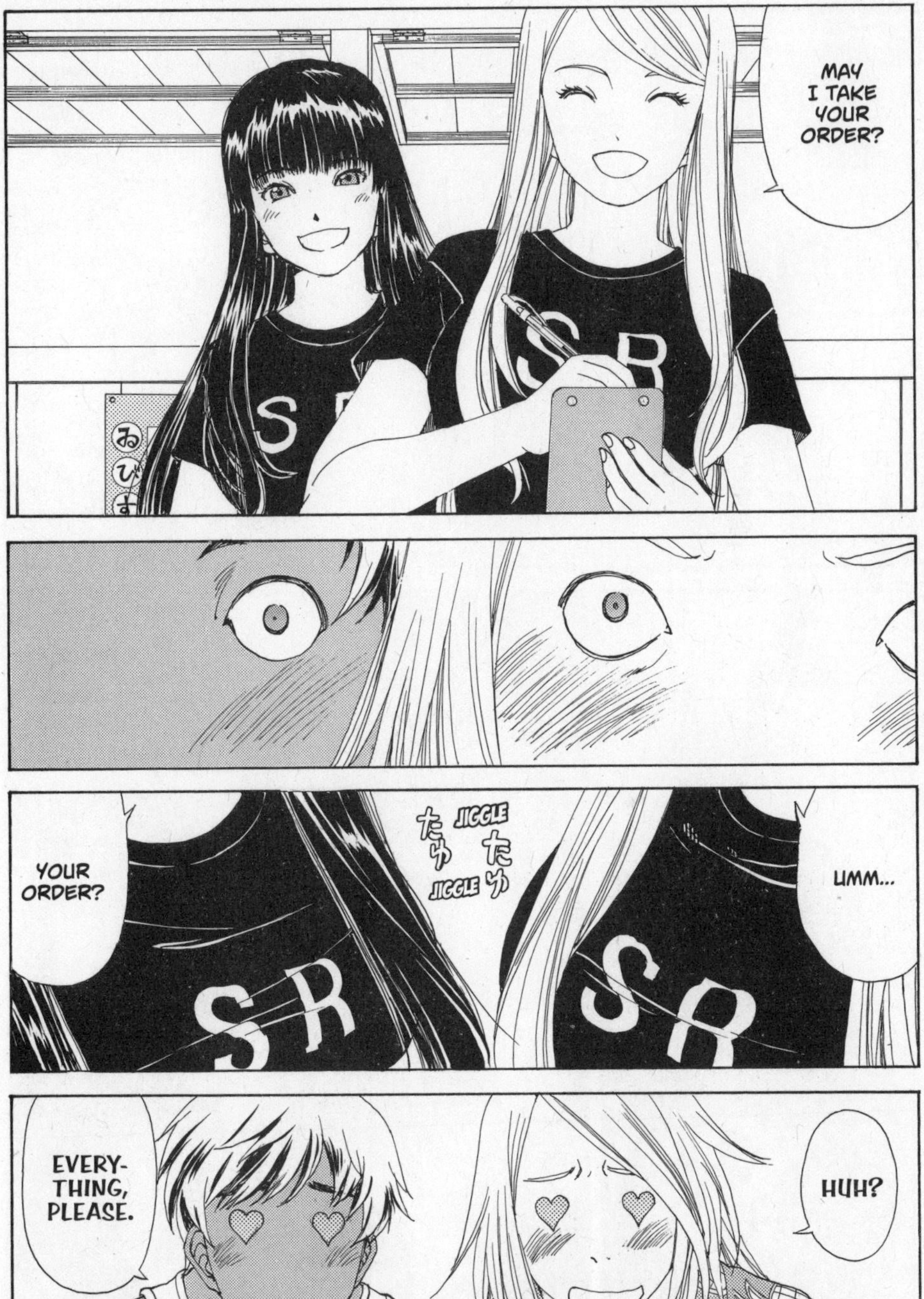
MAY I TAKE YOUR ORDER?
UMM...
たゆ JIGGLE
たゆ JIGGLE
YOUR ORDER?
HUH?
EVERY-THING, PLEASE.

Poster: Mohi-KAN (mohawk battleship) Girl

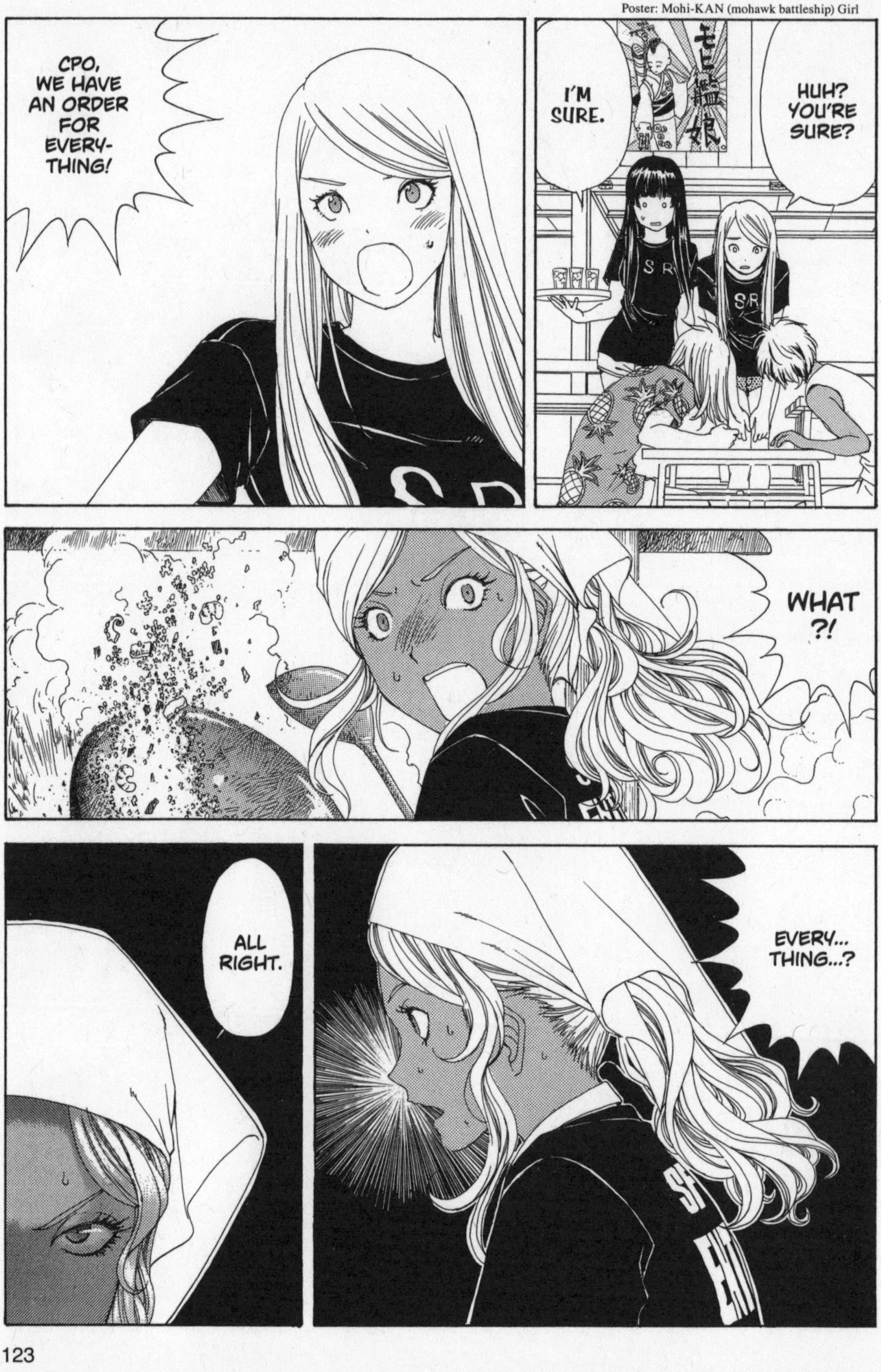

モヒ艦娘
HUH? YOU'RE SURE?
I'M SURE.
CPO, WE HAVE AN ORDER FOR EVERY-THING!
WHAT ?!
EVERY... THING...?
ALL RIGHT.

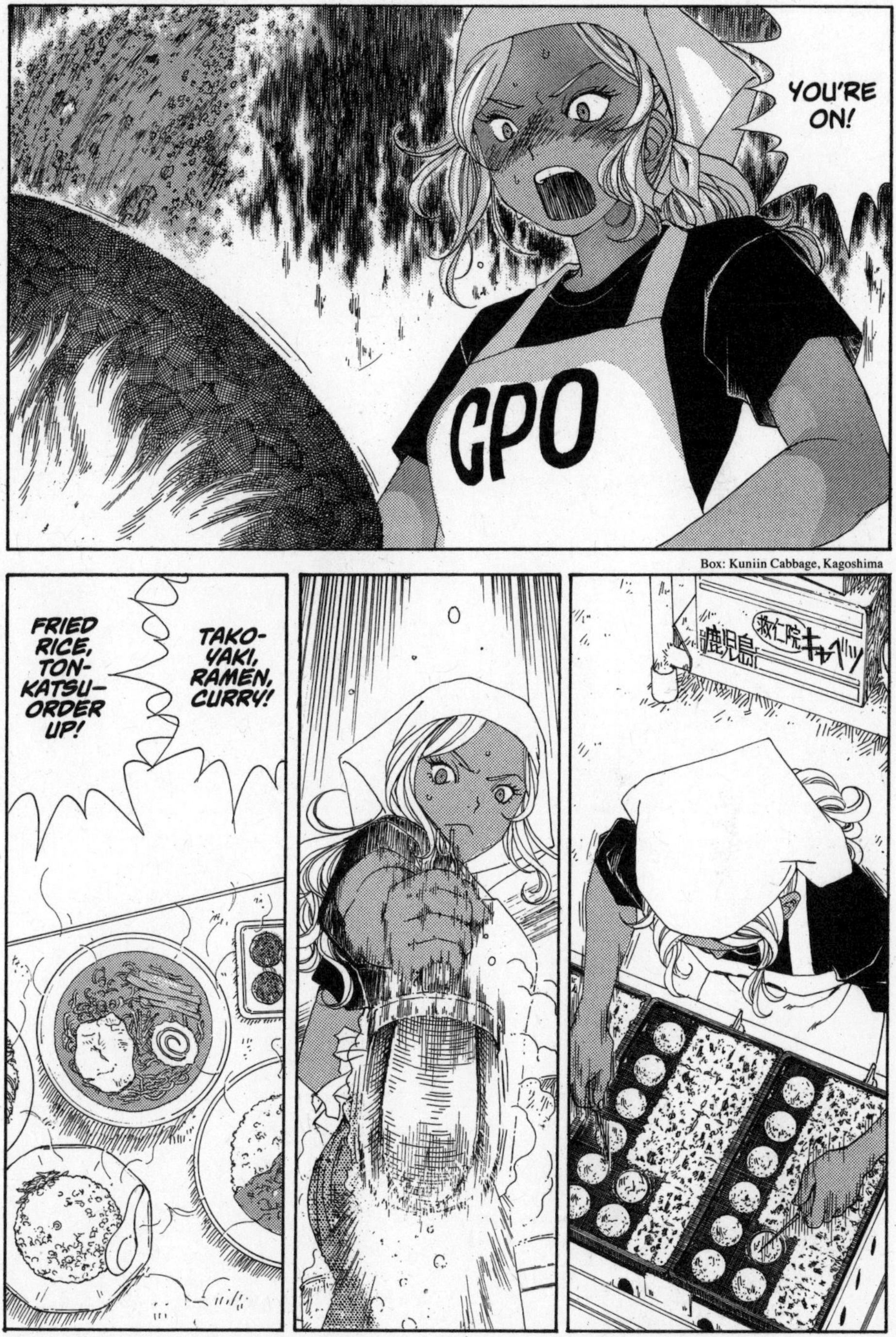
YOU'RE ON!
鹿児島
救仁院キャベツ
TAKO-YAKI, RAMEN, CURRY!
FRIED RICE, TON-KATSU— ORDER UP!
Box: Kuniin Cabbage, Kagoshima

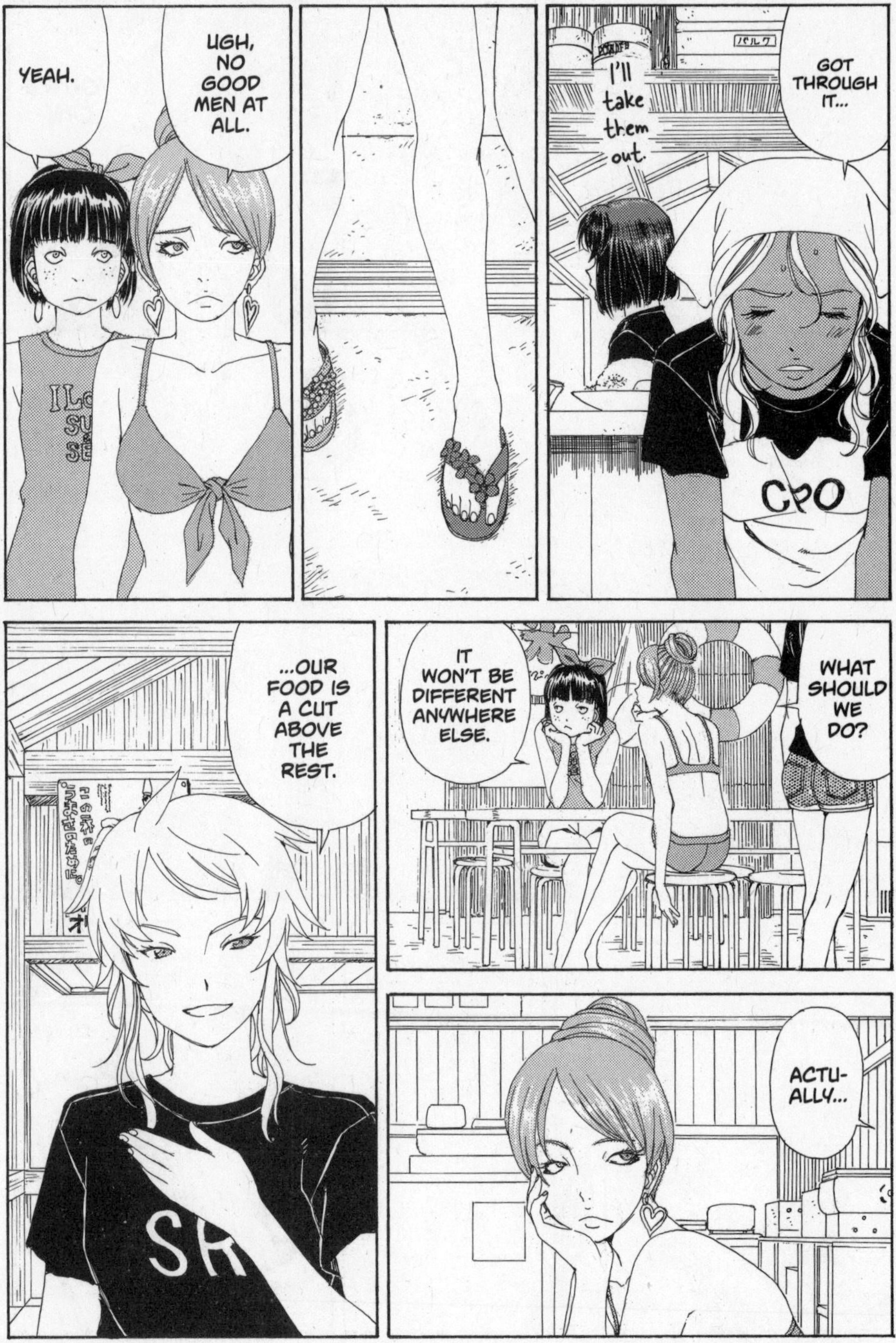
GOT THROUGH IT...
I'll take them out.
UGH, NO GOOD MEN AT ALL.
YEAH.
WHAT SHOULD WE DO?
IT WON'T BE DIFFERENT ANYWHERE ELSE.
ACTU-ALLY...
...OUR FOOD IS A CUT ABOVE THE REST.

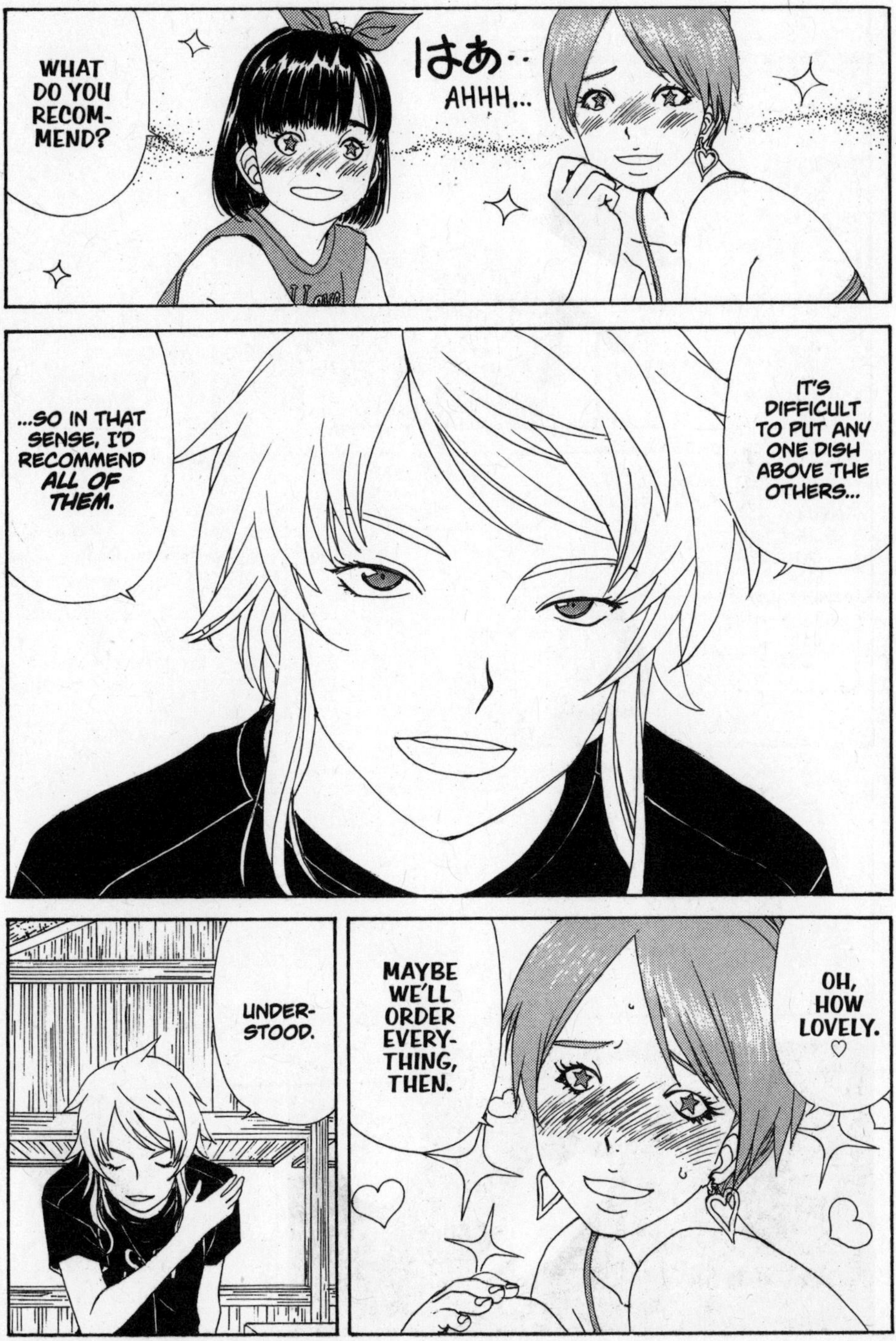
はあ‥
AHHH...
WHAT DO YOU RECOMMEND?
IT'S DIFFICULT TO PUT ANY ONE DISH ABOVE THE OTHERS...
...SO IN THAT SENSE, I'D RECOMMEND ALL OF THEM.
OH, HOW LOVELY. ♡
MAYBE WE'LL ORDER EVERYTHING, THEN.
UNDERSTOOD.

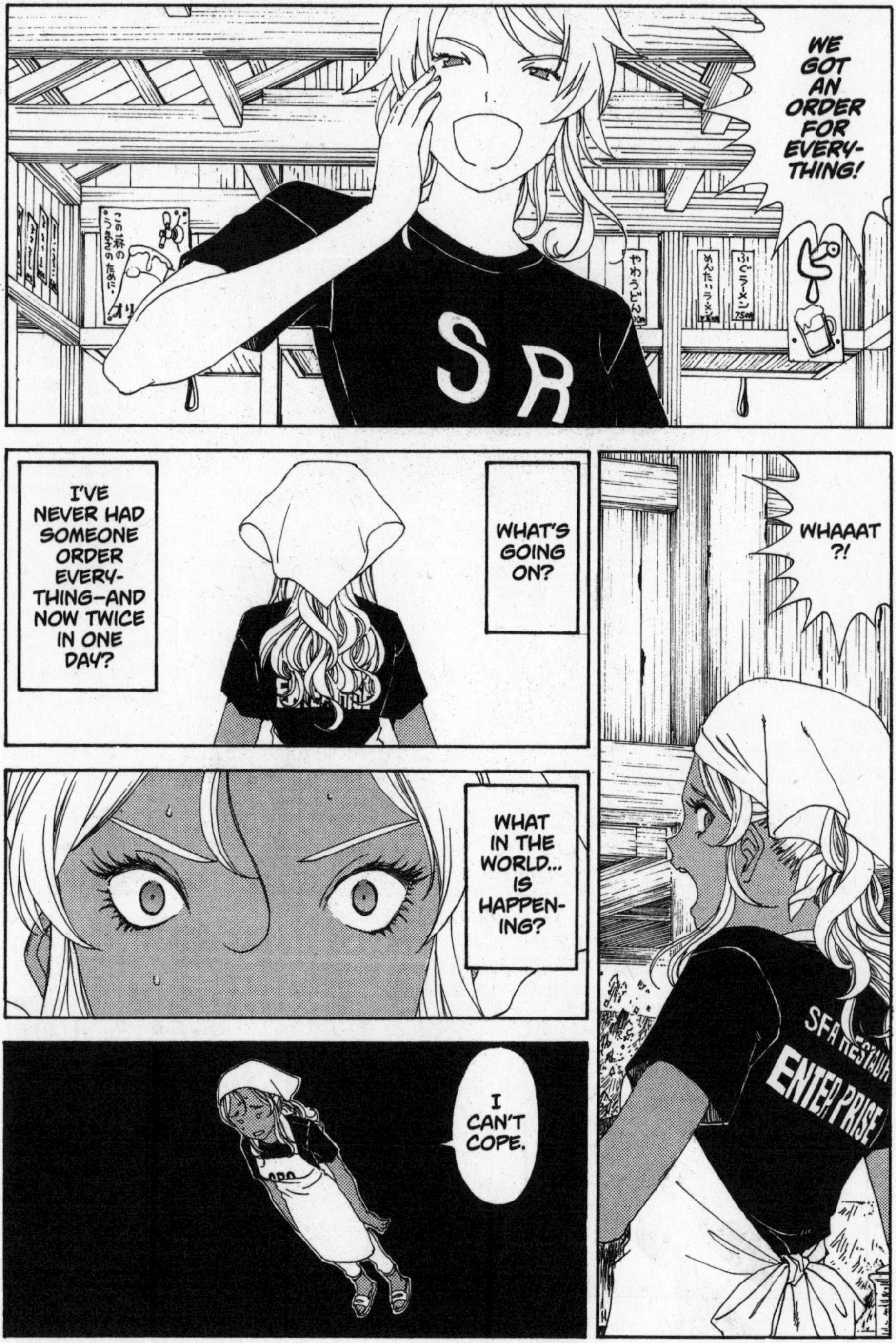
WE GOT AN ORDER FOR EVERY-THING!
やわうどん
めんたいラーメン
ふぐラーメン
SR
WHAAAT ?!
ENTERPRISE
WHAT'S GOING ON?
I'VE NEVER HAD SOMEONE ORDER EVERY-THING—AND NOW TWICE IN ONE DAY?
WHAT IN THE WORLD... IS HAPPEN-ING?
I CAN'T COPE.

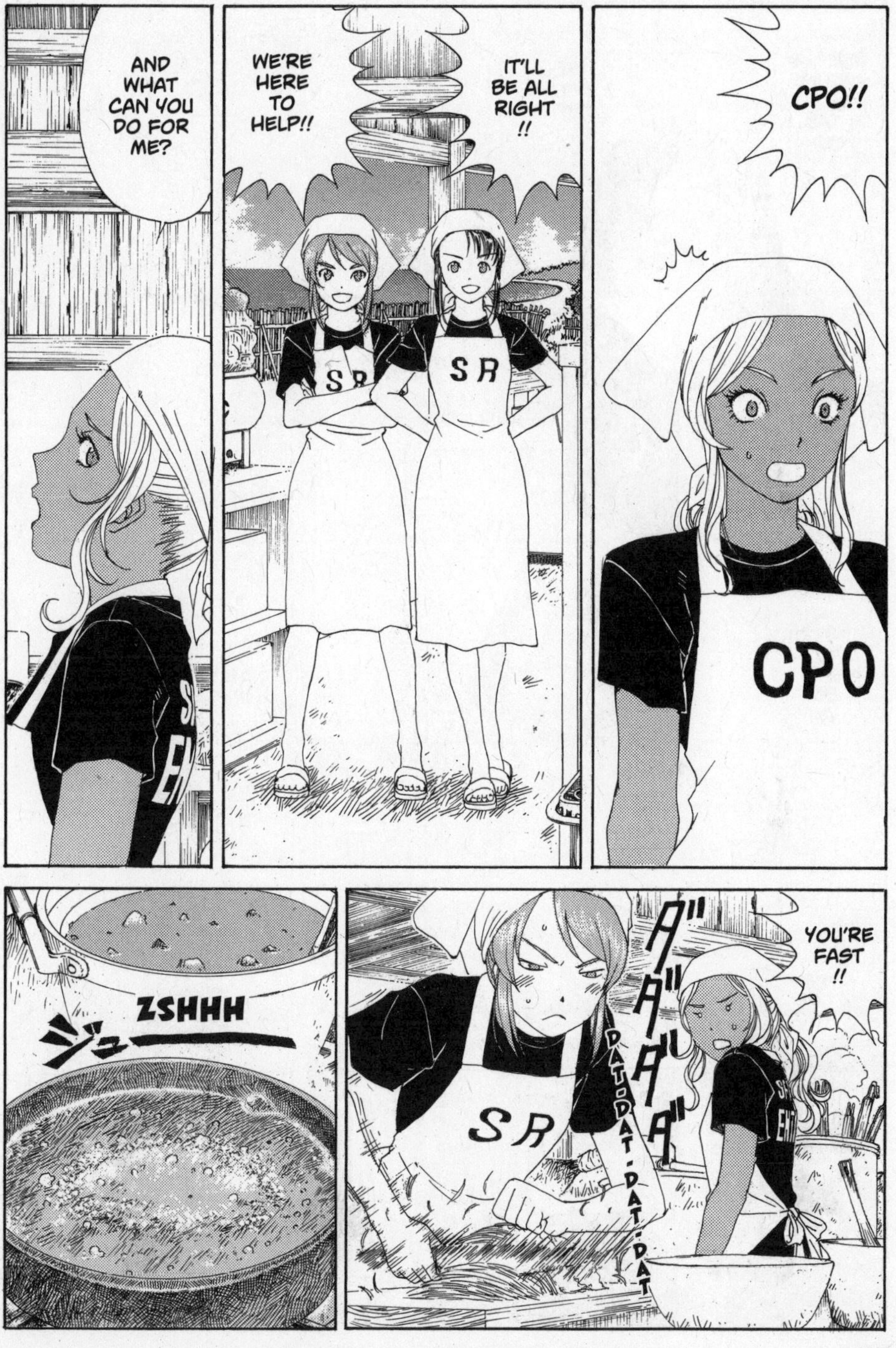
CPO!!
IT'LL BE ALL RIGHT!!
WE'RE HERE TO HELP!!
AND WHAT CAN YOU DO FOR ME?
YOU'RE FAST!!
ダダダダ
DAT-DAT-DAT-DAT
ZSHHH
ジュー

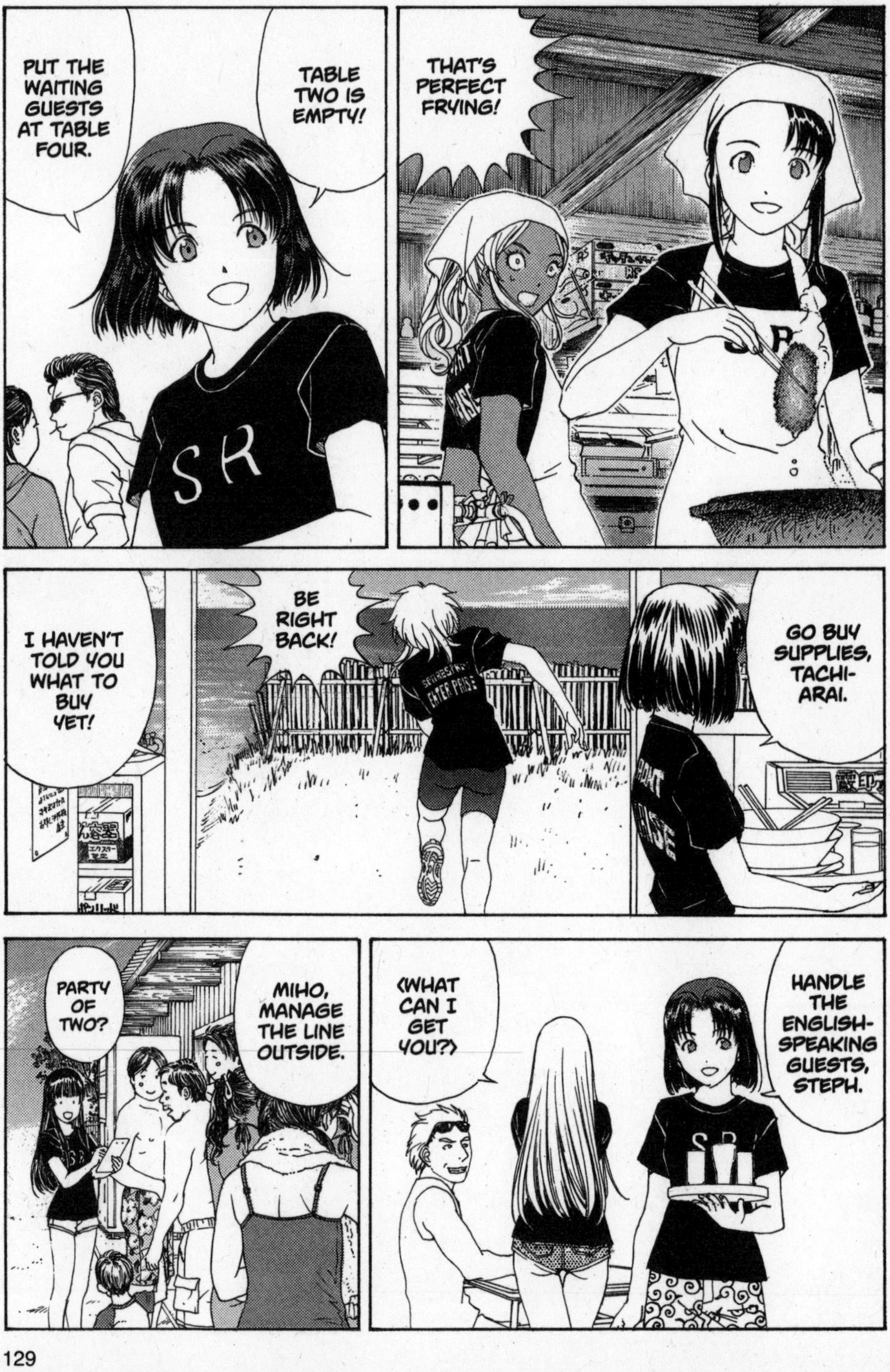
THAT'S PERFECT FRYING!
TABLE TWO IS EMPTY!
PUT THE WAITING GUESTS AT TABLE FOUR.
GO BUY SUPPLIES, TACHI-ARAI.
BE RIGHT BACK!
I HAVEN'T TOLD YOU WHAT TO BUY YET!
HANDLE THE ENGLISH-SPEAKING GUESTS, STEPH.
‹WHAT CAN I GET YOU?›
MIHO, MANAGE THE LINE OUTSIDE.
PARTY OF TWO?

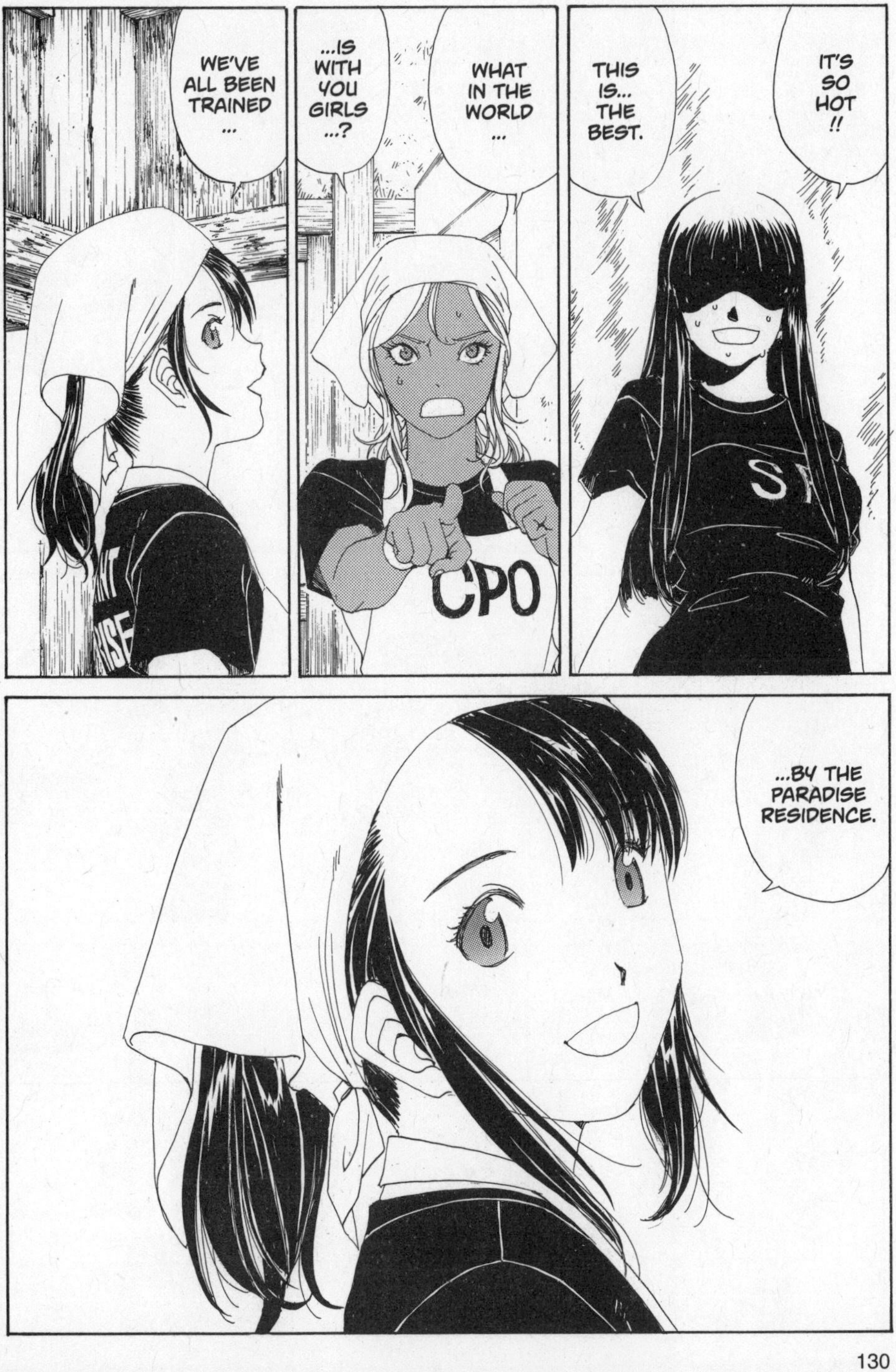
IT'S SO HOT !!
THIS IS... THE BEST.
WHAT IN THE WORLD ...
...IS WITH YOU GIRLS ...?
CPO
WE'VE ALL BEEN TRAINED ...
...BY THE PARADISE RESIDENCE.

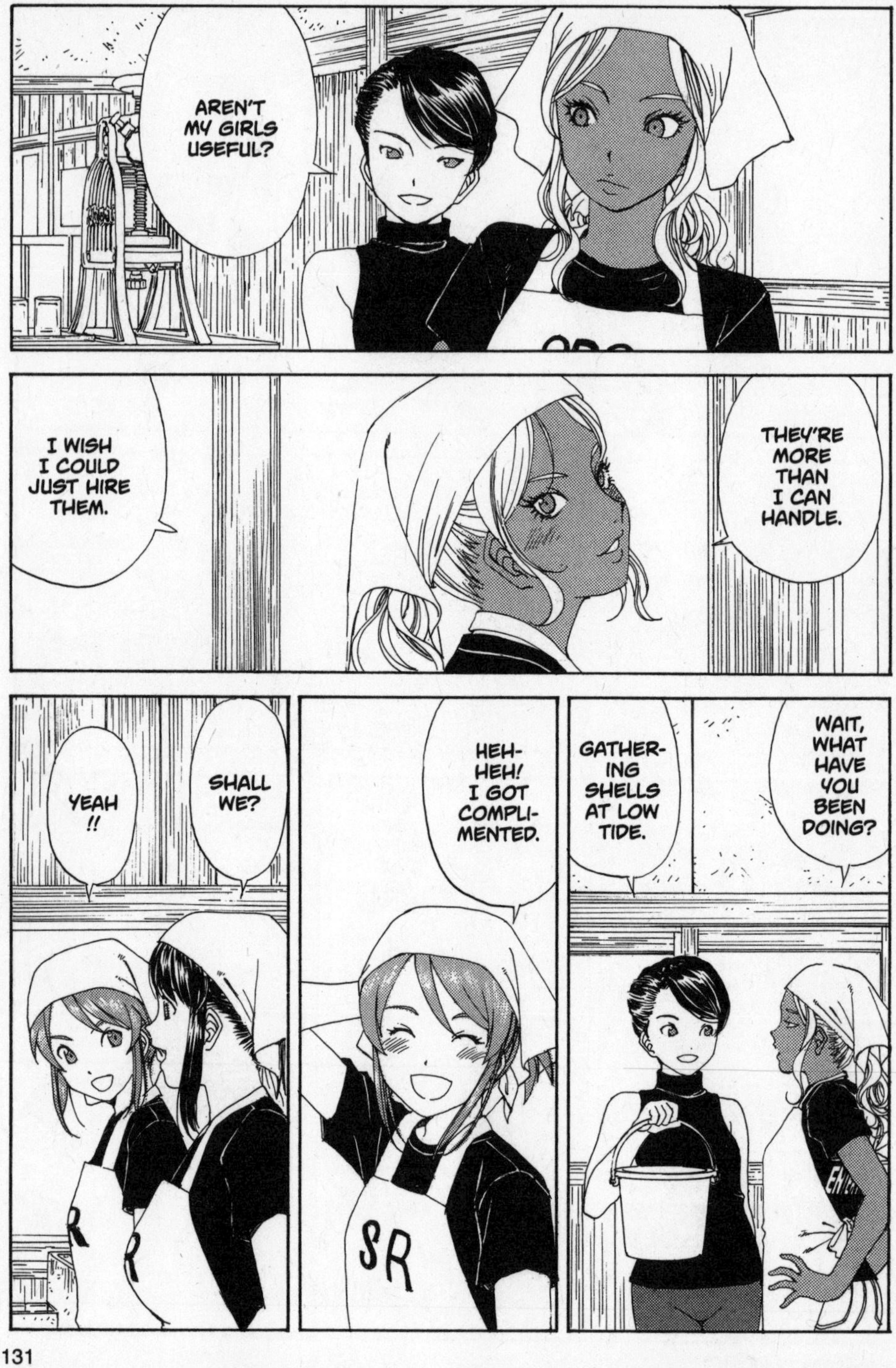
AREN'T MY GIRLS USEFUL?
THEY'RE MORE THAN I CAN HANDLE.
I WISH I COULD JUST HIRE THEM.
WAIT, WHAT HAVE YOU BEEN DOING?
GATHERING SHELLS AT LOW TIDE.
HEH-HEH! I GOT COMPLIMENTED.
SR
SHALL WE?
YEAH!!

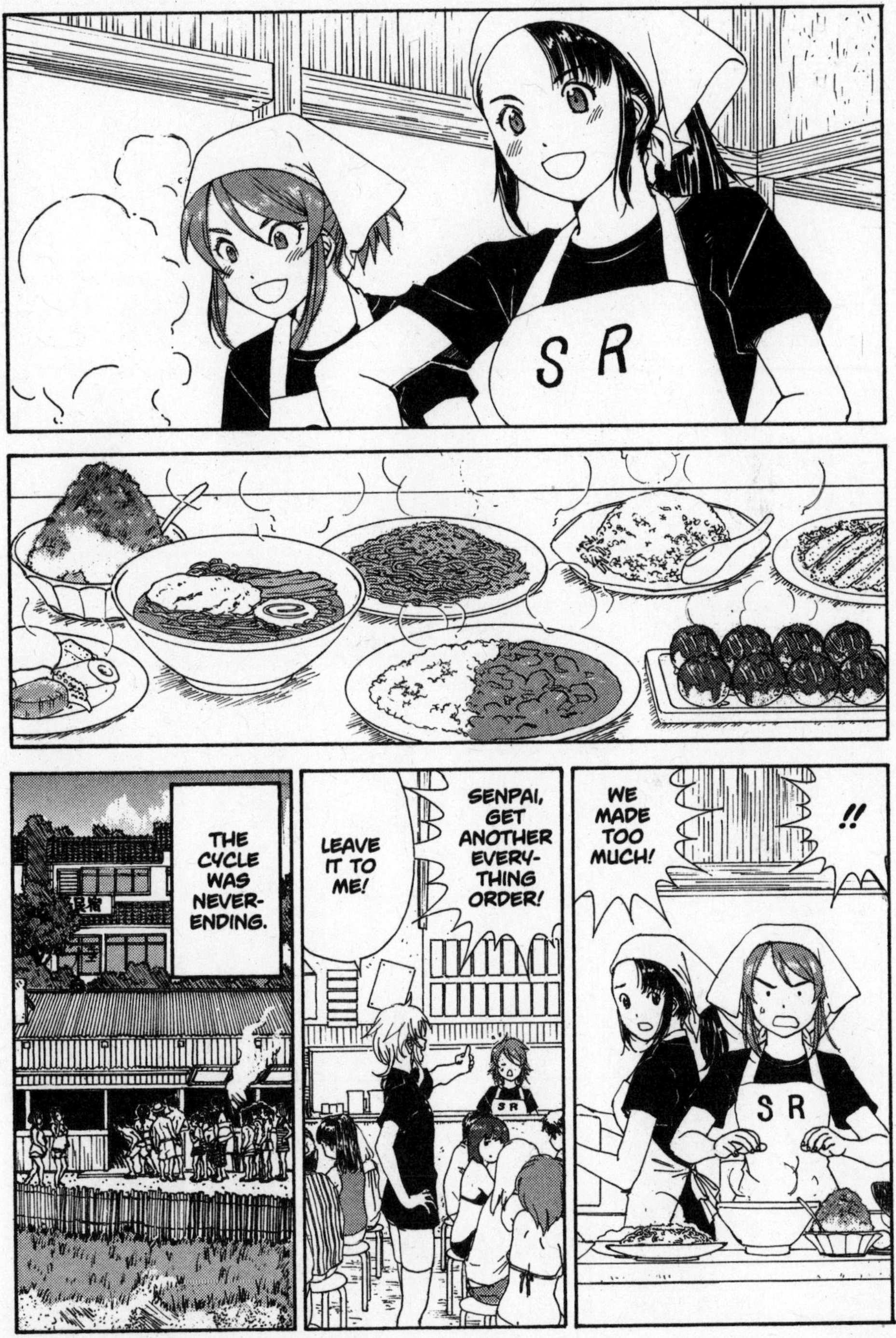
S R
WE MADE TOO MUCH!
!!
SENPAI, GET ANOTHER EVERY-THING ORDER!
LEAVE IT TO ME!
THE CYCLE WAS NEVER-ENDING.

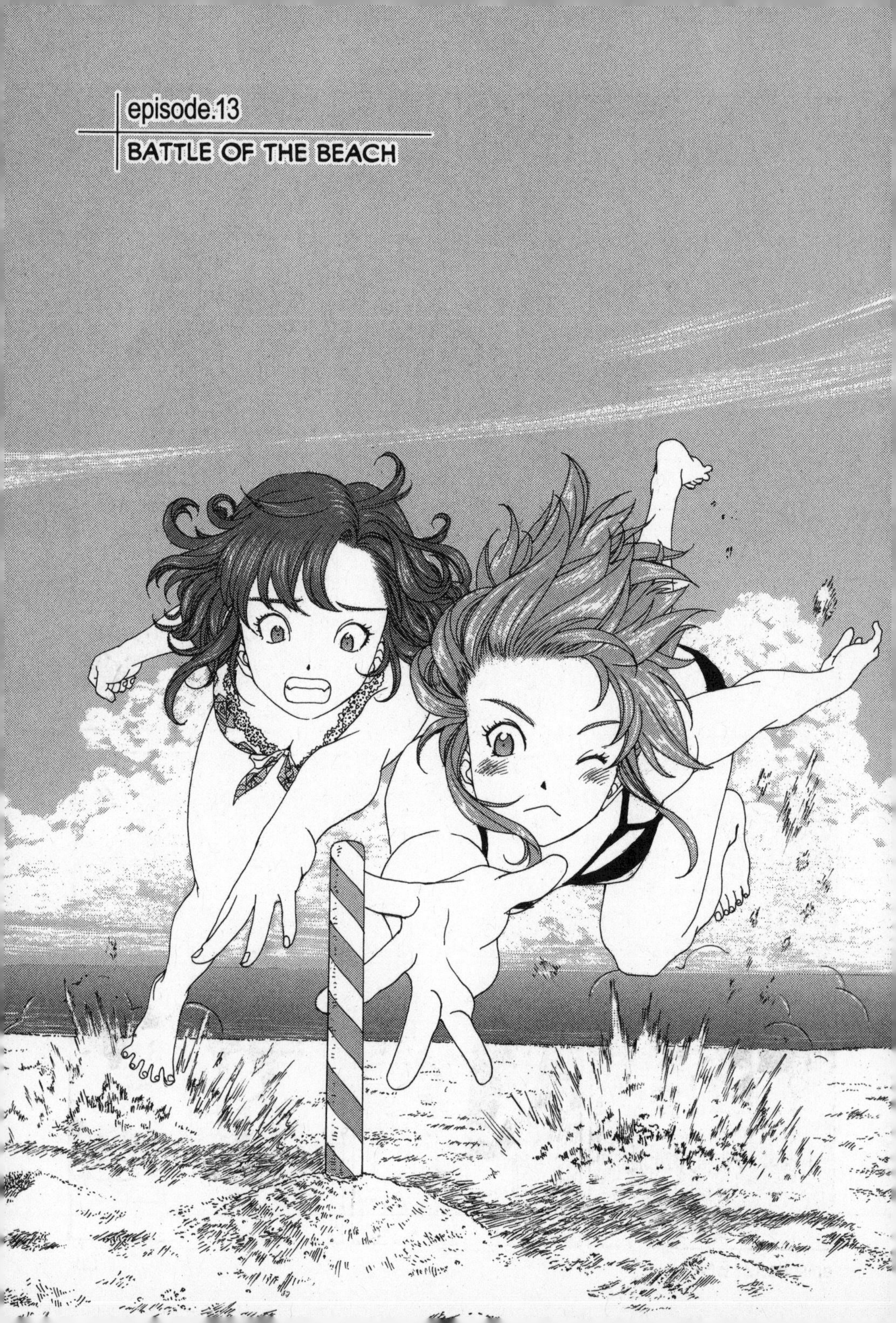
episode.13
BATTLE OF THE BEACH

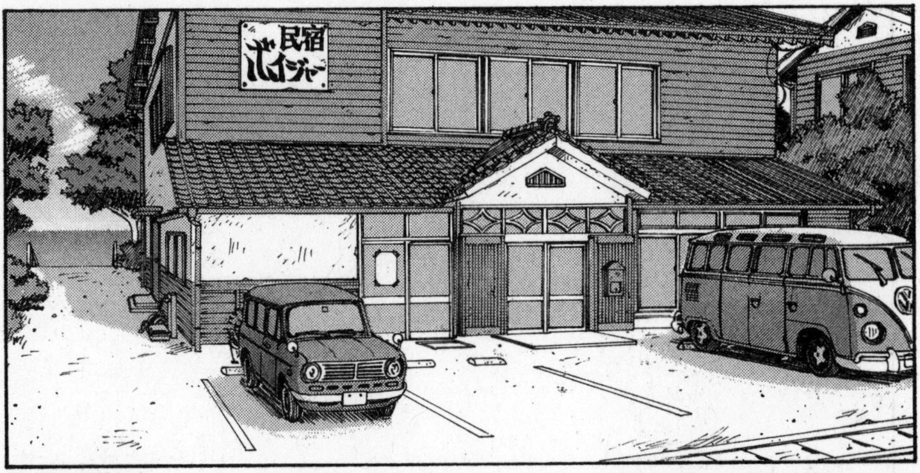
民宿
ボイジャー

Sign: Voyager Inn

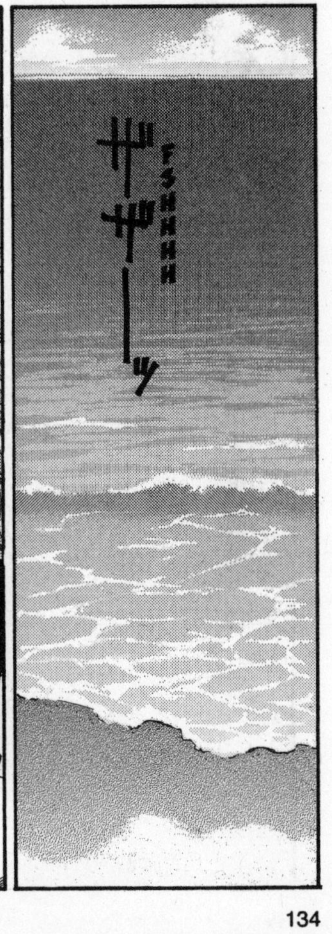
ザザーッ
FSHHHH

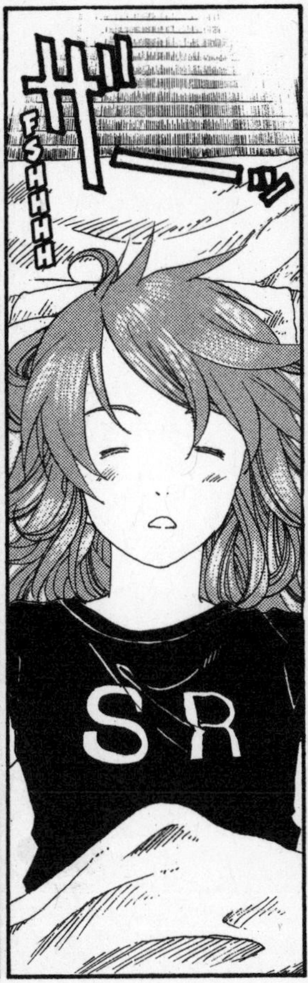
ザーッ
FSHHHH

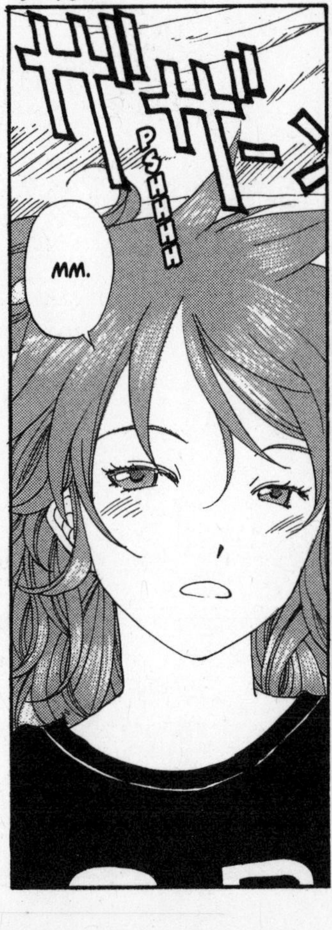
ザザーン
PSHHHH
MM.

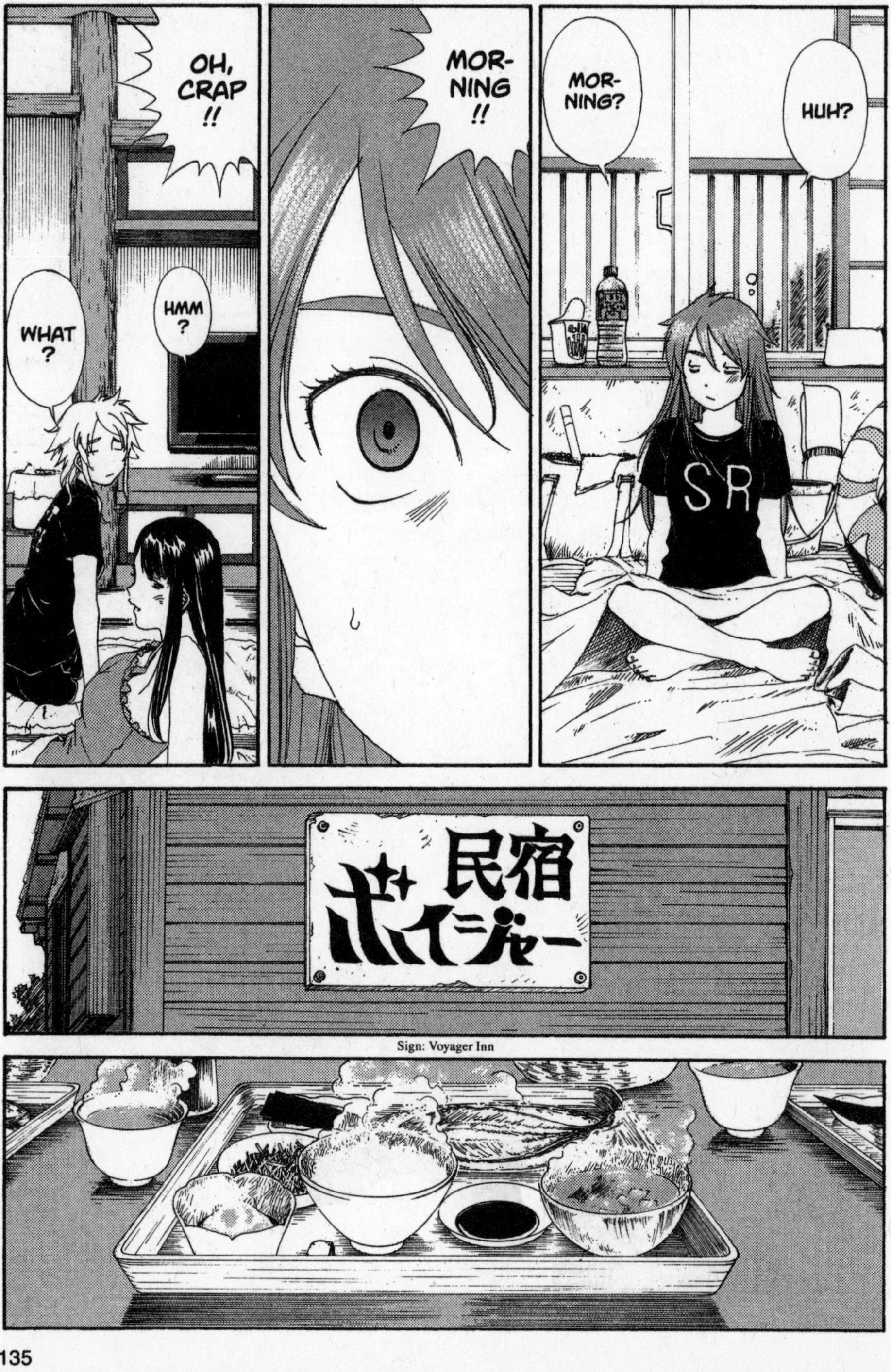
HUH?
MOR-NING?
MOR-NING!!
OH, CRAP!!
HMM?
WHAT?
民宿
ボイジャー
Sign: Voyager Inn

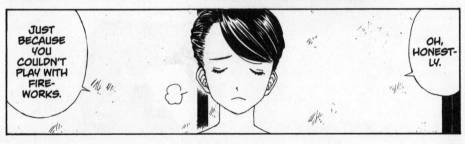

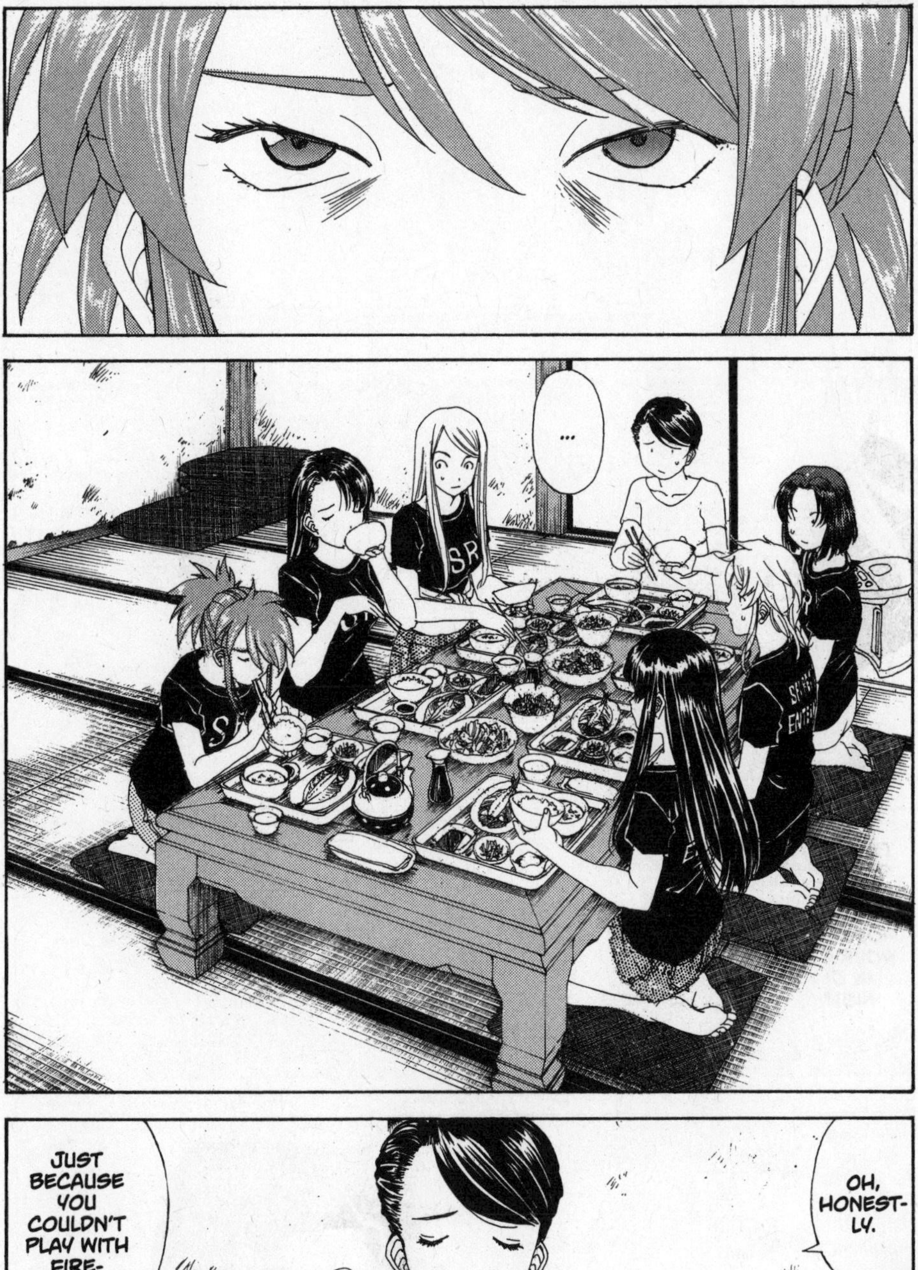
...
OH, HONEST-LY.
JUST BECAUSE YOU COULDN'T PLAY WITH FIRE-WORKS.

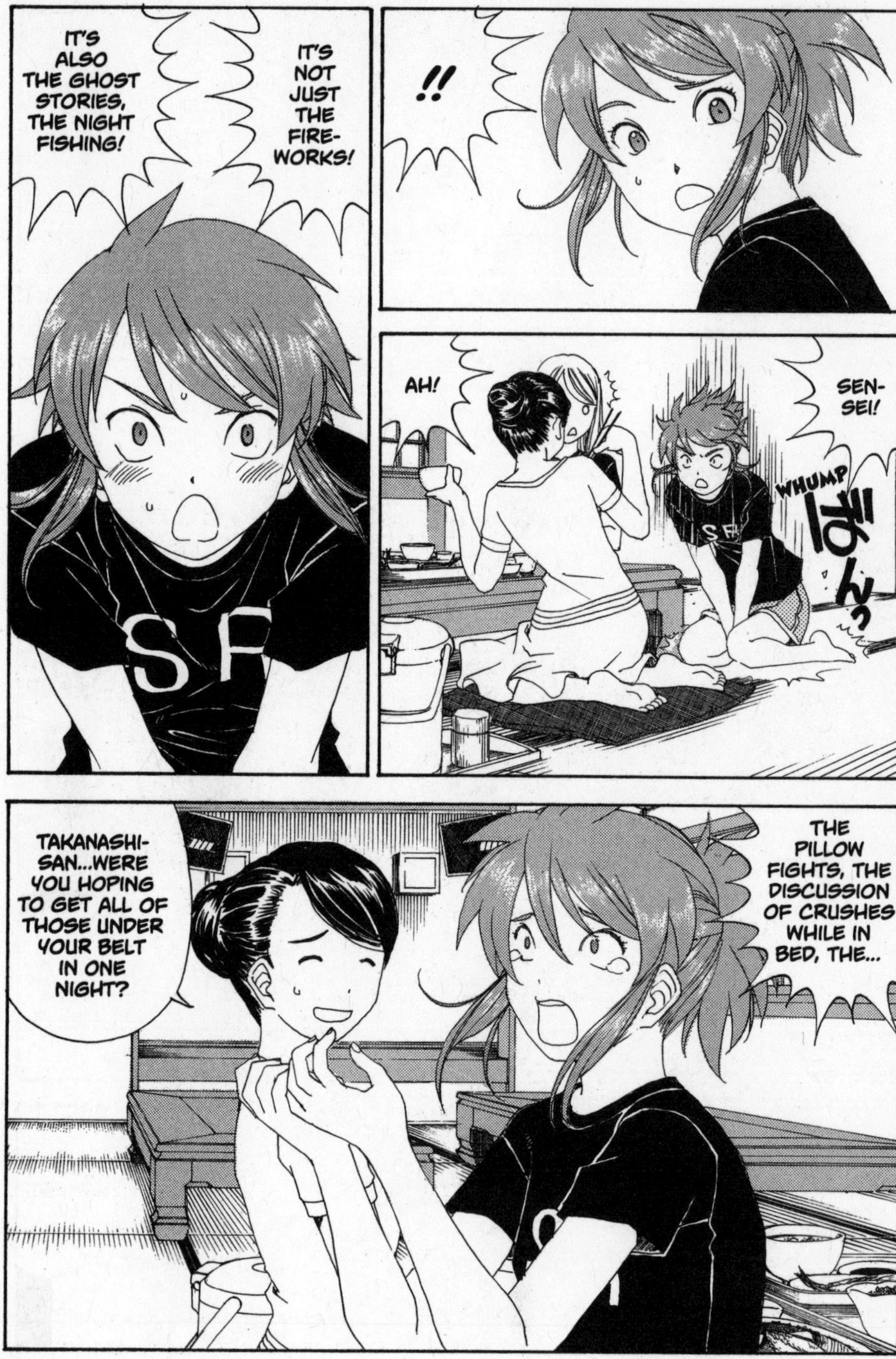
!!
SEN-SEI!
WHUMP
ぼんっ
AH!
IT'S NOT JUST THE FIRE-WORKS!
IT'S ALSO THE GHOST STORIES, THE NIGHT FISHING!
THE PILLOW FIGHTS, THE DISCUSSION OF CRUSHES WHILE IN BED, THE...
TAKANASHI-SAN...WERE YOU HOPING TO GET ALL OF THOSE UNDER YOUR BELT IN ONE NIGHT?

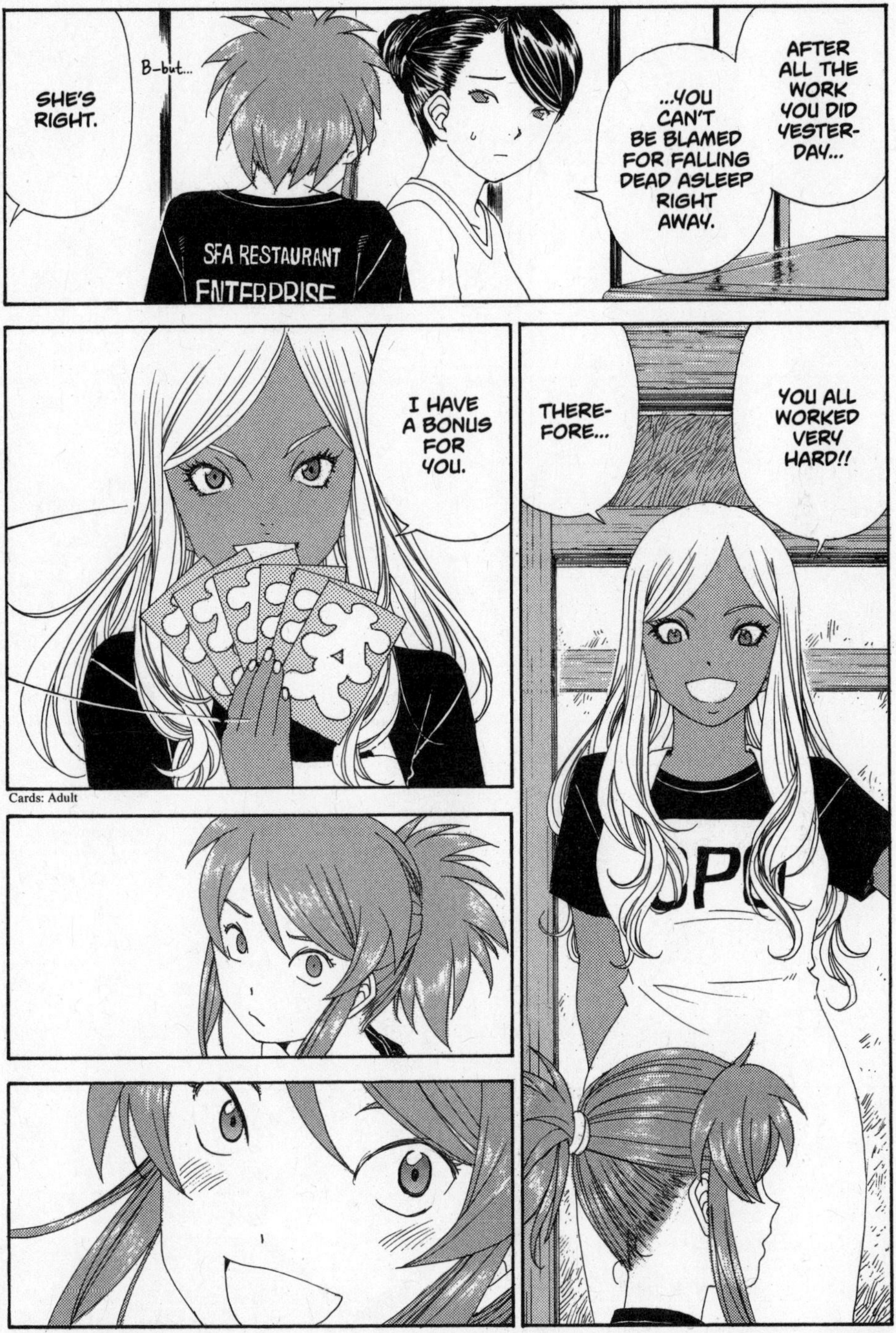
AFTER ALL THE WORK YOU DID YESTERDAY...
...YOU CAN'T BE BLAMED FOR FALLING DEAD ASLEEP RIGHT AWAY.
B-but...
SHE'S RIGHT.
SFA RESTAURANT ENTERPRISE
YOU ALL WORKED VERY HARD!!
THEREFORE...
I HAVE A BONUS FOR YOU.

Cards: Adult

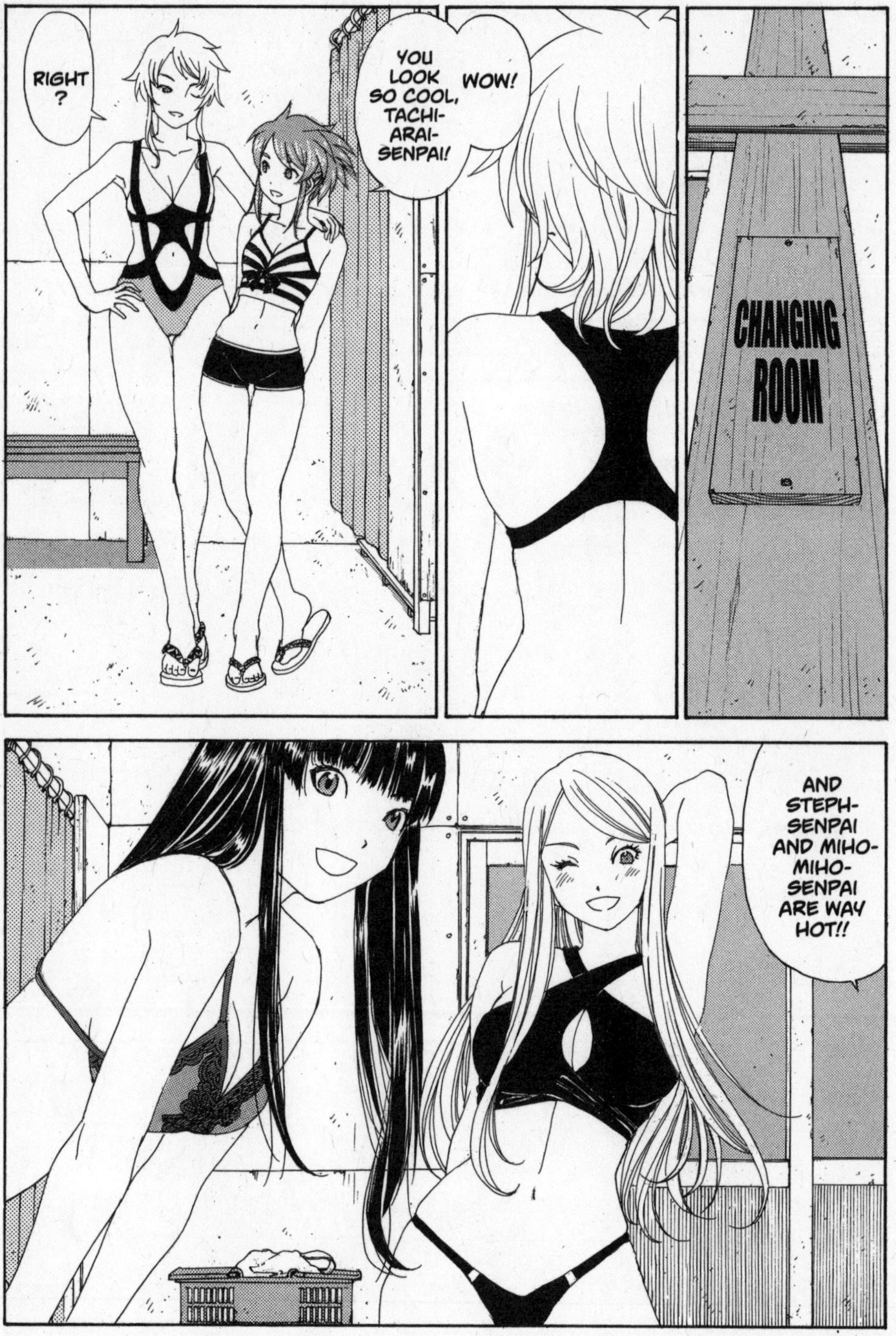
CHANGING ROOM
WOW!
YOU LOOK SO COOL, TACHI-ARAI-SENPAI!
RIGHT?
AND STEPH-SENPAI AND MIHO-MIHO-SENPAI ARE WAY HOT!!

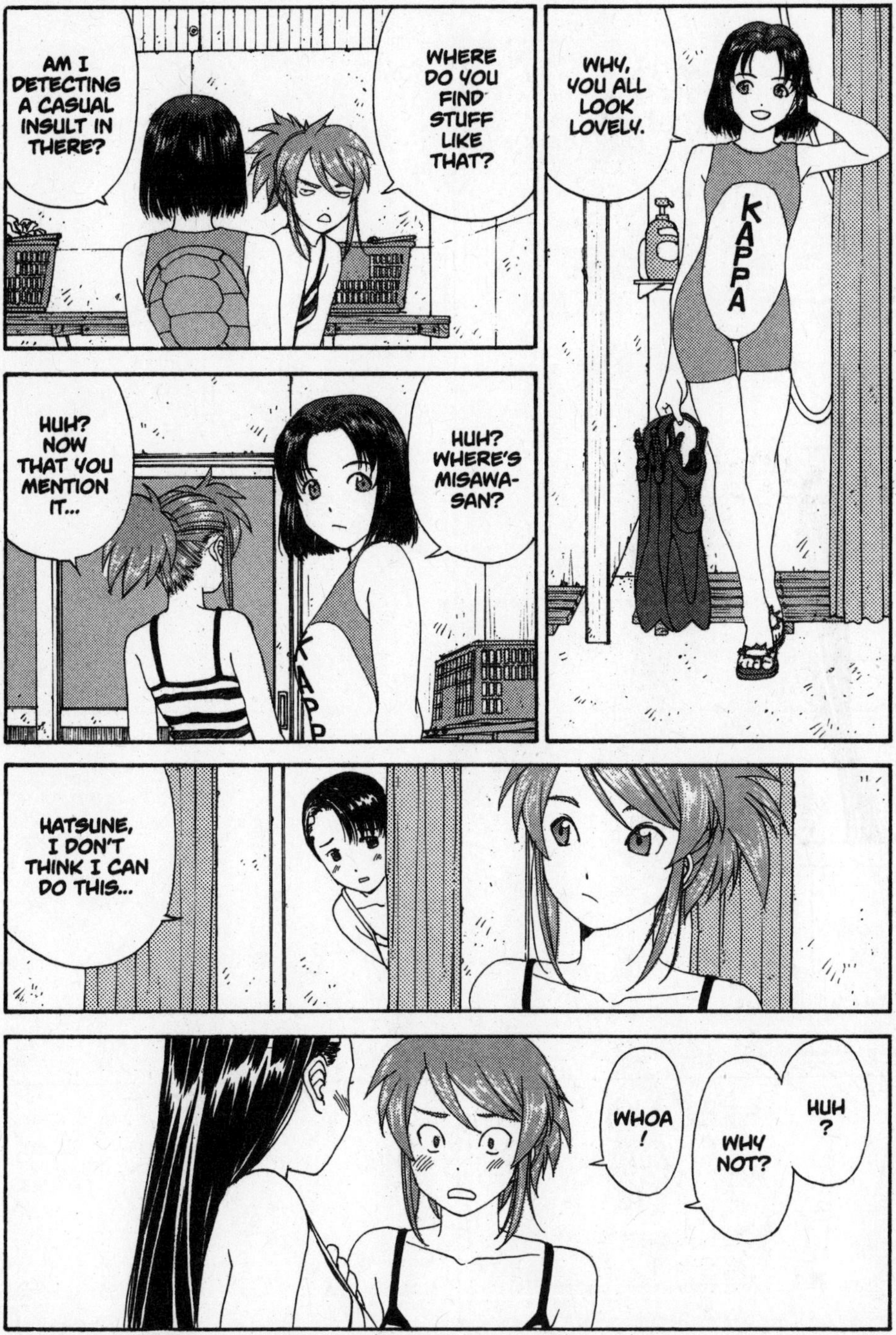
WHY, YOU ALL LOOK LOVELY.
KAPPA
WHERE DO YOU FIND STUFF LIKE THAT?
AM I DETECTING A CASUAL INSULT IN THERE?
HUH? WHERE'S MISAWA-SAN?
HUH? NOW THAT YOU MENTION IT...
HATSUNE, I DON'T THINK I CAN DO THIS...
HUH? WHY NOT?
WHOA!

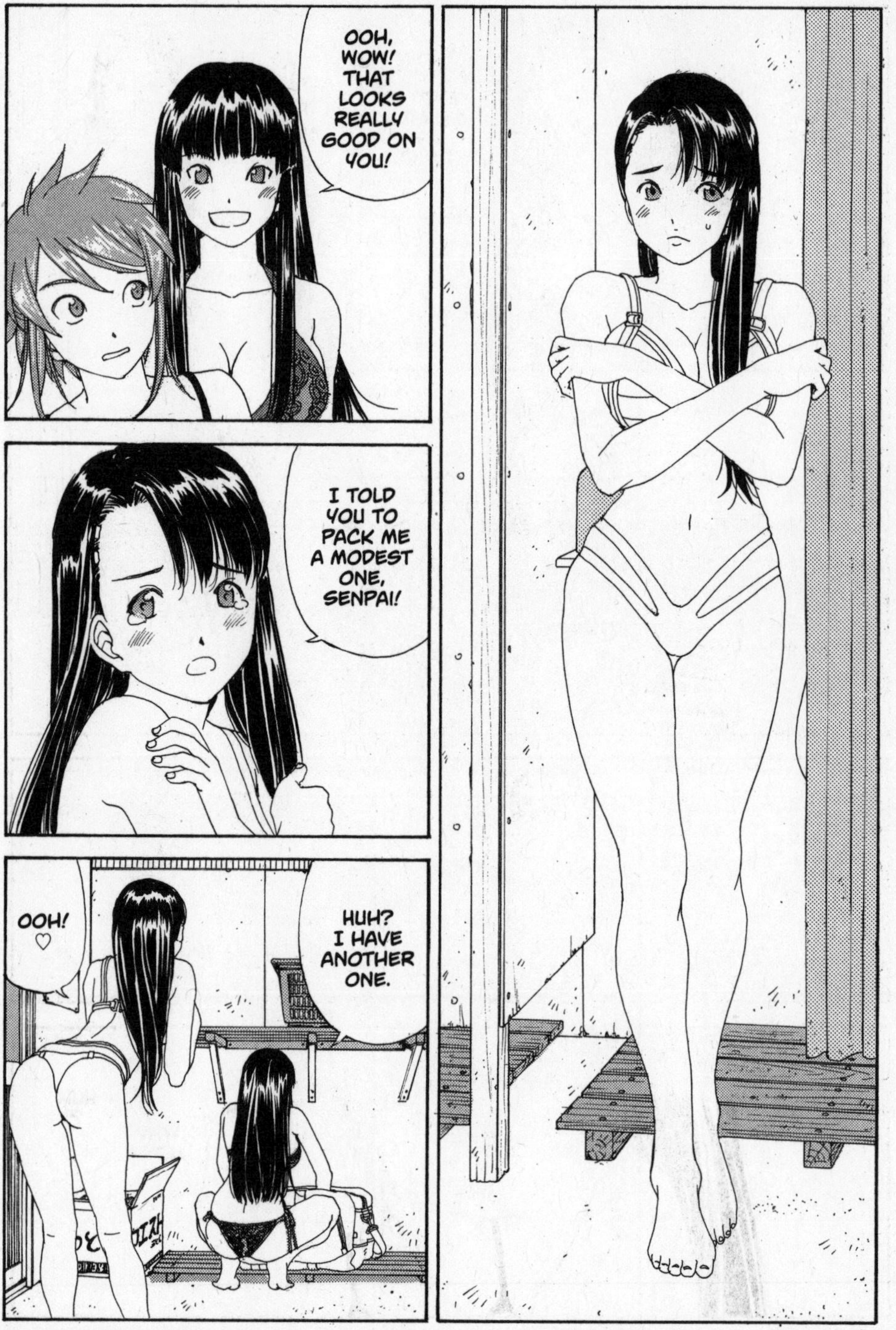
OOH, WOW! THAT LOOKS REALLY GOOD ON YOU!
I TOLD YOU TO PACK ME A MODEST ONE, SENPAI!
HUH? I HAVE ANOTHER ONE.
OOH! ♡

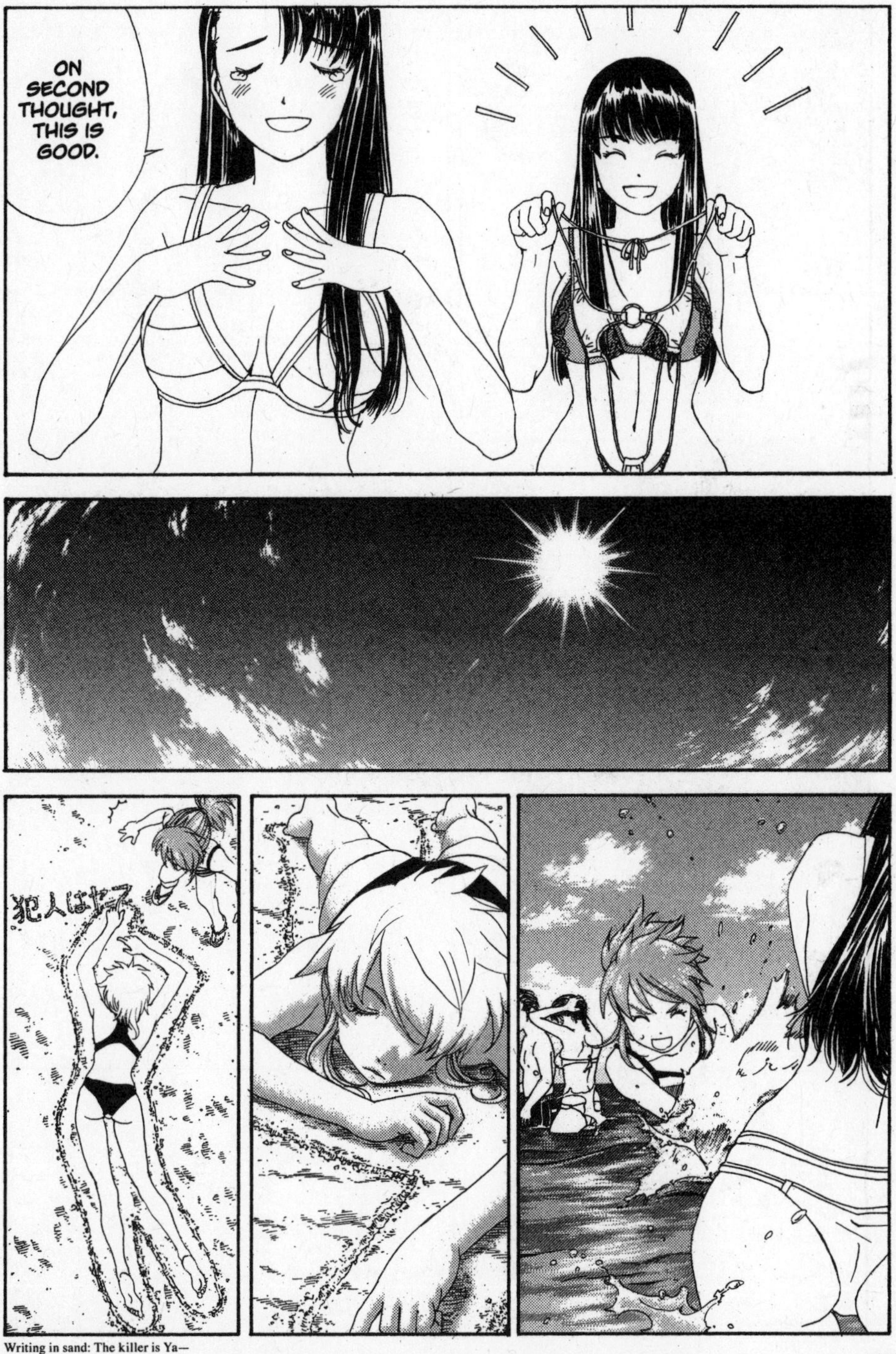
ON SECOND THOUGHT, THIS IS GOOD.
犯人はヤ

Writing in sand: The killer is Ya—

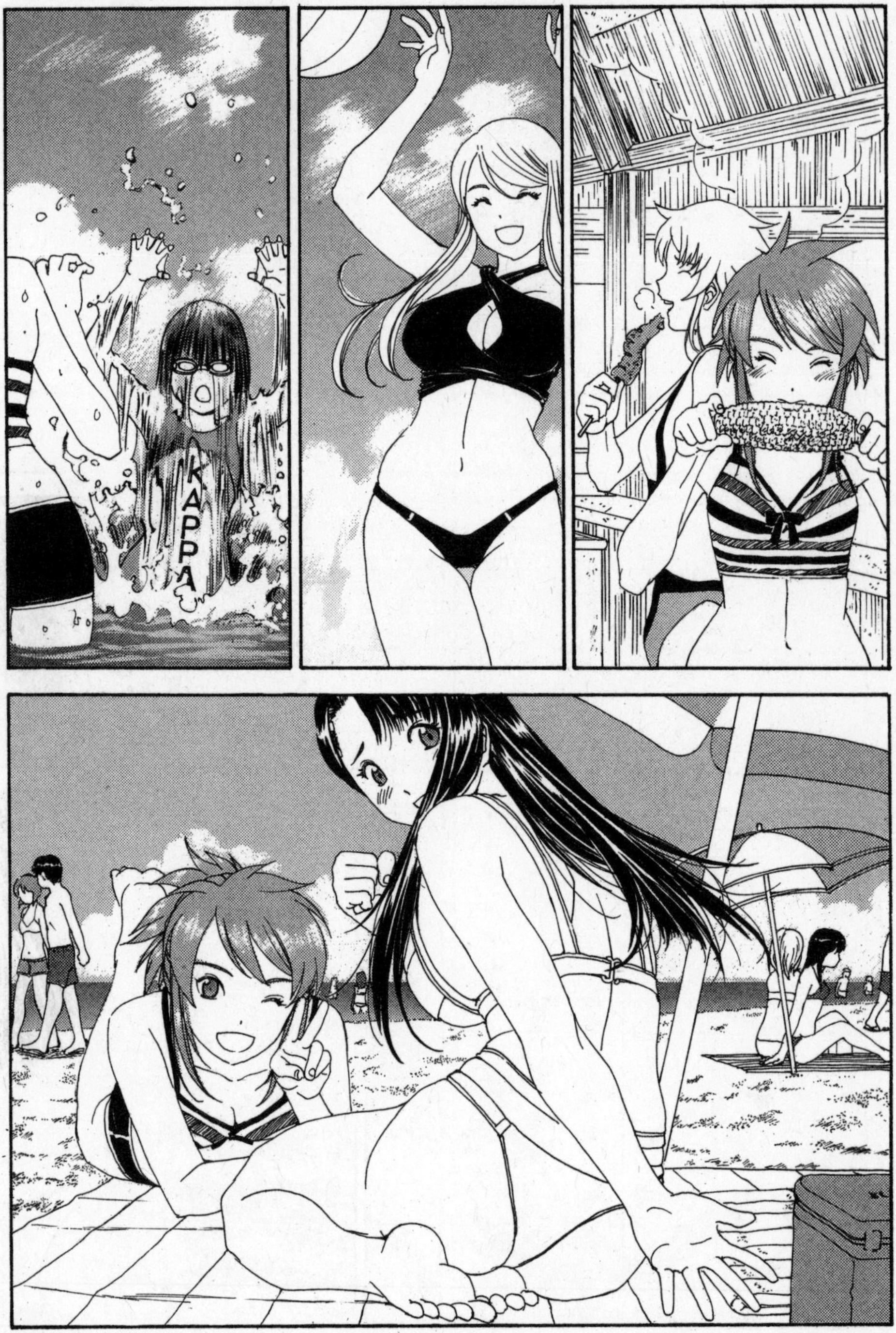
KAPPA

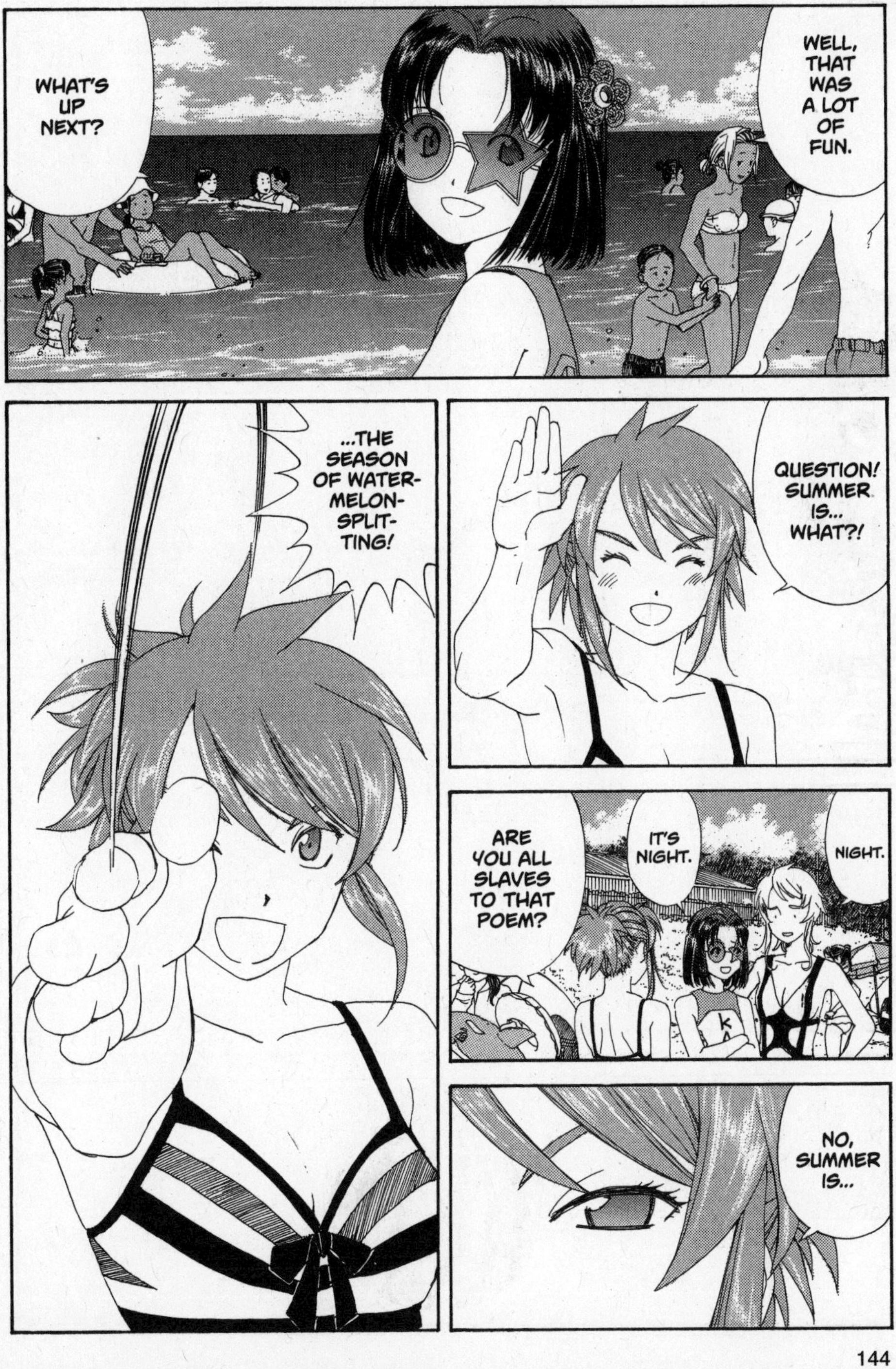
WELL, THAT WAS A LOT OF FUN.
WHAT'S UP NEXT?
QUESTION! SUMMER IS... WHAT?!
NIGHT.
IT'S NIGHT.
ARE YOU ALL SLAVES TO THAT POEM?
NO, SUMMER IS...
...THE SEASON OF WATER-MELON-SPLIT-TING!

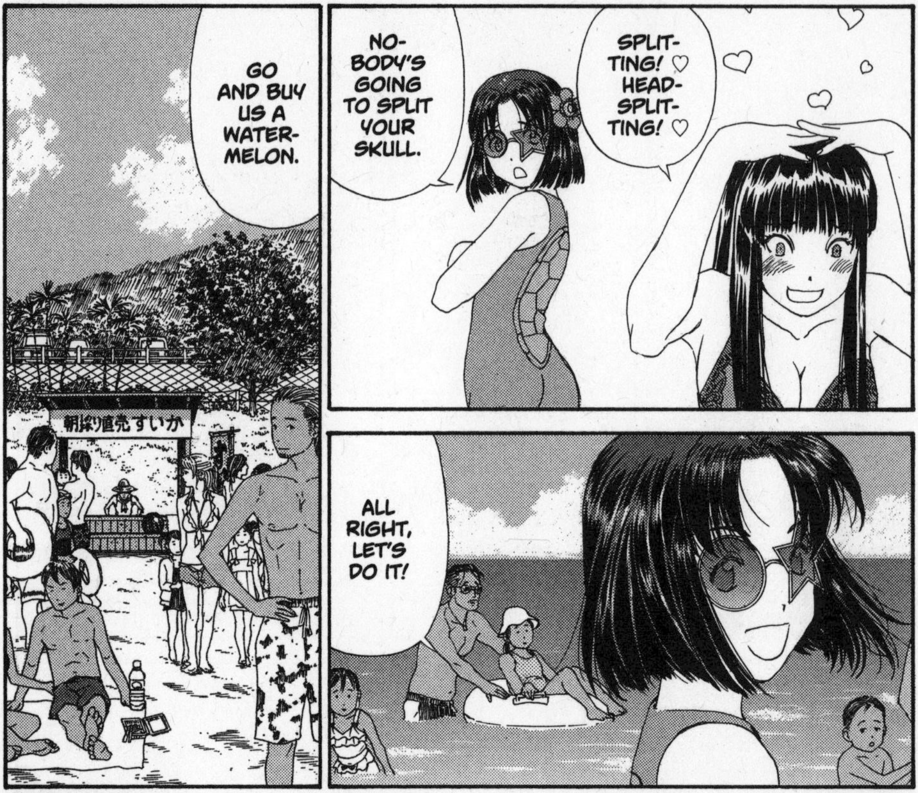
SPLITTING! ♡ HEAD-SPLITTING! ♡
NOBODY'S GOING TO SPLIT YOUR SKULL.
ALL RIGHT, LET'S DO IT!
GO AND BUY US A WATERMELON.
朝採り直売すいか

Sign: Fresh-picked Watermelon

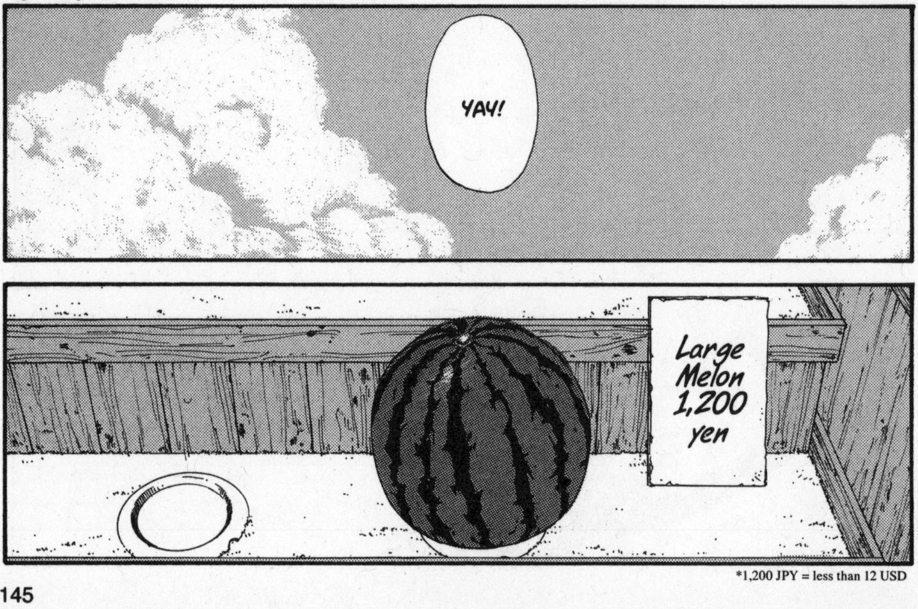
YAY!
Large Melon 1,200 yen

*1,200 JPY = less than 12 USD

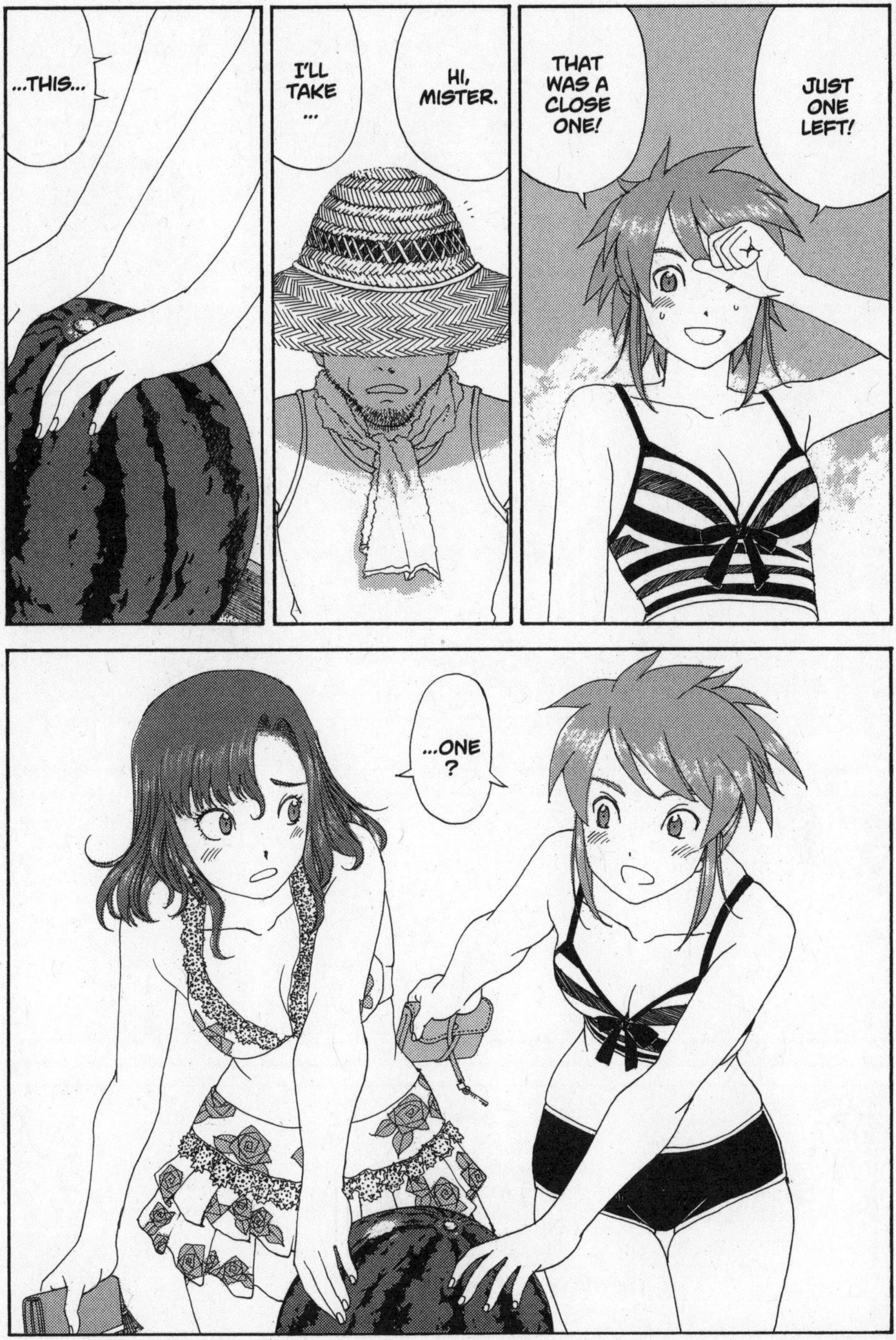
JUST ONE LEFT!
THAT WAS A CLOSE ONE!
HI, MISTER.
I'LL TAKE ...
...THIS...
...ONE ?

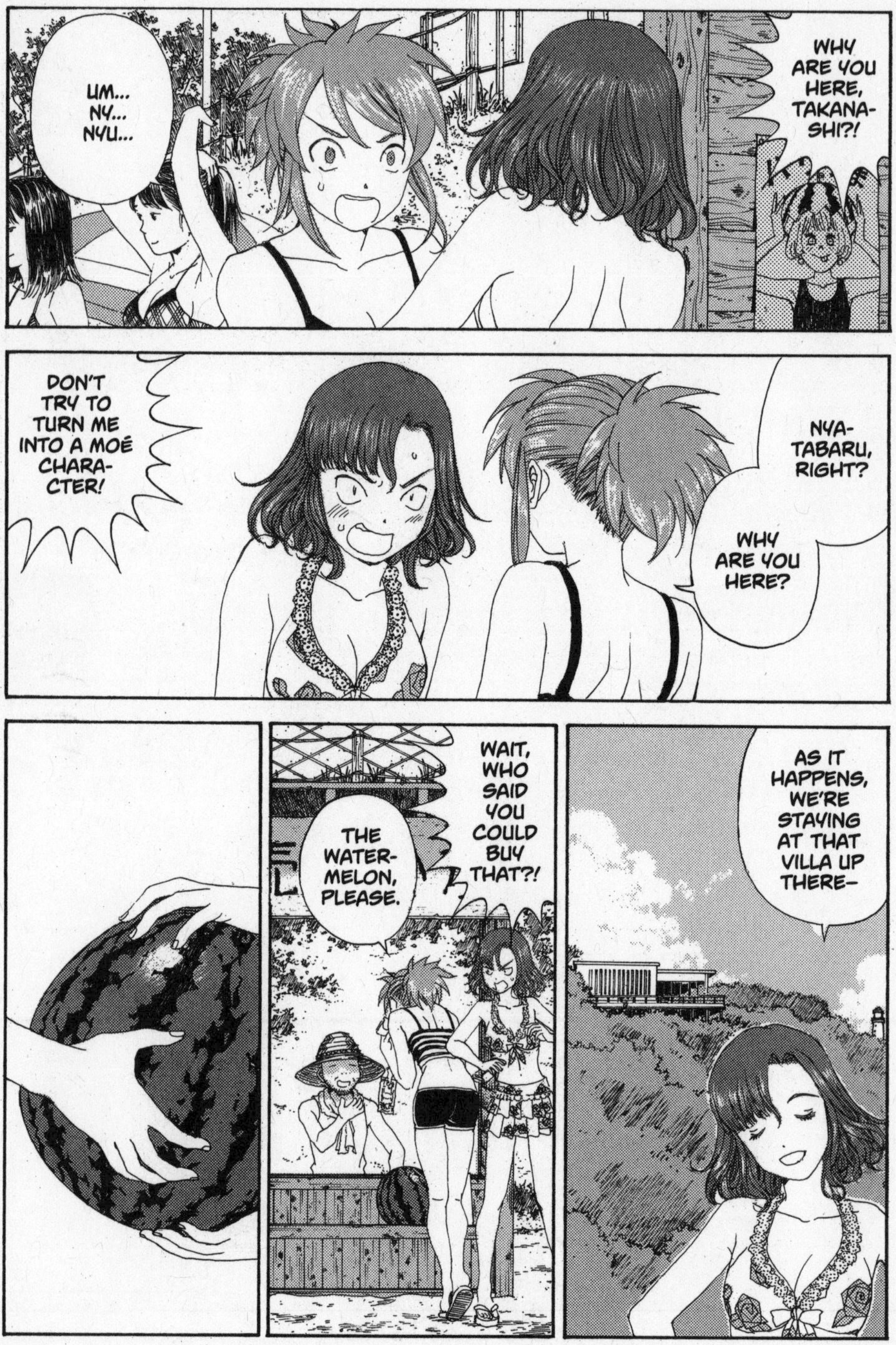
WHY ARE YOU HERE, TAKANA-SHI?!
UM... NY... NYU...
NYA-TABARU, RIGHT?
WHY ARE YOU HERE?
DON'T TRY TO TURN ME INTO A MOÉ CHARA-CTER!
AS IT HAPPENS, WE'RE STAYING AT THAT VILLA UP THERE–
WAIT, WHO SAID YOU COULD BUY THAT?!
THE WATER-MELON, PLEASE.

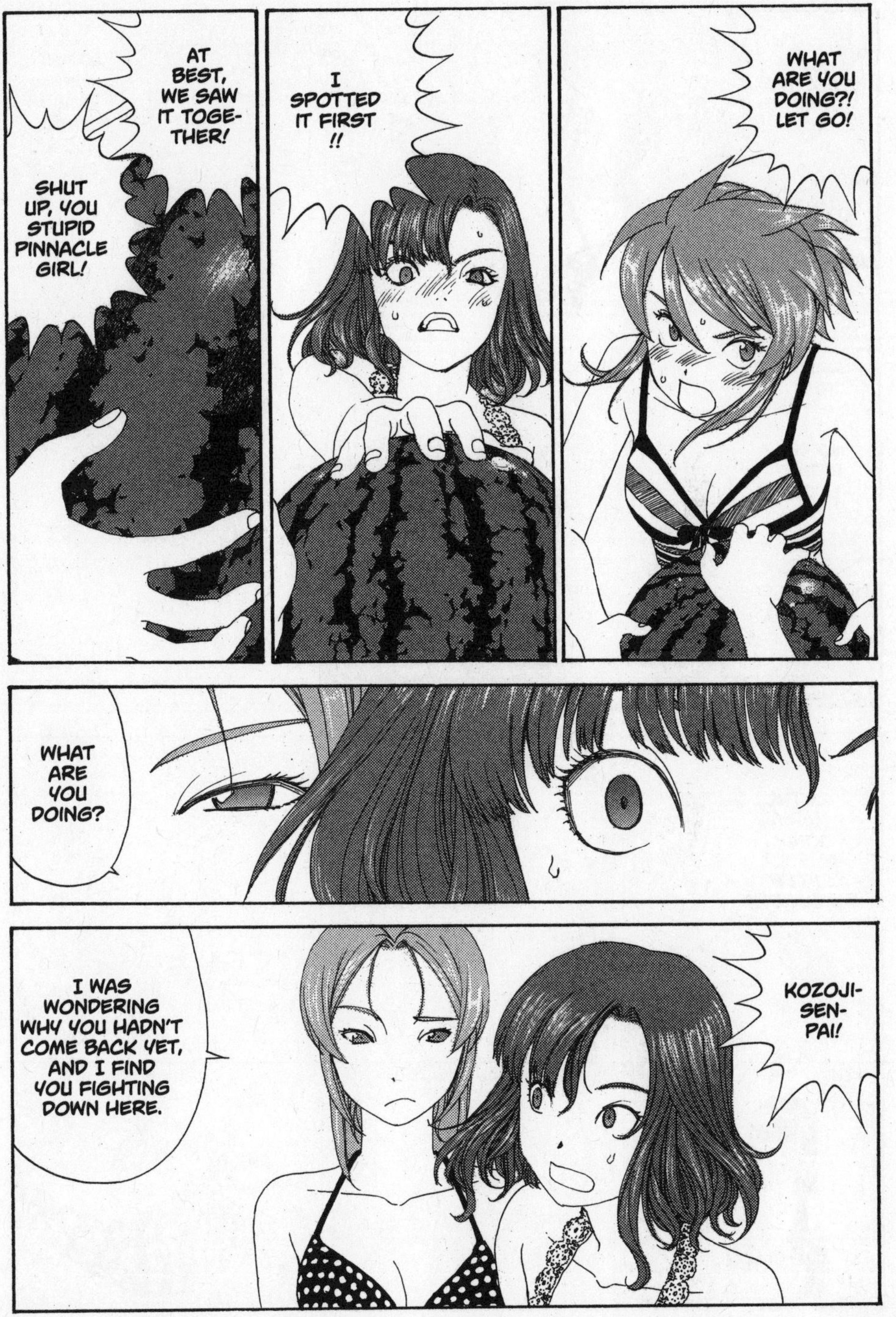
WHAT ARE YOU DOING?! LET GO!
I SPOTTED IT FIRST !!
AT BEST, WE SAW IT TOGE-THER!
SHUT UP, YOU STUPID PINNACLE GIRL!
WHAT ARE YOU DOING?
KOZOJI-SEN-PAI!
I WAS WONDERING WHY YOU HADN'T COME BACK YET, AND I FIND YOU FIGHTING DOWN HERE.

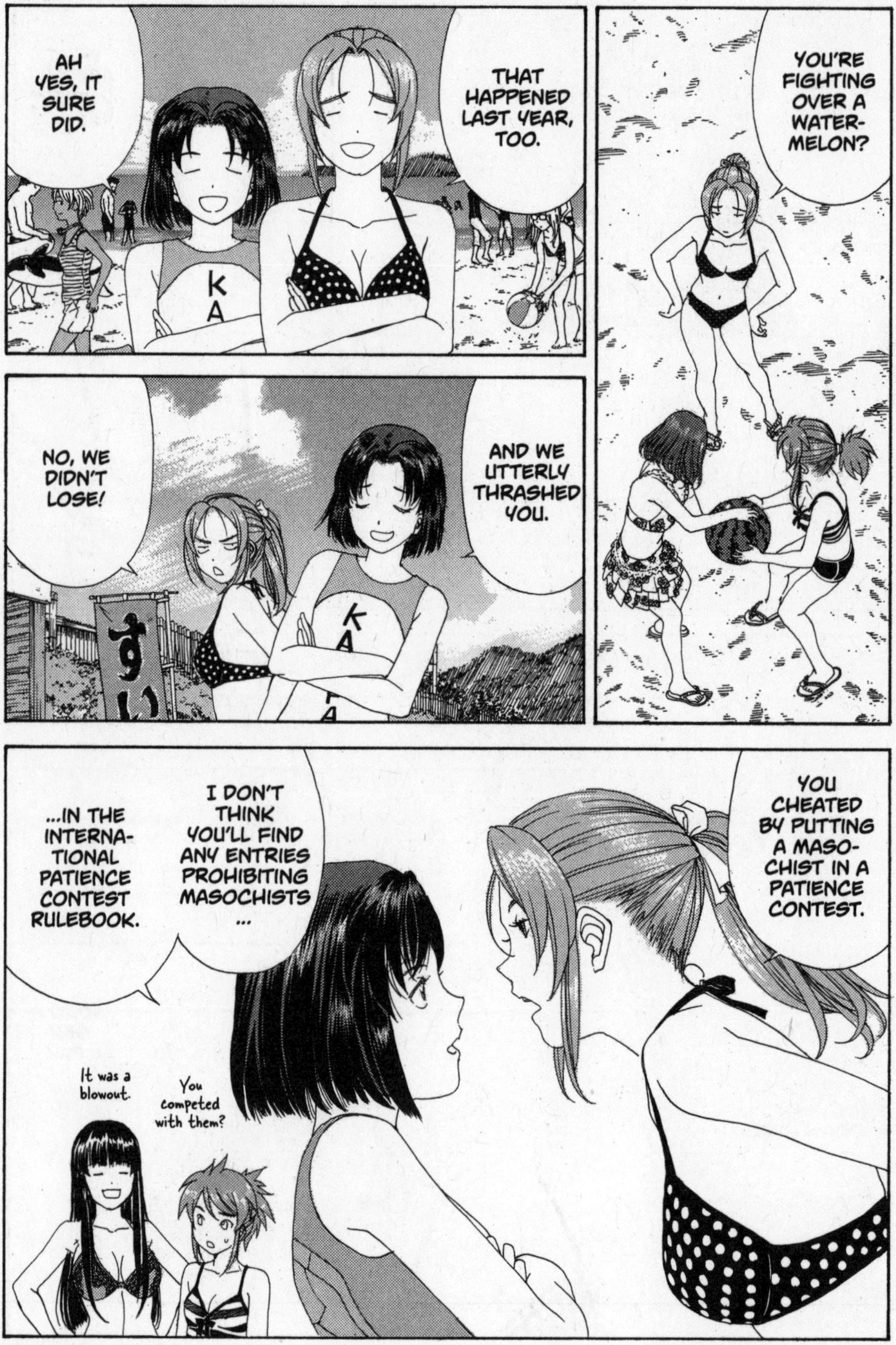
YOU'RE FIGHTING OVER A WATER-MELON?
THAT HAPPENED LAST YEAR, TOO.
AH YES, IT SURE DID.
AND WE UTTERLY THRASHED YOU.
NO, WE DIDN'T LOSE!
YOU CHEATED BY PUTTING A MASO-CHIST IN A PATIENCE CONTEST.
I DON'T THINK YOU'LL FIND ANY ENTRIES PROHIBITING MASOCHISTS ...
...IN THE INTERNA-TIONAL PATIENCE CONTEST RULEBOOK.
You competed with them?
It was a blowout.

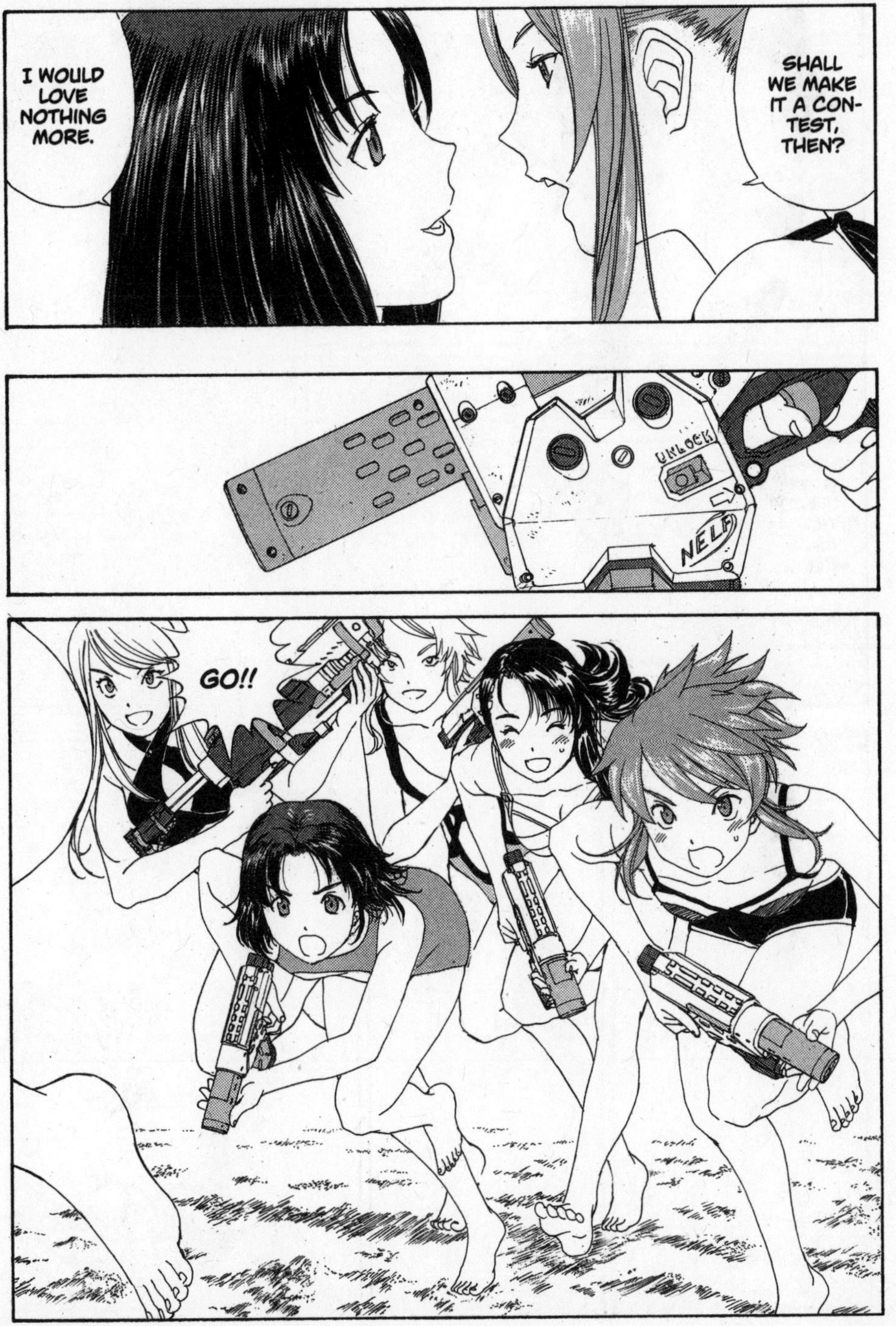
SHALL WE MAKE IT A CON-TEST, THEN?
I WOULD LOVE NOTHING MORE.
UNLOCK
OK
GO!!

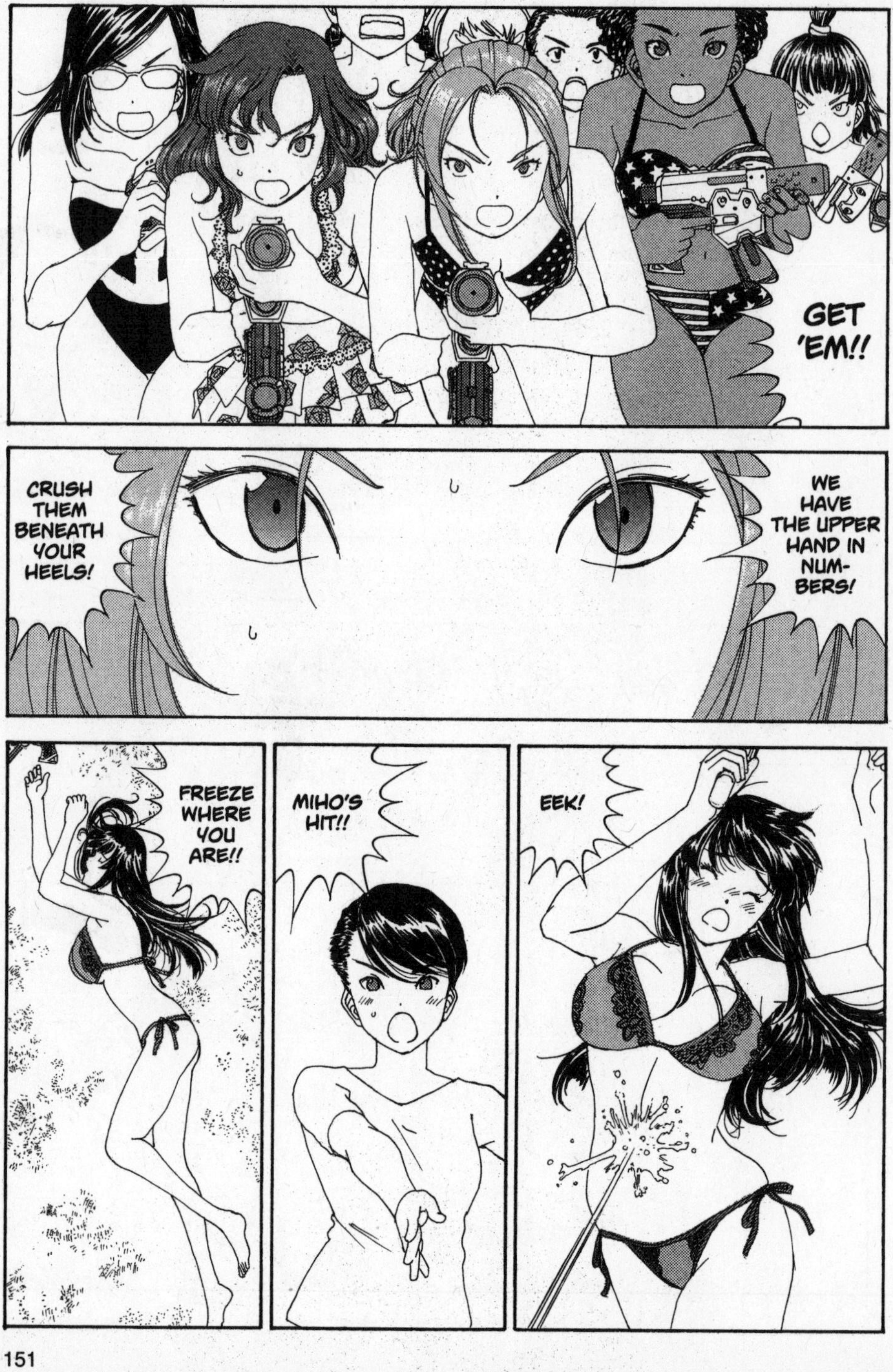
GET 'EM!!
WE HAVE THE UPPER HAND IN NUM-BERS!
CRUSH THEM BENEATH YOUR HEELS!
EEK!
MIHO'S HIT!!
FREEZE WHERE YOU ARE!!

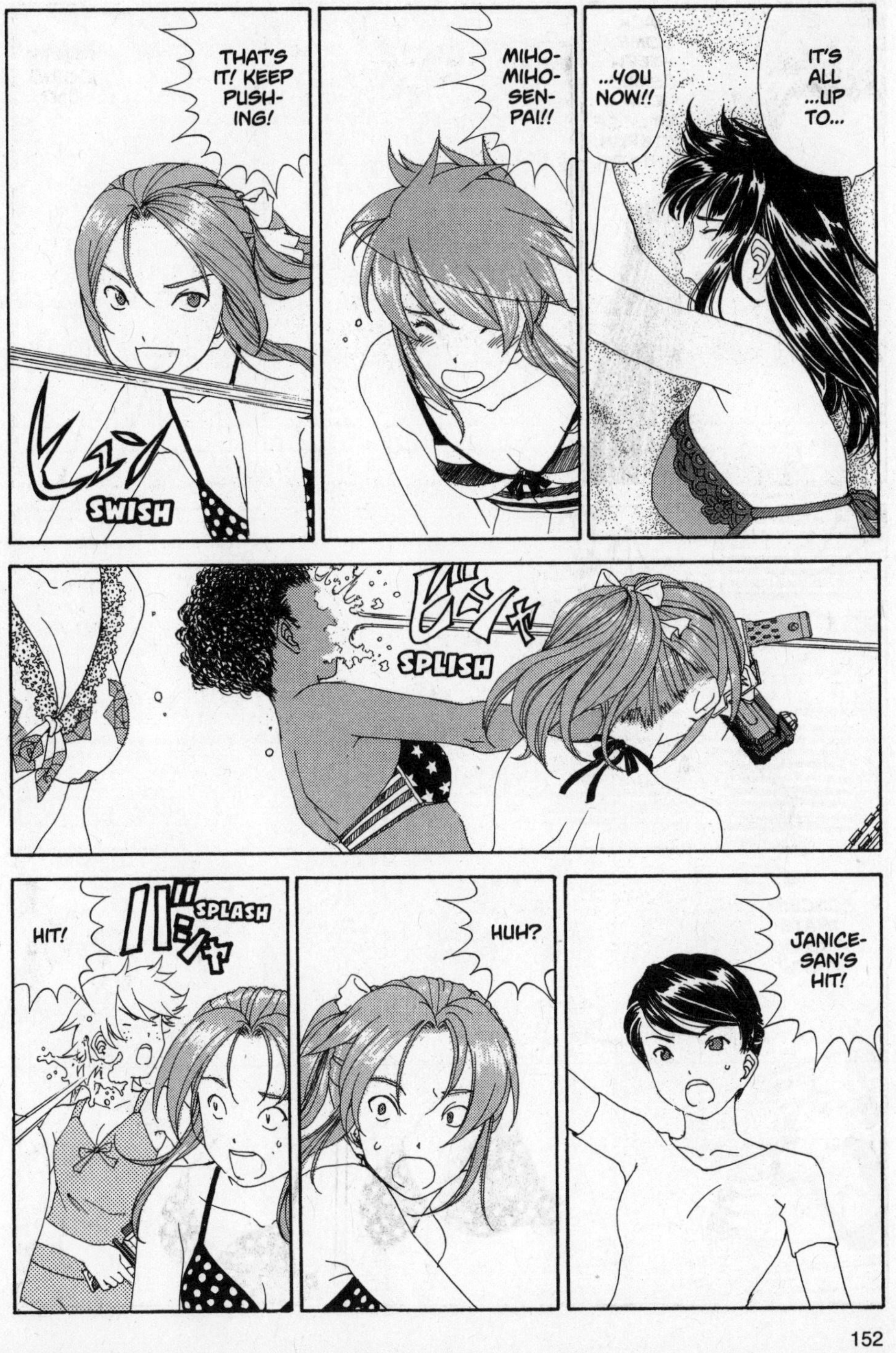
IT'S ALL ...UP TO...
...YOU NOW!!
MIHO-MIHO-SEN-PAI!!
THAT'S IT! KEEP PUSHING!
SWISH
SPLISH
JANICE-SAN'S HIT!
HUH?
SPLASH
HIT!

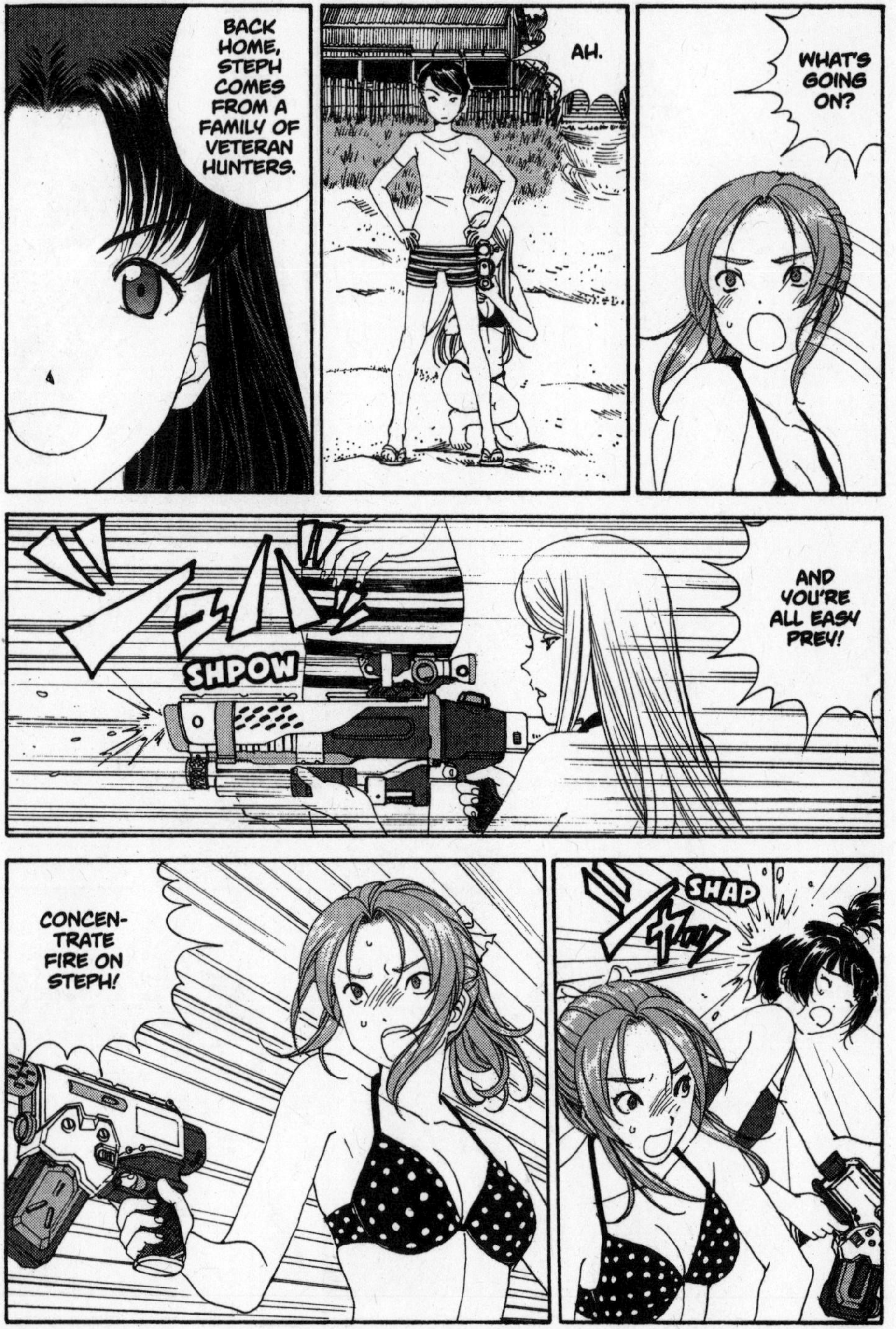
WHAT'S GOING ON?
AH.
BACK HOME, STEPH COMES FROM A FAMILY OF VETERAN HUNTERS.
AND YOU'RE ALL EASY PREY!
SHPOW
SHAP
CONCEN-TRATE FIRE ON STEPH!

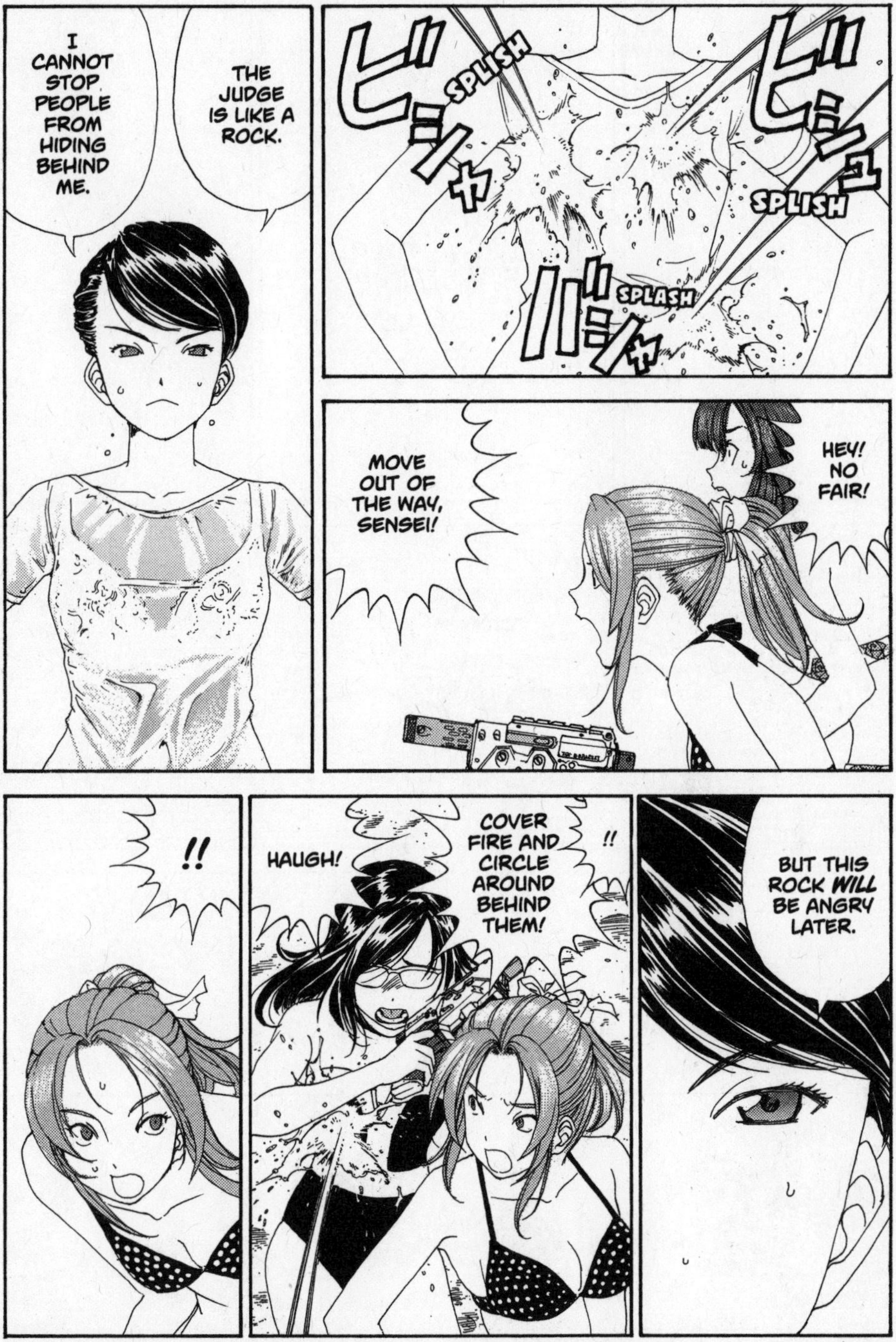
ビシュ
SPLISH
ビシャ
SPLISH
バシャ
SPLASH
HEY! NO FAIR!
MOVE OUT OF THE WAY, SENSEI!
THE JUDGE IS LIKE A ROCK.
I CANNOT STOP PEOPLE FROM HIDING BEHIND ME.
BUT THIS ROCK *WILL* BE ANGRY LATER.
!!
COVER FIRE AND CIRCLE AROUND BEHIND THEM!
HAUGH!
!!

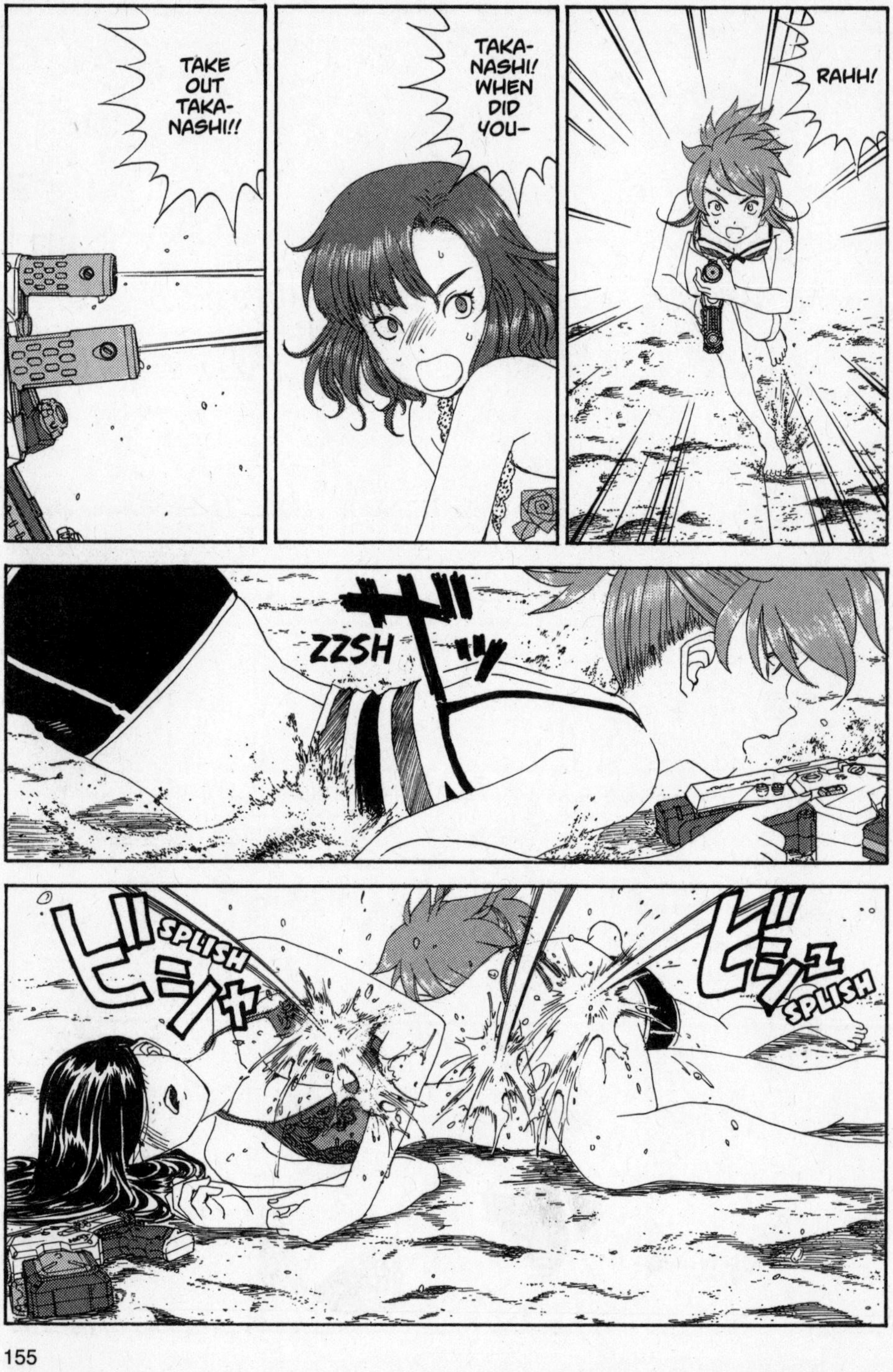
RAHH!
TAKA-NASHI! WHEN DID YOU-
TAKE OUT TAKA-NASHI!!
ザッ
ZZSH
ビシュ
SPLISH
ビシャ
SPLISH

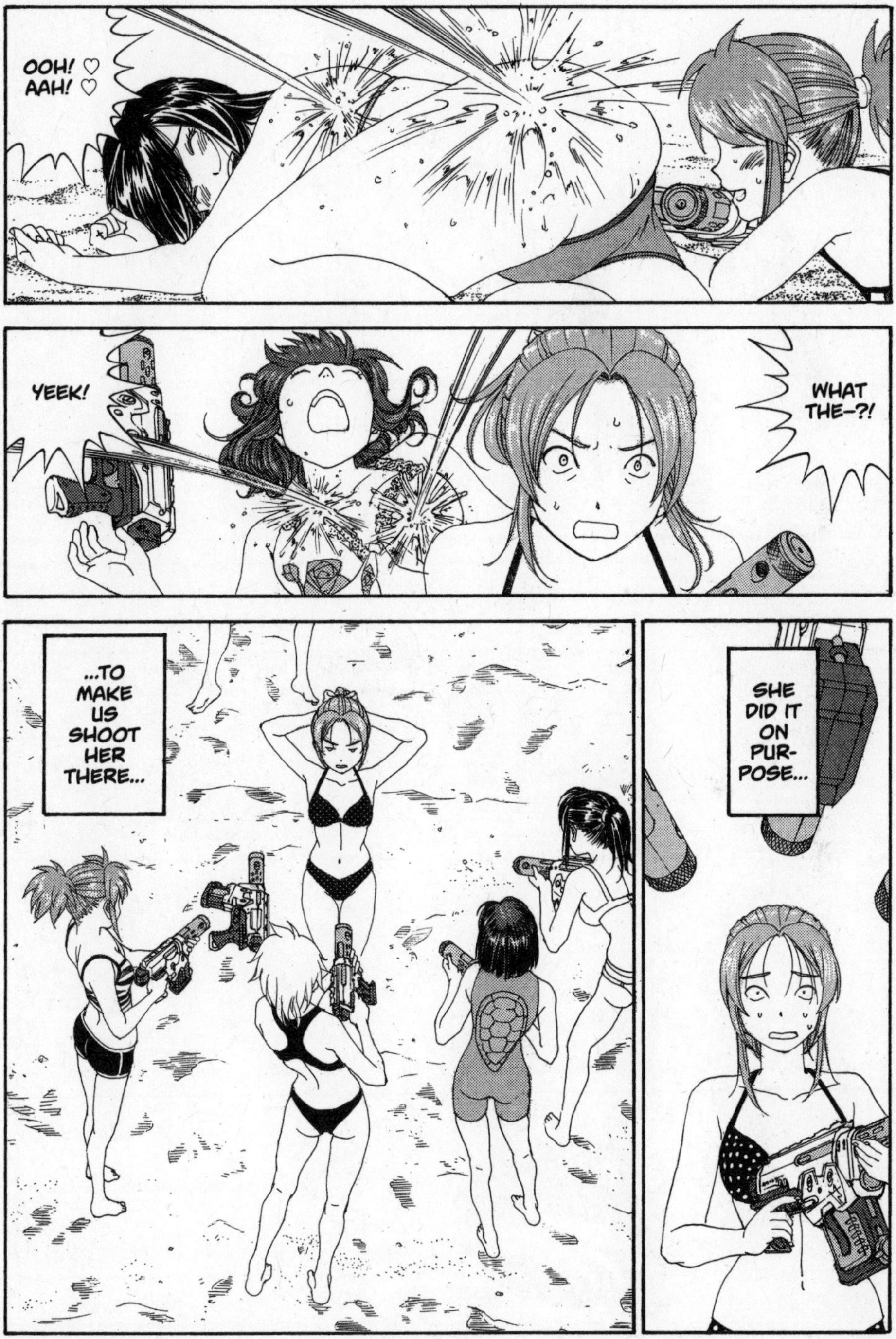

OOH! ♡ AAH! ♡
WHAT THE-?!
YEEK!
SHE DID IT ON PURPOSE...
...TO MAKE US SHOOT HER THERE...

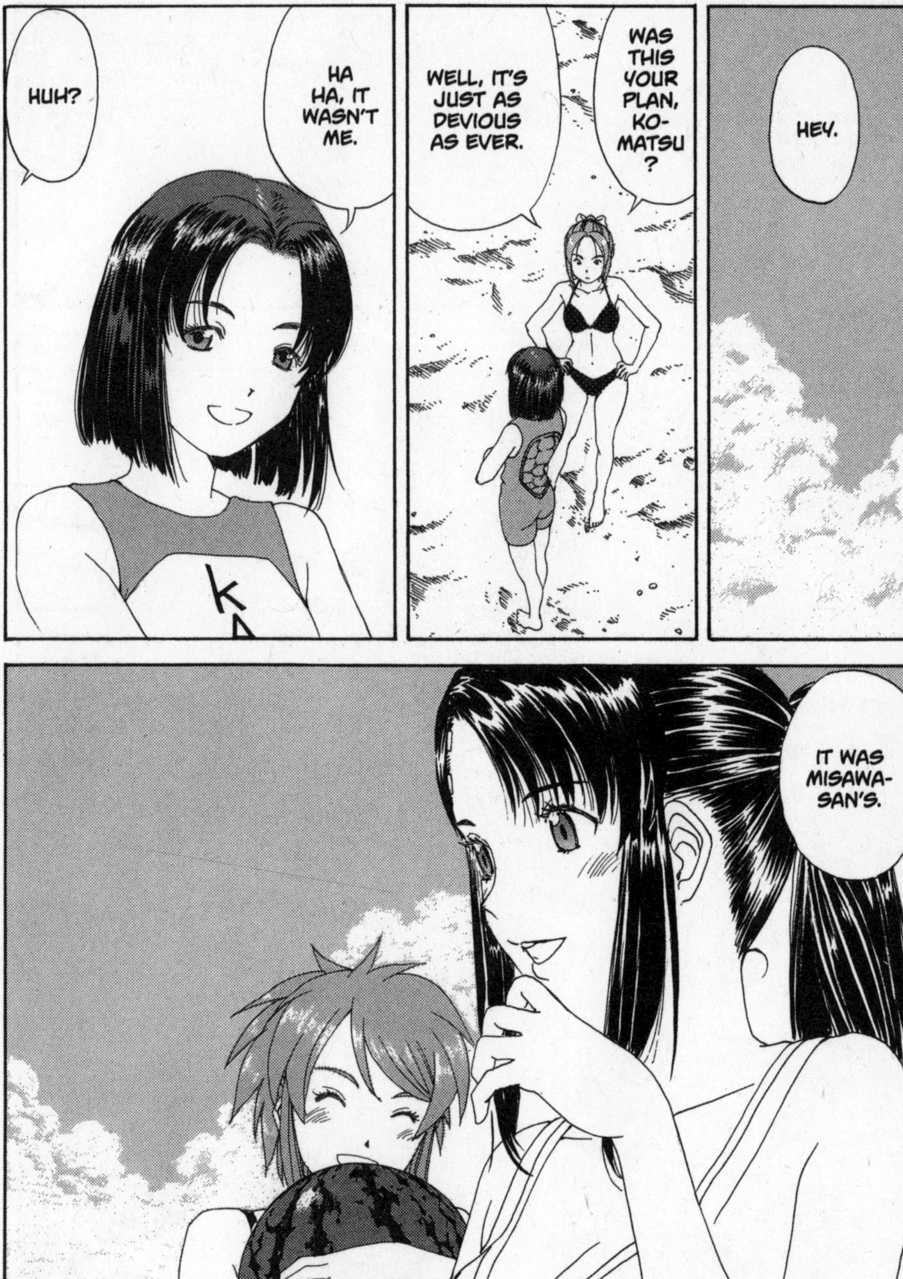
HEY.
WAS THIS YOUR PLAN, KO-MATSU?
WELL, IT'S JUST AS DEVIOUS AS EVER.
HA HA, IT WASN'T ME.
HUH?
IT WAS MISAWA-SAN'S.

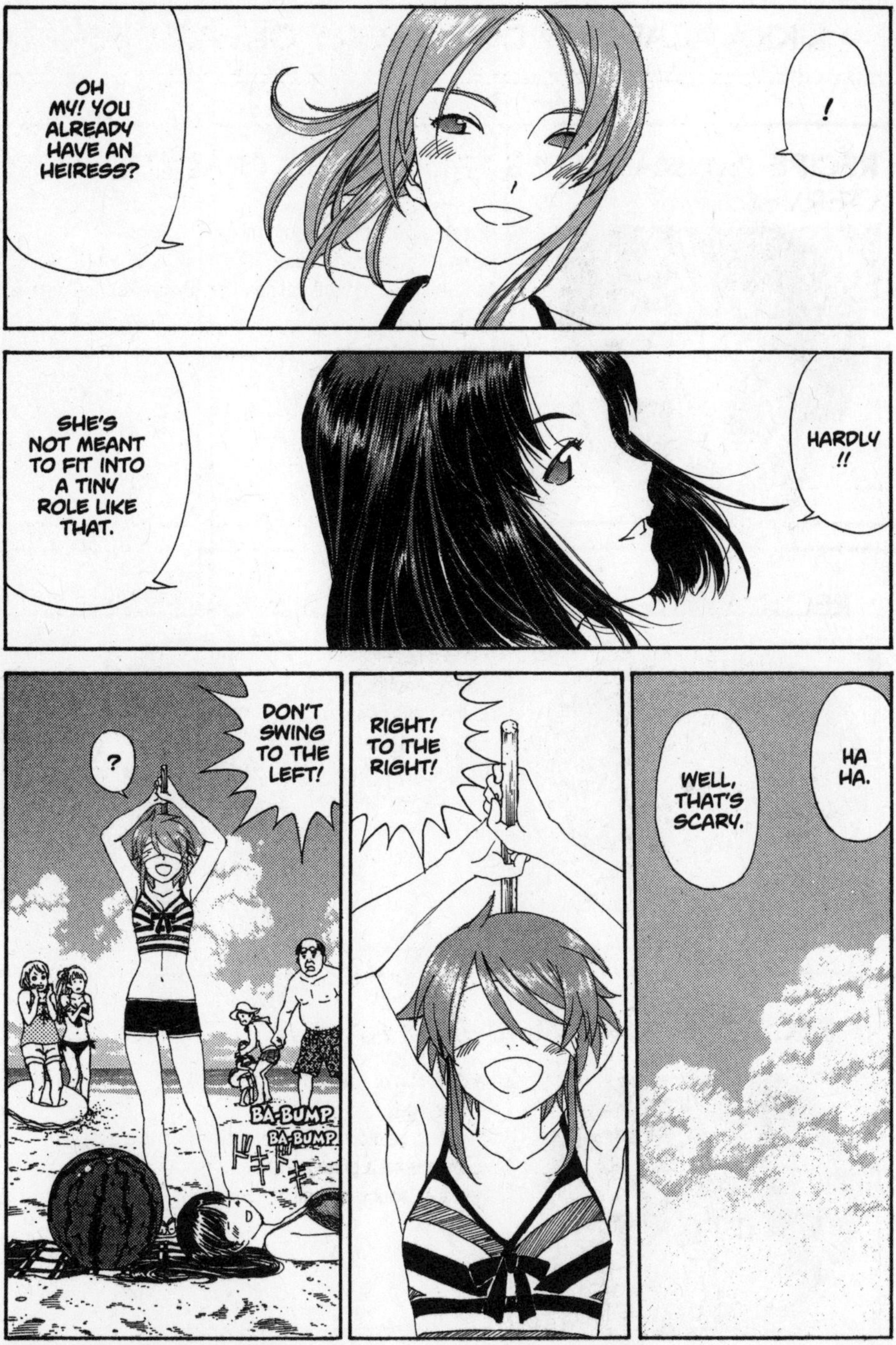
!
OH MY! YOU ALREADY HAVE AN HEIRESS?
HARDLY !!
SHE'S NOT MEANT TO FIT INTO A TINY ROLE LIKE THAT.
HA HA.
WELL, THAT'S SCARY.
RIGHT! TO THE RIGHT!
DON'T SWING TO THE LEFT!
?
BA-BUMP
BA-BUMP
ドキドキ

Paradise Residence 2 / **END**

○ KIKKA ACADEMY DORMITORY ONE KITCHEN ○

RECIPE 2: TAKANASHI'S FRIED SENBEI CRACKER SOUP (SERVES 1)

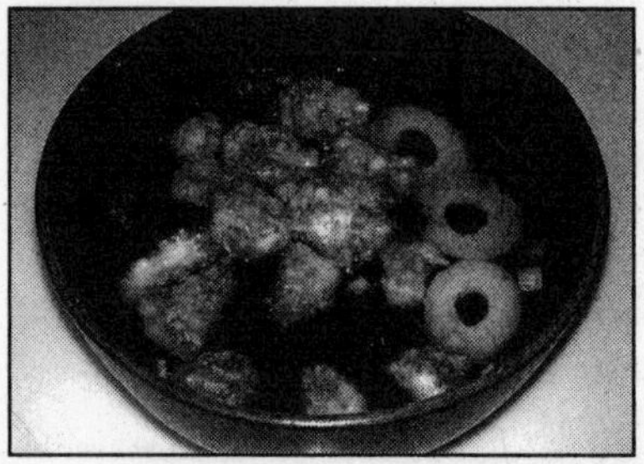

- One packet of soup broth mix
- One fried senbei cracker

Add hot water to broth mix and crush cracker finely before adding. That's all!!

RECIPE 3: STEPH-SENPAI'S SPAM BOWL (SERVES 2)

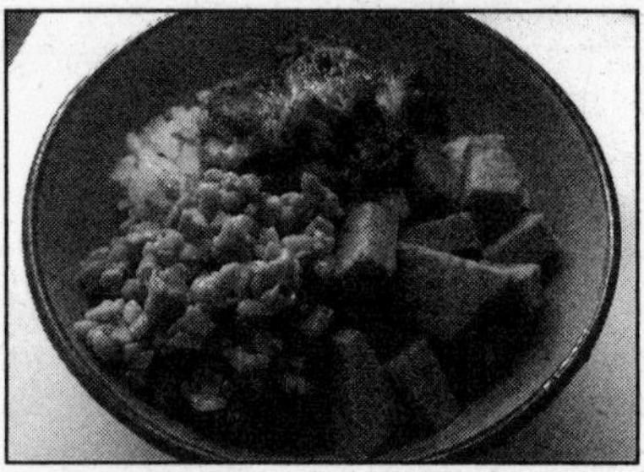

- 100 g spam
- 50 g kimchi
- One pack of nattô
- Steamed rice

Cut the spam to bite-size pieces, and heat in microwave, if possible. Place ingredients on top of rice and eat. Nori seaweed may be added to taste.

RECIPE 4: MIHO-MIHO-SENPAI'S RAW OYAKODON

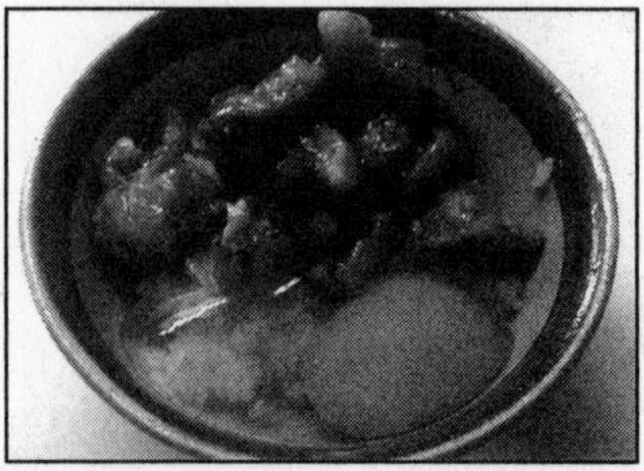

- One can of yakitori
- One egg

Heat up yakitori can in hot water, or place contents on a plate and heat in microwave. Pour yakitori, sauce and all, onto rice. Add raw egg and mix.

Translation Notes:

Japanese is a very different language from English, and translation is often more art than science. For your edification and reading pleasure, here are notes on some of the places where we could have gone in a different direction with our translation of the work, or where a Japanese cultural reference is used.

Oh! My Absence

The original Japanese title of episode 10 is "Ah Ssuketo SUMMER" (trans: Oh! Helper SUMMER) which sounds like the Japanese title of Kosuke Fujishima's previous manga, *Oh! My Goddess*. To tie this to the contents of the chapter while also mimicking the manga title as intended, "Oh! My Absence," was used.

Manager, page 15

While in English, the term "manager" in regard to sports implies someone in a leadership or coaching position, in Japanese sports clubs, the term manager refers to a role that is closer to a secretary or "team mom," a student who helps organize the team members, takes roll, launders uniforms, and so on. The manager does not participate in the competition.

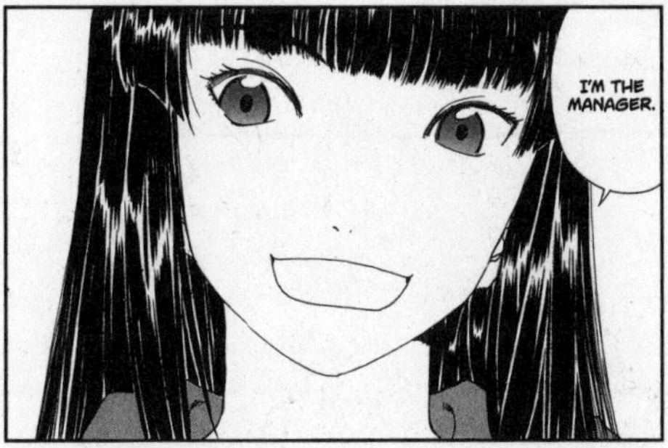
I'M THE MANAGER.

Monjayaki, page 17

A regional variant of the popular Kansai (Osaka/Kyoto) dish okonomiyaki, found primarily in the Kanto (Tokyo/Yokohama) area instead. Both dishes consist of savory batter and various toppings that are poured onto a griddle and fried like pancakes.

The Pillow Book, page 31

The poem quoted for this problem is the beginning of *The Pillow Book*, a collection of writing by Sei Shonagon, an 11th century contemporary of Murasaki Shikibu, the author of the famous *The Tale of Genji*.

Ankake, page 44

A type of heavy, rich sauce made with potato starch and soy sauce.

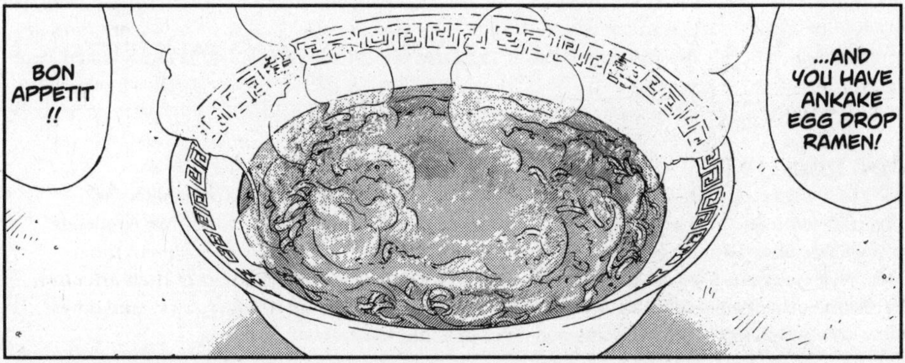
...AND YOU HAVE ANKAKE EGG DROP RAMEN!
BON APPETIT !!

Oyakodon, page 46

A dish of chicken and egg simmered and served on top of a bowl of rice. The name literally means "parent and child bowl."

Ochazuke, page 49

A simple dish of tea, broth or hot water poured into a bowl of rice, often with toppings like nori, pickles, wasabi or fish.

Tanuki, page 50

The descriptor for noodle or soup dishes with little pieces of fried tempura batter (known as "tenkasu" or "agedama") added.

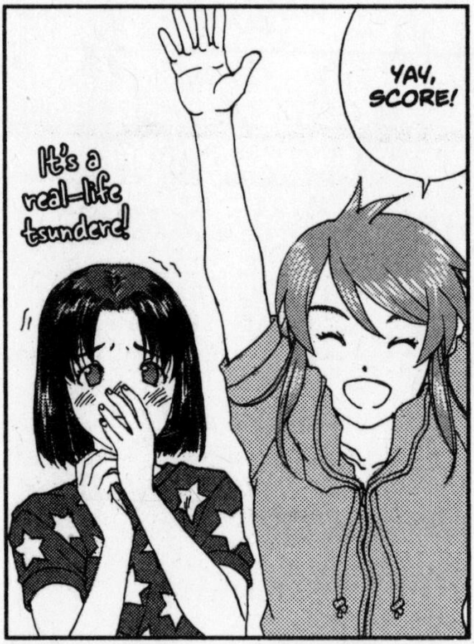
YAY, SCORE!
It's a real-life tsundere!

Tsundere, page 93

A character archetype found specifically in anime and manga. A tsundere typically has a secret crush or infatuation with another character, but puts up a cold and hostile exterior under most circumstances, so as not to reveal this fact, or feel vulnerable about it.

Katsudon, takoyaki, page 119

Katsudon is a dish of deep-fried pork cutlet (tonkatsu) and egg served over rice. Takoyaki is sometimes colloquially known as "octopus balls" in English, a dish of octopus pieces in a savory batter that is cooked in special spherical pans, then covered with a special sauce.

The Killer is Ya(su), page 142

"The killer is Yasu" is a meme that originated from the 1985 investigation adventure game, *The Portopia Serial Murder Incident*, for the Famicom Console. In the game, the player plays the role of a detective, trying to solve the murder of the president of a bank company. The player is a silent protagonist, so most of the commands are executed by the player's assistant named Yasuhiko (Yasu) Mano. The line "The Killer is Yasu" came from a late night radio show called "Beat Takeshi, All Night Nippon" where the host, famous comedian and director Takeshi Kitano, while playing the game live on the radio, says "The killer's this Yasu guy, ain't it?"

Moé, page 147

Moé is a slang term to describe a person or character whose appearance or behavior is extremely cute and endearing. The Japanese character for moe means "to bud" or "to sprout," perhaps because these objects of affection are often youthful. It is also a homonym for "to burn," so it is equally used as a verb when one's passion "burns" for the object of their affection. Oftentimes, the feelings of attachment to a moe character extend to their quirks and flaws, hence this moment between usual-rivals Hatsune and Nyutabaru.

Paradise Residence volume 2 is a work of fiction. Names, characters, places, and incidents are the products of the author's imagination or are used fictitiously. Any resemblance to actual events, locales, or persons, living or dead, is entirely coincidental.

A Kodansha Comics Trade Paperback Original.

Published in the United States by Kodansha Comics,
an imprint of Kodansha USA Publishing, LLC, New York.

Publication rights for this English edition arranged through Kodansha Ltd., Tokyo.

First published in Japan in 2015 by Kodansha Ltd., Tokyo, as *Paradise Residence* volume 2.

ISBN 978-1-63236-278-0

Printed in the United States of America.

www.kodanshacomics.com

9 8 7 6 5 4 3 2 1

Translation: Stephen Paul
Lettering: AndWorld Design
Editing: Ajani Oloye
Kodansha Comics Edition Cover Design: Phil Balsman